Be, Do, ai

The Trilogy of Human Achievement

By Scott Palangi

Winding Road Publishing

Be, Do, and Have

The Trilogy of Human Achievement"

Copyright © 2003 by Scott Palangi

All rights reserved.

No part of this book may be reproduced or transmitted in any form
or by any means, electronic or mechanical, including
photocopying, recording or by any information storage and
retrieval system without written permission from the author,
except for the inclusion of brief quotations in a review.

First printing - October, 2003

Library of Congress Catalog Card Number: 2003096298

ISBN: 0-9745297-3-7 (Trade paper)

Printed in the United States of America

Act as though it were impossible to fail. ~ Plato

You're a faker. ~ Jimmy Graesser

– First Edition Authors Note–

If you find typographical or grammatical errors in this book,
they're here for a reason. Some people actually enjoy looking for
them and we strive to please as many people as possible.

Other Products By Scott Palangi

☐ **Discipline Makes the Difference $12.95**
How to Get Mentally Tough... In Just 21 Days!
(Paperback Book, 112 pages)

☐ **Samurai Success - $14.95**
Principles of Warrior Excellence for Business & Life
(Paperback Book, 187 pages)

☐ **Bias for Action $24.95**
How to Get the Number One Characteristic of Success
(2 Audio CD's, 2 hours 12 minutes)

☐ **15 Minute Fitness $24.95**
How to Get Thin, Strong, and Flexible Without Weights,
Machines, or Cardio Classes in just 15 Minutes Per Day
(Illustrative/Instructive Book, 108 Pages)

☐ **Gold-Medal Thinking $10.95**
How to Think, Act, and Perform Like a Champion
(Paperback Book, 88 Pages)

☐ **Championship Habits $97.00**
How to Cultivate the Habits of Health & Happiness
(Live Seminar, call 1-800-PALANGI for schedule)

☐ **Insights Into Excellence $96.00**
Monthly Newsletter for Managers, Sales Professionals, and
Entrepreneurs. (for back issues visit www.scottpalangi.com)

Table of Contents

ACKNOWLEDGEMENTS

Great achievement are rarely accomplished alone.

Not that this book is a great accomplishment; nonetheless, it too, was not accomplished alone.

Big thanks go out to the Palangi Martial Arts Students for providing the laboratory for testing these ideas. Without you, the concepts presented in here would still be..."out there".

I would like to thank my karate instructor from afar, a man who served as the impetus for me to "get up off my knowledge" and organize these thoughts into a book. Thank you Master Hafner; you changed my thinking in less than three hours with a pen and a pad of paper!

To Tom Clifford, for continually encouraging me to speak straight from the heart; to ignore the Naysayer - and "Just Do It"; for years of great training and support while on my journey; for reminding me to laugh about human nature; and for teaching me that true charisma is not *"getting people to like you"* as much as it is *"speaking your mind."*

To Master Jimmy Grasser, who has personified what it means to be a genuine person; you are the *realest* of the *real men* in the world. Thanks for teaching me through your example alone... that we have to "Be" in order to "Do", and "Do" in order to "Have". Thanks for always being there no matter what. You have been a truly positive source in my life and taught me that *"tolerance always precedes happiness"*- in more ways than I can express.

To master copywriter Bob Bly, who let me into the "bat cave" and demonstrated a belief in me.

To master Tiger Schullman, who taught me directly that, "They can copy what you *do,* but they can't copy what you *are.*" Thank you for always keeping an open door for great training, and a huge "thank you" for setting an untouchable example for the entire martial arts industry.

To Chris Esposito for always believing in me over the past 15 years; for being close even while being far; for the best "love-hate relationship" I'll ever cherish; and... for making sure there was always an extra blanket and pillow around.

To Fred Gleeck who, over a cup of coffee on one Saturday afternoon in New York City, said, "Hey, why don't you let me teach you how to write a book?"

To Matt Serra, who taught me to conquer my innate fears without actually telling me *how* to do it.

To Herb Perez, for teaching me that our potential lies on the other side of our fears.

To my significant other.... whose time was shortchanged while I hammered out this book. Mindy – you're the best companion, and friend, a man could ever have.

Finally, to my parents, for offering me a great example of *courage* tempered with *consideration*.

And to all the other people who have contributed either directly or indirectly to the "Trilogy" of Be, Do, and Have. In fact, this is not my book. It is not even really a book, but rather, a record of observations from the many Masters, Entrepreneurs, Olympic Athletes, and of course... the best friends the world has ever seen.

You all know who you are. Too many to name.

Thank you for being, doing, and having... spent such quality time with me.

You have all taught me: In order to become happier... you must either change your goals -- or -- change yourself.

Scott Palangi

PREFACE

Life is a Do-It-Yourself Project!

One morning, a carpenter told his employer, a building contractor, of his plans to leave the building business so he could live a more leisurely life with his wife and enjoy his extended family. He would miss the paycheck, but he needed to retire. He and his family could *get by.*

His employer was sorry to see his good worker go and asked if he could build just *one more house*, as a personal favor. The carpenter said "yes" but it was easy to see that his heart was no longer in his work. He had lost his enthusiasm. He resorted to shoddy workmanship. He used inferior materials, "cutting corners," as he rushed to complete the "job." It was an unfortunate way to end his career.

When the carpenter finished his work and his boss came to inspect the house, the contractor extended his hand toward his carpenter and said, "Here" and handed him the front-door key. "This is your house!" he said, "My gift to you for being so loyal all these years."

What a shock! What a shame! If the carpenter had only known he was building his own house, he would have done it all so differently. Now, he had to live in the home he had just built... *And, none too well.*

So it is with us. We build our lives in a distracted way, reacting, rather than acting, often willing to settle for with less than the best. At important points, we do not always give the job our best effort. Then, with a shock, we look at the situation we have created and find we are now living in the "house" we have built for ourselves. If only we had realized, we would have done it differently.

Think of yourself as a carpenter. Think about your "house" *each day* that you hammer a nail, place a board, or erect a wall. Build wisely. It is the only life you will ever build. Even if you live in it for only one day more, that day deserves to be lived to its fullest potential, graciously, and with dignity.

INTRODUCTION

"Often times, men are anxious to improve their circumstances -- but unwilling to improve themselves."

~ James Allen

Deliberately living the life of your dreams is a concept that many people find inconceivable... *a "mystery."*

We find ourselves wondering, "What is it exactly that separates successful people from the non-successful people? The healthy from the sick? The happy from the *non-happy?"*

Is there some chromosome for success? A genetic link? Could it be that some people's DNA is simply more *predisposed* for high achievement than others?

Preoccupation with this question has spawned more industries than perhaps any other in the history of mankind. We have more and more "institutions" whose sole purpose is to assist people with their achievements, or their lack thereof.

We see an ever-increasing amount of social programs, educational programs, self-help books (including this one), tutors, and mentors -- popping up everywhere! All in the name of "assisting" people with improving their "quality of living."

Heck, even the personal trainers have personal trainers these days!

Of course there are some people, others, who could care less about *how* to improve their lives... Further, there are others who'd just as soon turn to tarot-card readers and psychics to find out "how things will unfold." They are more concerned with finding out *what* will happen *to* them, rather than realizing that they have *options.*

Although this success has been written about for thousands of years, the many responses to this question from so-called "experts" have, at best, only made us more confused, more skeptical, and in some cases, more apathetic.

To top it all off, we've also seen that even *"the experts"* have their hands full...*some are even struggling themselves.*

11

Well, I have some answers for you. I do not claim to have all the answers, but I do have a few.

Through teaching the martial arts for over a decade and practicing martial arts for two decades, I have found a link to human achievement that is so simple and so obvious, that it is usually overlooked.

There are *indeed* some solutions... some shortcuts, or "better ways" of attracting what you want into your life.

The best part is – these solutions are free! Of course, there *is* a price to pay to acquire these "success traits." But the price you pay to acquire these life-skills is not usually a monetary one. And, in the rare cases that it is, it's not *nearly* as high as the price you pay for *lacking these traits.*

You see, this is not one of those books that's designed to simply make you *feel good*... to give you a bunch of "good ideas"... or to give you something to "think about." This book is designed to help you *reach.*

Granted, you *will* get motivated, you *will* get some great ideas, and you *will* have plenty to think about. However, if all this book does is make you *"feel good,"* then I have failed as its author.

Great ideas happen... implementation is the tough part.

It is my goal that when you leave this book, you will have gained some actual skills--some *strategies*, and some *ways* of thinking, so that you can Be, Do, and Have everything you want out of life.

A Bias for Action

So what's this book really all about? I'll tell you, but first another story.

I was once attending a seminar for "positive mental attitude." The speaker was a highly-motivated and charismatic individual. Her presentation was about the power of *attitude*. She was trying to tell everyone that you first have to change your attitude in order to be happy. The message was: "Attitude is Everything."

I disagree. Well, to a point anyway...

You see, attitude, refers to how you "interpret" your circumstances. And yes, it's true, with some cultivation you can actually change your attitude under even the most dire of circumstances.

However, unless you take action – consistent action – you're only fooling yourself.

I am not impressed by "enthusiastic homeless people," if ya' know what I mean. Just being happy is great. But, damn it – let's *do* something, too!

Fact is, the quickest way to change your life, your circumstances, *and even your attitude* – is to *TAKE ACTION!!*

My point is this: There are many books out there that can anesthetize you. Over the years, I read many of them. Not much was gained other than feeling good for a bit and, of course - buying more books. I call those books, and that style of writing by the way – "mental-morphine".

You see, many books, instead of prompting you to achieve higher levels of self-awareness, attempt only to make you *feel "good"; to feel "okay,"* and/or to feel *"content"* about your current level of mediocrity.

Don't you be that naïve!

(While this "feel good" stuff is actually a good business strategy and sells books, it doesn't *help* you. They sell books; you feel good about the life you *have* instead of the life you *could have*; you fall in love with their work, and keep buying their books...*mental morphine*. My goal is to help you help yourself, not just massage your ego.

Don't get me wrong; most self-improvement literature *is* founded on fantastic universal principles. M*y* contention is that *they lack a bias for ACTION.*

Further, whereas some literature about success and achievement is like "Chicken Soup for the Soul," the book *you're* reading right now is more like **"Chicken Soup for the CHECKLIST!"** (Not that we neglect the soul, but I feel that the *most* spiritual improvement... comes from *getting off your ass* – not just sitting in a church – thank you very much.)

Martial Arts masters have known and practiced these principles for years. That's why, "back in the day", they were much sought-after for their insights and leadership qualities. Besides, after the need declined for their brute strength and hand-to-hand combat skills, the only thing these "masters" had to offer was their *wisdom* and their level-headed *leadership*.

What was it about these men and women that made them seem to possess so much higher knowledge? It was their desire for self-improvement, that and the deep-seated, genuine thirst for reducing "the complicated" into the *simple*.

Martial artists had no desire nor time for *fancy theories*, or mental morphine. "Give me what works because I have a job to do" was the order of the day.

Their lives depended on it back then... and the martial arts masters of today still live as if it holds true now. As you are about to read, your life has always depended on it.

Yet, this is not a martial arts book. It is about something more important than defending oneself from an enemy.

It's about personal alchemy. It's about becoming better at this "game of life."

The very fact that you are holding this book in your hands has moved you up a notch in human existence. I do not say this to pat myself on the back, but just look around you and see what other people are reading...that is, if they are reading at all!

A large part of this book was spawned from a discussion I had with one of my instructors who is, in my eyes, an enlightened being. One time, while studying under this man, I said, "Sir, this is really great stuff. Why don't you write a book?" He said, "I gave my message to you. Now, you go and teach it."

So then, *what's* in these pages that will make your life different, just by reading them? Glad you asked!

This book gives you, by way of insight, analogy, and *food for thought:*. specific ways to start THINKING about the things you want, the things that hold you back, and the things that will allow you to be, do, and have everything you want.

These new ways of thinking (commonly called paradigms or beliefs by many in the self-improvement world) will make incredibly good sense to you. But, as you are about to learn,

...what is common-sense is not always common-practice!

You see, the *thinking part* causes you to become, or as I like to put it, to *BE* different. Armed with a new way of thinking, we then will "cross the bridge" to focusing on getting stuff done... the "DO"ing!

Once you've got the proper mind-set, and are ready to go after your dreams, you need a *plan*. In this book, you will get the best ideas, methods, and strategies for designing, organizing, and EXECUTING *your* plan... and we are going to create it together right here in these pages!

Make no mistake about it. This book is going to change you just by reading it, and thinking about its message.

Now, here's where it gets tough. We've worked on the inner part -- the "being", the attitude, and the thought process germane to achievement....

And, then we've started taking action, taken some serious steps towards the things that we want; we're getting more done, more things accomplished...but, we haven't crossed the "great divide" just yet...

THIS IS WHERE 99% OF PEOPLE DROP THE BALL.

The trick now, friends, is to add some PERSISTENCE! You see, I am not going to be able to tell you anything you don't already know or give you something you don't already have. However, *I am* going to open your eyes to the one thing that has kept EVERYONE a hostage to his or her own freedom, a prisoner in one's own life, and kept each of them from being the master of their own fate: lack of "right **persistence.**"

Many of us are already persistent, but we are persistent at the wrong things!

As a side note, did you know that, until now, there has never really been a book about how to develop persistence? It's definitely a tough subject to analyze. I mean, we all know of its importance. Many books touch on the "inner work" that I call "being." Many books address only the *action* and *planning*, or what we are going to call the *Doing*...but then, they leave us hanging.

Fortunately, you don't need to find such a book now. I will teach you all you need to know about developing persistence.

Of course, we need to get good at ALL OF IT, right? The Being, the Doing, and the Having!

Ready for your journey? Let's get started!

PART ONE: SUCCESS DEFINED

In Order To Achieve Something You Must First Define It.

Problems arise whenever you try to discuss the meaning of success with other people. Many people have very strong opinions about what success "really is". And not only are their opinions strong, people will also get defensive if you try to persuade them to take a different point of view.

The funny thing is that the biggest losers of 'em all – will almost always tell you that you "can't define success."

Yeah, they'll tell you how "success means different things to different people."

And, they'll quote the most arbitrary adages such as, "Hey...to each his own." It's almost as if they want to be successful at avoiding the issue of..... Defining Success!

Why do you think that is?

One reason.

Fear.

See, if I let each of you believe that success has a specific meaning for you, then I can never say that you are – "Unsuccessful." Get it?

But, as soon as we try to "define" success, it invariably forces people to wonder if they're lacking some! (And that stings.)

But friends, we will only get confused if we try to "accept" all the different definitions of success. Therefore, right now, let's get something straight: *We must agree on a simple enough version of the definition of success if you are to get anything worthwhile from this book.*

With that in mind, let's take a look at some of the ways we delude ourselves by believing in subjective, passive, and "gray" definitions of success.

Success is not an opinion

Back in September of 1991, I started collecting quotes.

I would study different philosophers, masters, monks, theologians, CEO's, and so on – in hopes of gaining some insight into this definition-less goal that so many of us talk about.

The most frustrating bunch of people (if you don't mind me stereotyping them) are the unemployed yet well-educated. You know, the MBA type? People who have much schooling under their Gucci belts, but never really seem to make anything happen.

These individuals LOVE telling you that success is not "definable."

As soon as you mention the word "success," they instantly become defensive and start their shtick about "success is different for each of us." And sometimes, because they're such a well-read bunch, they have some good "material" that is difficult to refute.

They'll hit you with the ol':

"Hey, money isn't the only way to experience success."

"There are different *kinds* of success."

"Success is a Journey -- Not a Destination." (Hmmn, no wonder it takes so damn long!)

"Success is the pursuit of a worthwhile goal." (Gee, sleeping is worthwhile.)

"It's not about *getting* what you want -- but *wanting* what you have." (Well, I'd like to have some new stuff!)

"You are successful to the degree that you are happy." (Great, now let's join the Peace Corps and let those other fools run the shop.)

Have you ever heard these statements before?

Guess what folks... it is all B. S.!!

Contrary to popular belief, success is not an opinion... nor does it mean different things to different people. ALL success can be reduced to one simple principle (and it is simpler than you think). Here is the exact definition of success:

Success is the Ability to <u>Deliberately</u> Achieve
a Specific and Desired Result!

In a nutshell, "success" is about deciding to do certain things and, then, <u>getting those certain things done</u>!

It is the ability to achieve a specific, intentional, deliberate, and desired result.

So, if your ambition is to sit on the couch all day, watching television and eating potato chips.... and that's what your doing – yep, you're a success.

If you hate your life, and set a goal to hate your life – congrats, you're a success, too.

Conversely, if you have dreams and unfulfilled desires that still need accomplishing, you are not successful (yet).

See, it's all about the deliberateness of the achievement. For example, if you have a rich uncle who croaks leaving you millions of dollars, you are not successful (unless you murdered him). Why? Because there were no *intentions*. You don't get credit for what you didn't create.

Successful people can bring forth their "intentions" and their "plans".

Unsuccessful people lack that ability. (This is what this book is all about.)

Things happen to them, rather than they themselves creating the happening of things. Make sense?

Success is literally the ability to transform:

Thought into Decision…

Decision into Plan...

Plan into Action...

Action into Persistence... and then finally,

Persistence into **Desired Results**!

Until you master these five steps... which govern all achievement, you are fooling yourself if you think you'll ever accomplish anything significant with your life!

But, what do we see all too often?

The exact opposite...

We see people floating aimlessly, living day after day commuting to dead end jobs. We see people with no definite **wants, dreams, or goals** to speak of... No **clear direction** or **sense of mission**.

And, although these same people cannot tell you what they **want out of life,** they are *real-quick* to point out all the things that they don't want... You know the type, they're usually:

Too busy complaining about what they **don't have**.

Too busy complaining about what they **don't want**.

Too busy complaining about how they were **wronged, cheated, taken advantage of...** and **GOT A BAD DEAL**.

Until, in the end, they have lived an entire lifetime without even scratching the surface of their potential.

Isn't that sad?

But, that is the cycle that is so commonplace today.

Now, I know reading the above paragraphs sort of "struck a chord with you."

How do I know? I know because it did so with me too, when I started to wake-up! You see, there was a time when the person you just read about above -- WAS ME!

That's right. We have all been, at one time or another, in that lousy rut before! But the real danger is, the next thing you know...

It actually becomes 'normal' for us!

Well, guess what friends... It doesn't have to be this way anymore.

A solution exists, and it's easier than you think!

A solution you can learn through studying the principles presented in this book.

That's correct. I learned all the stuff <u>you</u> are about to learn by studying successful people, reading success literature, attending all the seminars, and then finally... failing several times over within a ten-year period only to finally, to eventually, and to painfully, **get it right!**

My journey led me from New York, to Miami, to Los Angeles, to Chicago, and eventually... to Seoul, South Korea!

I have lived with self-made multi-millionaires, entrepreneurs, gurus, theologians, you name it... I studied it! Heck, I even lived in a Buddhist temple in hopes of discovering the "missing link" to achievement! I've read all the books, heard all the tapes, and attended all the talks.

And, here is what I discovered...

You cannot **do** what successful people do and **get** the same results they get until you **<u>learn to think</u>** the way that they **<u>think</u>**. And, when you learn to think the way they think, you'll be able to do the way they Do, and then you'll be able to achieve any identical, or specifically-desired result! (Have what they have.) See? Be, Do, and Have.

You see, it isn't only about doing more.

And, it isn't about having more...

It's about *becoming* more.

<u>Be</u> is the key.

Listen, I once had a mentor, who said,

"Don't wish life was easier -- wish you were better!"

And when we talk about **Being**, we are really talking about **Thinking**, aren't we?

Successful People Think Differently...

High Achievers Think Differently...

Now, here's where it gets good; think about this for a minute:

My teachers taught me that there are **formulas** for success. Apply the right **formula** -- reap the **right result**.

You see, once you have the correct formula - or the "strategy" as I like to call it - then you have the power to break down the barriers of your own self-doubt and limitations. Consider this for just a moment:

All people, at one time in their life, fall into one of the FOUR "life-categories" below. See if you can identify with any of them.

- I don't know what I want...

- I know what I want -- but I don't know how to get it...

- I know how to get it -- but for some reason **I still never get it!**

And finally,

- I always get it -- but I am still not happy...

So then, which category do you sometimes find yourself slipping into?

Many people float back and forth from one category to another. What's even sadder is, most people are totally unaware of their life-category rut and could care less that a solution exists!

Well, what if I told you there was a way where... you could sort of "step into" a successful person's mind and **borrow** their way of thinking! Their "mind-set" if you will. Wouldn't that be amazing?

I mean, just imagine facing an obstacle, say a huge career goal... And, instead of getting upset, confused, or intimidated by the goal, **you actually started to think** like a Michael Jordan, or a Bill Gates, or any other person who would look at the same situation as if it "were a breeze" or a "Piece of cake."

Wouldn't that be a valuable skill to have?

Well, that is what this book is all about. Each passage is linked to a topic that's guaranteed to turbo-charge you on your path to success! (That is, to create your own deliberate and desired result.)

Hey, I'll bet you've heard it said that, "success is a state of mind," right?

That's close – but it's not complete.

By our definition here, success is *indeed* a state of mind. But, it's a state of mind that **prompts** you into taking **action** which, of course, allows you to **attract** that which you **desire**. It is NOT simply a state of mind.

Something Is Missing

"The unexamined life is not worth living."

~Plato

What is it that makes some people successful?

Well, there are two big questions that need answering.

The first one is: <u>What is it that makes some people seem to magnetically attract success, health, and happiness?</u>

I don't know if you've ever considered it before but, how is it that two people – from similar backgrounds, similar upbringings, and identical families, and so on – *wind up* in two *totally different places years later?*

One happy and one sad. One person: prosperous and enjoying great relationships; making the miraculous occur. The other person: *broke...* both financially, emotionally, and dare I say – spiritually?

Is it "luck"?

Is it "ordained"?

Fate?

Look at your own life right now. Think of someone who just seems to "get it all." What's going on there?

Is it possible that they know something you *don't*? Or that they do something you *can't*?

24

Or, better yet... Is it possible that they *are* something you *aren't?*

Based on the title of this book, you know that I believe it has more to do with this last one.

I believe *we* can create our own circumstances, just as we can pick up a pen, drive a car, or comb our hair, or do any other seemingly mundane or daily activity.

The hardest part here is accepting that this is true. It is difficult to say, "I did this to me." So, before we go around placing blame and trying to figure out this missing link to achievement, lets go on to the second question:

How can I become one of them?

How would you like to live the life of the person you've most admired? Sometimes, we think of what it must be like to have "rock-star" status or what it would be like to live the life of a Michael Jordan, a Madonna, or a Bill Gates. Or have the personal power of a Mother Theresa or a Gandhi.

What you are going to learn from the trilogy of Be, Do, and Have, is that, at your current level of thinking, even if you had the chance to walk a mile in their moccasins -- you might still miss out on what's really important. And that is: *how they think.* How they look at life, how they look at people, and how they feel about the way the world operates. To put it bluntly:

What separates the great from the ultra-great is not so much what they *do*, but the <u>way they *think*</u> <u>about what they *do*.</u>

The Secrets of Success

What is "a secret" anyway? Is it something that only a few people know? Is it something that only a few people do? Or, is it... something that only a few people do...that very few actually *know* they are doing? Stick with me on this...

Whenever you say to people that there are secrets to success, they always look at you a little funny. But I ask you... *what exactly is a secret?* Well, it's not what you think.

Usually, people think of a success secret as a "hot stock tip" or some "magic potion" found in the Himalayas. Really, secrets are much more subtle than that.

Webster's defines a secret as, "something not apparently obvious." Most success secrets are like that. They aren't necessarily *profound,* but they are in right in front of you, right under your nose. (If you glean one thing from this book, let it be that the *obvious stuff* is always what people "miss out" on.)

Therefore the first secret is that *there are* secrets to success!

You see, if I know something that you don't know... to you, that thing is pretty much a secret (no matter how simple it may be). Take it even deeper. If I know something you don't – and I *also take action on it* – guess what that's called? A huge secret!

So get this: Just because you know something, and it sounds simple, it does not mean you understand it. A success secret is never surprising; and when you realize how subtle they are, you almost feel foolish for not "getting it."

Take magic for example. If I were to show you how to do a card trick or show you the "secret" to an amateur magic trick, you would say, "Oh, of course... *that's how* it works"... but until you learned the "trick," you were no closer to "figuring it out" prior to my having shown you.

I am not going to tell you anything new in this book. Some of the insights will definitely be new to *you* because I've not read about them anywhere else and got them straight from my teachers. Many of the strategies will make you go, "Wow!" But by and large, most will make you go, "Hmmn." (By the way, "Hmmn" usually precedes, "Wow.")

Speaking of simplicity, did you ever tell something to somebody (something simple) and they give you this quick response like, "Yeah, yeah, I know. I know!" But then... you notice that they don't *do anything about it?* And there you are, thinking to yourself, "I thought you said you *knew?*"

Well, if you hear about something that sounds familiar in this book, but it is something you are *not currently doing*, stop right there. Try to re-learn the principle as if it's your first time learning it. Here's why...

To *know* and not *to <u>do</u>* is really, *not to know.*

That's worth repeating: To KNOW and not to "DO" is really not to know, at all!

For example: You can say that "you know" you should exercise, but if you are not currently exercising – you really do not "*know.*"

One of the most obvious examples of this is when someone tells you, "It's a good idea to save 10% of your income." You think to yourself, "I've heard that before, what else is new? Tell me something I don't know?" What happens is you don't even realize that you don't *know* because you AREN'T "*DO*"ing IT!

Had you truly known the value of saving that 10%, you would be doing it already, and you'd be able to talk about its significance!

So rule #1 is *Do not overlook the obvious. Every success secret is a little obvious.*

The Danger of Simplicity

"Before enlightenment – chop wood, carry water; After enlightenment – chop wood, carry water."

Zen Koan

Again, everything you are going to read in this book... is simple. In fact, if you are to acquire one simple concept from this book, let it be this:

All of the best stuff is simple.

The danger implied here is that you're going to read something that sounds simple and dismiss it as unimportant. That's part of the problem with success; often times we miss out on success because it doesn't *feel* like success is happening to us.

For some strange reason, we miss out on success because it doesn't feel PROFOUND. Another reason is because we associate success as something that requires some COMPLEX process. But it is not. Success is always simple -- but not easy.

Here's an example: You may read something like: Success is the ability to reduce to complex into the easy. And because it sounds like something you've heard, you may think, "Right, I got it; success is simple."

✳ Therefore rule #2 in this book is *Do not dismiss ideas because they are simple.* ✳

The reason we think success is something complex is because we haven't yet attained it. So naturally, we think it is because we lack some knowledge or know-how, some *skill*.

Again, achieving success in any and all areas is done by accomplishing the simple things over and over with no let-up.

How I Stumbled Upon These Principles

My background is martial arts.

Perhaps one of the greatest benefits of this training is that there isn't much "luck" involved with progress! No one has more than they deserve, or less. I'm talking about skill here. If you practice martial arts and you're doing your side kick, you've got the exact side kick you deserve to have. This is probably one reason that people who practice martial arts have an innate sense of personal responsibility for their results. In martial arts, it's pretty apparent that you have to literally *make* the "first creation" in your mind.

What I'm saying here is:

You never do a martial arts move better than the way you see it in your mind.

This is not a book about martial arts, so I will try to make as few references as possible. However, it is sort of rudimentary that one must create "within" before seeing "without".

So it is with success principles as well.

You must *think*... before you *do*. If you *do* without thinking first, the end result is usually pretty lousy, meaning... your techniques may have been horrible. With the help of a good instructor, you learn that the more often you mentally create what move you want to be able to do, the better, faster, and more precise you will be able to execute the technique. Success!

This would later serve as the foundation of the Be, Do, Have material.

Studying martial arts requires that you do basically two things very well.

1) Pay attention to detail.

2) Take action!

These two aspects of discovery are paramount for any achievement. Thos knowledge caused to me to really look past the mere results that successful people were getting and ask WHY they were getting them.

Paying attention and taking action would soon lead me to seek out successful people and study what were doing. ALL of what they do - the, *behind the scenes* stuff, if you will. That's where the real value is. Don't look at their wallet; look at the *way* they hold it.

I thought, "Could it be possible that successful people follow a similar process? Creating their outer circumstances first in the mind and then, in physical reality?"

So, I did not invent any of these methods, nor did I, and I will not claim to have discovered them. I merely observed thousands of examples of "the process of achievement." Then, I tried techniques in my own life and got *lucky enough* with the results to get *excited enough* about organizing them into sensible practices.

Therefore, it could be said that the Be Do Have strategies are not *original* so much as they are *effective*. I don't care *why* they work, only *that* they work.

Like any other thing that catches on, it first starts with one person saying, "Hey, have you ever noticed, A, B, and C before?" And then the person you're talking to tells their friends. They say, "Hey, that's good stuff – we should write this down!"

Next thing you know, it grows. All of the sudden, they're calling you a philosopher because you have the ability to make sense!

The rest is in your hands.

Here's Why Success Seems So Elusive

"Luck is a matter of preparation meeting opportunity."

Oprah Winfrey (B. 1953) Talk show host, actress

We all fluctuate between greatness and lousiness everyday of our lives. The main problem is that we tend to spend more time on the *lousy* side. In this section, I want to devote a few moments of time to examining why success in any field of endeavor seems to elude us. First, let's take a quick look at why some people never even come close to discovering these secrets.

8 Reasons People Don't Know The Secrets

You discover a secret through experience. Therefore, until non-successful people experience success, they may be oblivious to the fact that these secrets exist. Thinking success to be some complicated process, people are not even aware that they are practicing some of the very thought patterns which serve to keep success *from* them.

Most people, in fact, 8 out of 10 people, are subject to some of the following types of thinking. Below, as you read the examples, you may see yourself, your family members, and definitely some of your close friends.

Reason #1) They Are Too Lazy

Yes, believe it or not, some people would rather not even entertain the idea that they could improve their lives. And, it's not just because they doubt it's possible -- they are just too lazy! They are caught up in the cycle of "I want someone else to take care of me; I don't want to accept the idea that success is a possibility." Interestingly enough, they don't even realize it – can't even see it.

"Just give me job, and/or some stuff to do, and I'll be fine," is their motto. It's okay, though! To some degree, we need people like this to keep the world going around, so they actually are necessary... even though it seems on the surface.

The very thought of more responsibility scares them to death! Fortunately for these folks, they will never have to experience the fear of failure... because they won't even get up to bat!

Cool, more room for the rest of us who want to swing for the fences!

Reason # 2) They Don't Believe There *Are* Secrets to Success

Yep, some people think that there *are* no secrets. I am not sure what this crowd *does* think it takes to make it because, upon interview (meaning, when I am actually able to get them to openly discuss the subject of success), they shut down and say stuff like, "Isn't it a nice day?", "So, did you see the news last night?," and "I like trees; do you like trees?"

Getting past the normal pleasantries is tough to do with the non-believers. Books like this one are like kryptonite to *them*! When they hear someone speak with enthusiasm or confidence, they want to get out of the room. Secretly, they want to get jobs as professional skeptics! (But then, they wouldn't feel sure if that job would last either!)

31

Good topics to discuss with them are: Psychic readings, astrology, the lotto, and the latest trashy novels. Then, perhaps you might follow up with questions like, "Do you think Elvis is really raising pit bulls down in Mexico...? Should we legalize marijuana, etc?" Anything *except*, "What would it take for us to become more... happy, healthy, successful, prosperous, and effective!"

Reason # 3) Fear of Criticism

Less excusable is the fear of criticism. Heck, even among high-achievers criticism is everywhere. It just seems to be part of human nature to want to make someone aware of their flaws. If you are in the habit of criticizing others, this book will definitely help you. Let's take a closer look at the fear of criticism.

People don't know these secrets because they never get to apply their strategies. In the case of criticism it works like this:

Let's say that me, you, and two of our friends are on a bowling team. Nothing really competitive -- just for fun. And then one day, one of our friends comes to us and says, "You know what gang? I am going to start getting to the alley a little early and see if I can straighten out some of my throws..."

What do you think some of our reactions might be -- even though we are all teammates? Probably, "Hey, what for? We're just having fun! Why do you have to go and get all serious on us?"

Anytime you go to improve yourself in some way... The "crew" will always be there to remind you of where you came from.

In his book On Writing, Steven King recalls his days in high school, days that would later serve as the foundation for the plot of Carrie. Steven tells of this one girl who would come to school dressed in rags – and the entire school abused her. It didn't matter that she already had nothing. Her peers wanted to take that, too! To quote directly he said, "She wore the same thing every day... you could see her shoulders trying to escape through the worn-out threads that came from wearing the same clothes to school every day."

After winter break however, this disheveled girl came back to school in a brand new, red dress!

But the "crowd" (who'd made quite a sport of her by this time) was having none of it. The ridicule got worse. The crowd was not going to let her escape this neat little box they'd worked so hard to place her in.

Of course, you know the rest. She kills everyone and gets the last laugh! Lucky for you, I've outlined advice that'll eliminate the need to kill anyone in these types of circumstances, and... *you'll still get the last laugh!*

Your-self / Their-self

You see, anytime and *every time* you try to improve yourself, you unintentionally cause others to look at themselves.

And that stings. That's just the way it is. Get used to it. And whatever you do, do not hide your efforts. Never apologize for making strides to become better as a person.

You probably have some friends or family who, if they saw you reading this book right now, would say something like, "What are you reading that for? Are you greedy or materialistic or something?"

Whenever you challenge the status quo, many of your acquaintances or friends may feel alienated. That's because you will seem like an alien to them. But YOU are not the one alienating them! They do it to themselves.

There have been a lot of people, millions of people, who could have made the world a better place, but when they met with that criticism – they slid back down into mediocrity! They make excuses along the way like, "Aww, I didn't really want it anyway."

Reason # 3-A) *Perceived* **Criticism.**

THIS IS THE MOST DEADLY OF CRITICISM! Look out for this one! Perceived criticism is more powerful than real criticism

33

because our imaginations have a tendency to run wild. Usually, perceived criticism happens in one of two ways.

You're thinking about setting a goal to do something you've never tried before... but as you dream about what it will be like to live up to your full potential, **you imagine people criticizing you behind you back** (or maybe even to your face!). Fueled with the negativity of these feelings, you don't try, or even take any action. I have three words for you: Get over it.

Or, you believe that if you do try to succeed and "Do" not, the "gang" will criticize you. Once again, get over it!

The reason my Get Over It mentality works best is because your perceived fears about what "they" will say or do are actually pretty good instincts! As you think, dream, and act upon new goals – people will always be there to criticize you!

I guarantee you that if you work in job with peers and, all the sudden after reading this book, you realize that the benefit of applying yourself will make you a *high performer* – and you start busting your hump, there is going to be somebody saying, "Hey, slow down. You're making us look at ourselves; you're making us all look bad."

Isn't that sad? But it's life.

The Crab Factor

Crabs offer a great example of this concept. Did you know that if you want to go crab hunting -- you have to put two crabs in your bucket to actually keep ANY crabs? It's true! Put just one in there... turn your back... and it's gone – outta' there!

But when you put in two crabs, something weird happens... Something miraculous... Something... HUMAN! As soon as Crab A reaches the bucket's rim and has the possibility of escape, his dear friend, Crab B, pulls Crab A back down into the bucket!

The crabs will do this to one another until finally they both give up and decided to laze in the bucket. (Then they probably go out and get a few drinks and yuck it up about the old days.) Sound like anyone you know? I know of no greater example than this Crab Factor to illustrate the nature of many people we know. Do not stand for this!

Now, there is a different group of people...

...the people up above you. Not "better" than you, but better at supporting people in their dreams than you might be. I decided to become one of those people. One of those people who, no matter what, no matter how down and out I might be... will ALWAYS say, "Good for you! Go for it! Don't slack off! Go get em!"

And here's the irony.... Here comes another dose of simplicity:

The only way to escape the "Crab Factor" is to become the kind of person who lets others climb on your shoulders to get out of their own bucket of self-limiting beliefs!

As soon as you become the person who lifts up other people, YOU instantly become "discourage-proof."

Want to get away from the idiots who keep you down – lift them up!

Reason # 4) Fear of Failure

Everything you want is...ON THE OTHER SIDE OF YOUR FEARS.

Rest assured, that any goal you have, any goal that is that is significant... encompasses fear. Period. A GOAL THAT "Do"ES NOT "Have" FEAR ATTACHED TO IT, IS NOT A GOAL... BUT AN ACTIVITY!

The fear of failure goes hand in hand with fear of criticism. Whereas with the fear of criticism, you may be gun-shy of giving something your best effort only to suffer the scrutiny of peers in the event that you fail... With the fear of failure, it's worse.

The fear of failure is about you yourself not wanting to find out that you might be inadequate.

God forbid you discover you are inadequate at something. The psychology here is that IF I NEVER FIND OUT I CAN'T "Do" SOMETHING... AT LEAST I'LL KNOW THAT I DIDNT FAIL AT IT!

Here it is again with no caps: "If I never find out I can't do something, at least I'll know that I didn't fail at it."

Simple right? And powerful too, because you know you've been there.

Now, before we go any farther, I ask you:

Can you tell me one thing you can fail at?

Name one, and by George, if I am wrong I want you to email me the thing you can fail at so that I may learn because I have not found any one thing at which one can fail.

Why do I say this? Because... As long as you can keep on trying, you simply cannot fail. "Can't" is an animal to lazy to try. There is not one thing that you can not step up to the plate for and take yet, another swing!

The fear of failure is not real but it will always be there when you start something new. And, odds are, if you still have some "music left" in you, you'll feel this way again the next time you move outside your comfort zone.

What is the best way to overcome the fear of failure? Well, that is one of the fundamental objectives of this book – to isolate, examine, and overcome this "false idea" of failing. But, let me first say this...

The fear of failure loses its power when you stop trying to make it disappear. By accepting that it's just part of "the game," it will no longer have a stranglehold on your potential. Each and every time you move outside what is regular, normal, and easy or "comfortable" for you, *the fear will always be there!*

Reason # 5) Fear of Moving Outside Their Comfort Zone

Ask anyone if they are afraid of success and you will almost always hear, "Of course not! Why would anyone be afraid of success?" Well, there are lots of reasons. Although the reasons are not legitimate or "real," the fear is present just the same. Everyone has a certain level of "success" that, no matter how 'uncomfortable" it might seem, that is VERY comfortable for them.

Whenever you think of success, the first obvious thing that will happen is change. Change causes a natural "response" which we associate with fear. But really, it is just the body preparing you for the road that you are about to travel. What exactly is this "preparing" that the body gives us?

Consider what happens when you almost have an accident while driving. You're driving along going about your daily routine. Traffic lights, turns, it all seems usual...Then, suddenly a HUGE GARBAGE TRUCK in the lane next to you starts to veer into your lane. Even though you manage to swerve around this truck, avoiding the accident, when you finally come to the next traffic light, you notice your heart is pounding...

Coupled with this, your legs feel heavy. You are now sitting in an upright position, totally alert. Totally aware. Why? There is no danger. You know you're safe. Yet still, the body doesn't know it.

All that's going on inside of you at that moment is for self-preservation. Had you really gotten into an accident, your reflexes would have been much more ready to "save you" if it were necessary. Fear, in this sense, is your friend.

It's the same with success: The unsure, insecure, and doubtful feeling that we get when moving outside our comfort zone is actually just the body's intelligence telling us that it is ready, and WILLING, to adjust to the forthcoming changes.

But, since we sometimes are not used to putting ourselves through this experience, **we mistake it for fear, and lack of confidence**. In a sense, we fool our nervous systems so much that we no longer gravitate towards change. And subsequently... success.

All along, that uncertainty we felt was nothing more than the body getting us ready for the next challenge. The feeling of fear was actually there to assist us. Who do you think will be more successful: the person fear paralyzes or the person fear PROPELS?

High-level athletes are used to this feeling and await its arrival. They think to themselves, "Yes! Here it comes! Now I am ready... BRING IT!"

It is my goal through these pages to NUDGE YOU OUT OF YOUR COMFORT ZONE REGULARLY!

Reason # 6) Self-Limiting Beliefs

Welcome to the #1 reason people haven't lived out their dreams.

Self-limiting beliefs are subtle. You may be operating based on these beliefs without actually being aware you are being bound by them! They are always "verbal" in nature, in that they creep up on us as soon as we even *think* about making our lives better.

They are like knee-jerk reactions. At one time, we actually "learned" them. But, we had to install them; otherwise, we wouldn't have them.

There is a two-step process to eliminate them. They are:

1. Identify them (or admit that you have some self-limiting beliefs).

2. Act in *spite* of them (prompt yourself to take action).

That's how they disappear. First, you come clean with yourself and admit that you have a few of them holding you back. Then, almost in an arrogant fashion, you test their validity by taking ACTION against, and in spite of them.

Samples of Self-Limiting beliefs are:

- I can't be successful because I am undereducated.
- I can't be successful because I am over educated.
- I can't be successful because I don't have a family.
- I can't be successful because I "Do" have a family.
- I can't have a family because I am not successful enough.
- I can't start to _____ until I have _____.
- This town is too big for someone like me to "make it."
- This town is too small for me to "make it."
- I am too fat.
- I am too tall.

- I am too skinny.

- Successful people don't have any friends.

- Successful people have too many friends.

Identifying YOUR OWN self-limiting beliefs.

I have found only one way to truly identify self-limiting beliefs. And, that is by using a system of self-discovery that I will teach you in this book.

You see, no one else can tell you about your self-limiting beliefs. Now, obviously, they *can* tell you, but it's my experience that the only way you can actually change and work *through them, is* by finding them *yourself.* Now, this does not mean that you can't see other people's self-limiting beliefs; you can. Someone else "telling you" or pointing fingers about your shortcomings, even if true, *does not* facilitate change. Change happens only when *you* find *your own* restraints and say to yourself, "I can't believe I have been letting this thought hold me back!"

Here's what's interesting... Discovering your personal self-limiting beliefs happens only when you *dream big dreams.* (Something *most* people are too afraid to do.)

When you go about your daily activities, just doing the regular and the mundane, it's tough to pinpoint your belief systems.

It is only when you begin to *"want something"* - that you come face to face with the mental chains holding you back.

In a later chapter, we will go through a step-by-step process that will blow you away...

You will kill two birds with one stone. We will identify your self-limiting beliefs while, at the same time, create a blueprint for your future.

You will literally see the beliefs enter your mind and you will become entertained at how simple it is to point them out and then conquer them!

Now, let's look at the final reasons people don't know these things...

Reason # 7) They don't care that a solution exists.

Apathy. Some people simply do not care about their future. They have no interest in introspection. No interest in the world. They look at life as if it is a burden. Helping these people is beyond the scope of what I know; and quite honestly, I do not care much for helping them.

I freely admit that I've never made it my objective to help those who want to destroy their lives... Rather, I want to help those people who are willing to raise their hand and say, "I want more out of life!"

Reason # 8) They Believe In "Destiny"

Now, the buck stops here.

So far, I've been pushing a little "ideology" on you. I've tried to subtly get you to agree with the concept of "all the best stuff is simple."

I've shared the "The 8 Reasons People Don't Know These Things" hoping it'll make sense to you. I've also told you how I had this "awakening of the obvious" through martial arts training.

Here's where you are going to either throw this book in the garbage or keep on reading.

People who believe in destiny – usually fail to become happy.

Right now, as you read this, there is a very large group of people out there who believe in this concept of "destiny." They go around saying and believing things like:

- "Everything happens for a reason."
- "That's just how God wants it to be"
- "What can ya' do? … such is life."
- "If it's in the Lord's will, so be it."

And, of course... the granddaddy of 'em all:

"It's just my (your, the country's, the universe's) destiny."

On the surface, it may seem that these people have a healthy perspective on life. I'll grant them this: It's certainly a better approach than the attitude of the "Why Me"-ers – which is one of total abdication of any responsibility for their results. Nonetheless, the "Destiny" believers will not make much progress either.

In fact, you're about to learn how closely the two are related.

This is where the hate mail starts pouring in…

The "Destiny"-ers will fly under the flag of "destiny" as a form of self-control. They will pretend that things don't bother them, i.e. "Don't worry; It'll get better." "Every cloud has a silver lining," etc.

At the same time, they will recognize the power of taking action. But what they fail to miss is that, *by believing that "everything happens for a reason," they are, in the same breath, saying that there is some "power" outside there – outside of themselves that controls their circumstances more authoritatively than they do.*

And that, friends, is the problem. Look, I know it sounds practically blasphemous, but think about this for a moment.

If there is something "out there" that can "override, alter, or change" your consequences, do you think you can EVER truly make an assertive effort in your life? Do you think that you'll ever know what your "best shot" or even effort, really is? No.

Why? Because every time you meet with lackluster results, you will think either consciously or subconsciously, "Oh, it's my destiny."

Get it? You can't think like that. It sounds good in theory, but is the one single factor that will have two hidden traps.

1) You will not be able to "attack" your problems full throttle. Partly because, with the "destiny model", you'll believe you actually deserve what you're getting right now. You'll believe that your best efforts will be weakened because, deep inside, you believe that "if it was meant to be" it would already "be".

Do you see how dangerous this "destiny" thinking is? It's so plain as day for me. Yet, I don't know of anyone else who has written about this. I've observed it so many times that I am shocked more people don't get it!

Many will say that my philosophy is anti-god. Quite the opposite.

In fact, if there is a god, She is certainly thrilled with people who "Do" NOT believe in this destiny stuff. This leads me to #2.

2) When you choose the destiny belief system you are in fact saying, "God, get to work!" As if the creator of this magnificent universe hasn't done enough! Not only did our creator put this universe together – but he installed a perfect system of "cause and effect" into place so that we could leave him alone, get busy, and ultimately – FIND HAPPINESS!

Pretty much everyone agrees that the complainers and the whiners have a poor perspective.

At times, even the best of us have been blinded by one or more reasons for "missing out" on life's best rewards. Not anymore, you don't. Be on the lookout for these "modes of thinking." Don't slip up and fall into their traps.

I hate to get "religious" so early in the book, and I will make only this reference to "God": Our Creator's work is largely done. He put the world together and, fortunately for us, attached the law of "cause and effect" to it, so we can navigate it effectively.

This is the best gift He could ever give. (Or "She"… who really knows?)

I'll bet you God gets upset when people bother Him with stuff like "Lord, only *You* have the power to get me out of this one."

When all along, we used our own power - the same power we're expecting Him to "give us" - to get into our woes in the first place. And that power is the *power of choice*.

The Be Do & Have Trilogy

"Vision is the art of seeing things invisible."

Jonathan Swift (1667-1745) English satirist
<u>Thoughts on Various Subjects</u>

There is a process to all achievements.

I don't know if you've ever thought about this before, but there is a 3-step process to everything that is manifest in this universe.

This process I call Be, Do, and Have. You have already used this process to create your successes as well as any of your perceived failures.

Let's first take a look at the past few hundred years of man's search for happiness, okay?

At the most primitive level, humankind's quest for happiness was largely a focus of "Have". If you "had" the best stuff, you were happy. But that philosophy rapidly became short-lived. It quickly became clear that one couldn't simply have "everything," so then we (man) focused on having better stuff than our neighbors.

As long as we could keep up with "The Jones's" (or even better, beat them), we were not necessarily "happy" but we were – "Happy-er!"

Unfortunately, even now, most of us have not transcended this *race to accumulate* to "Have."

Back then, the focus on "Have" became so powerful at times that, when one couldn't recognize the force that the "Havers" were using to *have,* people succumbed to using its next best form of manifestation: theft.

The "Have" model suggested that "He who dies with the most toys wins."

Still, happiness, and the feelings of success and fulfillment eluded those who focused solely on "Have." Sometimes we were happy when we got our hot little hands on the material good we coveted

– sometimes not. Sometimes, when we were given things (for free), we were less happy than had we earned them ourselves.

Clearly, the event of "Having," even if one could do it at will, did not by itself make you quote unquote "Happy".

To make matters more complicated, there were many people who were clearly *happy* – people who had not even a pot to piss in, nor window to... you get the idea.

Enter psychology.

Soon enough, philosophers, sages, and various masters started coming out of the woodwork.

They taught us that, "Happiness, Success, and Achievement were feelings that one en

This ideology is at work whether you recognize it or not. And, the way you think about the "order" of this process, reveals a lot about your personal philosophy, the actions you will take and, of course, the results that those actions will produce.

To illustrate this, I want you to consider something simple:

Let's say, I were to ask you to put this book down... You would probably just *do it*. But what you may not realize, is that a mental process actually occurred in order for you to do that.

First, you thought about doing it; you looked at the table to make sure there was room for it; then, you decided to take action...

Second, your brain sent a signal to control the muscles in your hand... to move your hand in a way that would place the book down;

Third, the book makes its journey toward the table and, *as long as no obstacles are present*.... it arrives, as planned, and just as you had pictured it (although subconsciously).

Sounds simple right?

Well, what if I told you that there was a way you could actually make all of your other achievements... just that easy. It can happen. **But not until you start to notice the subtleties of ALL the other similar, simple, and apparently insignificant accomplishments.**

Everything has these three elements. First you think ("Be"), then you take action ("Do"), and eventually... you get ("Have").

Let's isolate the finer points to deepen our understanding.

Be

Be, or Being-ness, refers to the state you are in before any "DO"ing happens. It encompasses your:

Thinking, Intellect, Emotions, Attitude, Feelings, Awareness, Outlook, Disposition, Confidence, Clarity, Intentions, Decisiveness, Concentration, and Consciousness.

Put another way, and perhaps more understandably, the Be is the real you. Not the *"you"* that goes on job interviews, or meets the parents, or goes to church, and so on.

Be is the part of *you,* <u>that is *you,*</u> when no one else is watching.

So then, why is this important?

It is my observation that if we focus on Be before we focus on "Do," our doing will be much more effective, more sincere, more genuine, and ultimately: more do-able too!

Do

"Do", is the part everybody likes. Why? It keeps you busy! You feel like you're doing something. It also serves as a distraction from Be, at the very least. And, because it makes us feel like we are making things happen – we tend to place a little more focus on Doing than on anything else.

For example, have you ever gotten so busy doing something that you didn't realize what direction you were headed in...? Only to find yourself saying, "Wow, what did I do that for?" or, "How did I not see that coming?"

We all have. Guess why? Not enough focus on Be.

Under the umbrella of *Do*, I am going to give you specific strategies for becoming highly skilled in all that "Do"-ing entails. For starters:

Planning, Organizing, Prioritizing, Decision Making, Discipline, Motivating Yourself, Interacting with Others, Dealing with People and Problems, Self-Management... and pretty much anything else that requires action!

Doing is where the rubber meets the road. Once the inner work of Be has been done, you'll find you have so much enthusiasm that it prompts you to take action. It's like you're soaking in so much Be that you can't contain yourself... you just have to get moving -- but in a deliberate direction. See, that's the key. Not moving just for the sake of moving, which often time leads to disaster, but moving in a direction that you intend to go.

Superior Methods of Doing

Remember that phrase, "There's more than one way to skin a cat?" Hogwash.

We are now in the new millennium. We have evolved. There *are* better ways of doing certain things. My objective is to clue you in on some more efficient ways of - *doing your doing!*

We must master this "execution phase" so that we can enjoy the "Have". Trying to focus on just "Do" - with no deliberate strategy - is like climbing the wrong mountain: you get to the top and say, "This sucks!"

Follow the simple insights of the "Do" section of this book and you can't go wrong. You will wake up each day with an agenda of how you want to live, and how you'll go about doing it. Yes, your discipline will improve, too. Yes, people may say, "Hey, what's gotten into you lately?"

You will find yourself putting you head down on the pillow at night knowing that tomorrow has a plan. And, more importantly, you feel good about it.

Doing works best after you've adopting the correct state of being... then clarifying exactly what actions you need to take, taking out a pen and writing them down, and <u>then</u> *taking those intended actions!*

46

Have

Now, here's the tough part... You decide you want more out of life. You buy this book. You get motivated. You discover that success is simple, but not easy. You decide to make some decisions. You make those decisions. You clarify what you want. You take action...

But then, you don't get what you want so easily.

You've done it all. You did the Be part - you became genuine; you did the inner work. You got up off your knowledge (technical word for butt) and went out in the world to stake your claim. But then you discover, *it isn't all happening so quickly.*

Instead of Be, Do, & Have... Now it seems more like Be, Do, ...and finally – Have!

It seems to take forever.

What's the solution? Perseverance.

You see, everyone at one time or another has been a great starter but a poor finisher.

We are going to conquer that quitting reflex. You're going to learn how to revamp your outlook, your state of *being* about the persistence obstacle.

Fact is. You have, at one time, amazed yourself with a great start. But then you got sidetracked. I will teach you that:

PERSERVERENCE IS A STATE OF MIND. (Not a feeling!) PERSERVERANCE IS A VERB... NOT A NOUN.

You will literally learn how to *reprogram yourself* so that any goal you have will manifest if you follow the simple insights. Again, do not overlook this factor just because it is simple.

PERSERVERENCE IS A STATE OF MIND. It is a SPIRIT that you can literally *catch* by doing the *inner work.*

47

Let's face it. Even though you may not have been a big dreamer in the past... and even if the goals you have seem small... one fact remains:

All of your unfinished goals are unfinished due to lack of PERSERVERANCE - not lack of intelligence, lack of know-how, or lack of ambition.

Trust me, ambition and smarts are VERY OVER-RATED when compared to ACTION and PERSERVERANCE!

Once you start making these shifts in your thinking, you may get embarrassed when you discover how much of a quitter you've been in the past.

In addition, there are some other characteristics that you need to develop to master this gap between the doing and the having. They include:

- ✓ Persistence
- ✓ Focus
- ✓ Perseverance
- ✓ Positive Mental Attitude
- ✓ Visualization
- ✓ Friendships
- ✓ Your Outlook on Time
- ✓ Consistency
- ✓ Composure
- ✓ Mental Fortitude

All of these skills are within your reach now and available for you to attain.

Just keep reading and you'll be internalizing them already.

Gradually... through reading and doing... you will open yourself to more and more possibilities. You will be able to pinpoint where your quit-point is, BREAK THROUGH IT and MOVE PAST IT!

Imagine if you had all the skills you now possess plus the perseverance of say, Greg Lamond - who rode for 23 days on his bicycle to win the Tour de France. Wouldn't it be great to "borrow" the mind-set, and the *persistence level* of someone who seems to have the "bulldogged" persistence necessary to succeed? Well, you can!

Listen, if I wanted to change a light bulb and I couldn't reach it, couldn't I get a ladder or some other tool to make the job easier? Of course. So it is with the goals you set. You can learn to use perseverance as a tool. Exactly like a ladder.

Here's Why Be, Do, and Have Is Considered a "Trilogy"

<u>Webster's Dictionary</u> defines a trilogy as: *"a series of three dramas which, although each of them is in one sense complete, have a close mutual relation, and form one historical and poetical picture."*

The balance of these three areas is crucial for achieving and maintaining long-term success and peace of mind. Imagine if someone focused only on "Be." Meaning that their primary focus is mainly on doing just the "inner work" of being genuine, sincere, and mindful in their ways. Let's say, in addition to that, they also have the "Have" part mastered; they can persist and have strength during tough moments, etc.

What would happen if they lacked the "Do" part?

Now, what you've got is high-performing person who just can't perform!

I liken these people to those who spend years in a cave trying to become enlightened... only to wake up one day and realize they didn't do anything with their wisdom. This is similar to the person who's always going to school – learning, and learning, and learning, but never establishes a career. What a waste right?

Now, imagine a person who has high-octane action! They can START ANYTHING... Their motto is: "FIRE, AIM, READY." These folks are always busy... talking on their cell phones, making plans, going out, doing stuff. They may seem like shakers and movers – but if you look closer, you'll see a series of one burned bridge after another.

Focusing only on "Do", the action part, these folks may find themselves in the wrong relationships, working with the wrong firm, selecting lousy mentors, etc. And, to make matters worse – they have TONS of PERSERVERENCE! Ahgg! Such a waste!

They never focus on "Be", but keep sticking to a plan that they damn well know... isn't going to work. And, hence, they continue getting the same results. Instead of having 10 years experience, they have one year's experience TEN TIMES.

Steven Covey, author of the <u>Seven-Habits of Highly Effective People</u> calls this, "climbing the ladder to success... only to realize it's leaning on the wrong wall."

Next, and more common, is the person who's aware of the need for the "inner work" and even have the "action" part down pat, too. But, because they lack wisdom of the "Have" dynamics... the persistence... they continuously "pull the plug" too soon! They quit.

Why? Because they lack the wisdom of the process of "Have."

So, what's the secret?

Balance.

I'll say another thing about the balance of this trilogy: if you are going to err, err with the "Do" part! That way at least, you'll be making some progress that is measurable – even if it's in the wrong direction.

What Stands Between You and Your Goals?

If your personal order of "Be, Do, and Have" is mixed up, or worse – *backwards* – you'll find it tough to achieve a lasting level of success and happiness. Yet, many people fail to recognize that life's speed bumps are actually a result of a *dis-order* of Be, Do, and Have. These people have strong opinions about what stands between them and their goals. Usually, these opinions are inaccurate.

First, people will spend hours trying to defend the idea that "success" is defined in many different ways.

Instead of talking about the principles of success, they'd rather discuss that success, like beauty, is in the eye of the beholder.

I am often left with nothing else to say but, "Well then, what do you think stands in between you and your goals?"

A majority of people will say that their deficiency stems from some sort of action they need to take (Do).

Others will say they need to *get something* before they accomplish their goals (Have). They feel that everything would happen for them if they only had *this thing* or *that thing*. They are basically saying the answer is external, i.e. beyond them.

Remember these people? The largest crowd I mentioned earlier... the bunch I've titled "The Destiny-ers?"

The destiny-ers think they'll just wake up one day and it (success) will be handed to them.

Lastly, there is a more responsible group. Its members believe they are exactly where they are supposed to be based on the decisions they've made... and the actions they've taken in the past. These people have learned that they need to work on the inside stuff. Also, they recognize that *action*, though essential, is most effective when it stems as a direct result of one's inside condition (Be).

When we realize that the things standing between us and our goals are qualities of *character*, our circumstances begins to change. It is not actually life that changes – it's *us* that changes. Life simply obeys.

When people have the order of Be, Do, and Have mixed up (knowingly or not), they begin to experience poor results... everywhere.

Ask someone, "What do you believe stands between you and your goals?" and listen to the answer. The answers that you'll get are much like "tells" in gambling. Their answers reveal their own personal "order" of Be, Do, and Have.

Take a moment and observe the diagram below. See if you can do the "mental math" of what might happen when you are *out of order.*

The Different Possibilities of the "Order"

1.) Do Have Be

2.) Have Do Be

3.) Be Have Do

4.) Do Be Have

5.) Have Be Do

6.) Be Do Have

Your ability to succeed depends on
how you "see" the order of be, do, and have.

The Cycle of Accomplishment

There Is a Bridge to Your Success

In between where you stand right now – and where you want to go, there is a "bridge." We are all on this imaginary bridge whether we realize it or not. Usually, people simply focus on what's on the other side of the bridge. Or, better put, they focus on how far away they are from arriving at the other side of the bridge. Others, may remain fixated on their present position. They are stuck in the "now," also feeling frustrated.

What's more important, however, are the proverbial "mile-markers" we encounter while *on* this bridge of ours. We'll get to this in just a second. First, let's look at this bridge of ours.

We are all on a bridge...

but, where are we going?

On the left is a person. You. This represents where you are right now. The other side, where the question mark is, represents... nothing. Whenever your life looks like this, and sometimes it will, you'll feel confused, indifferent, and maybe even depressed. It's just how we humans are. We function best when we are working towards something.

On the other side, hopefully, is a deliberate creation of where you want to go.

You Must Identify a
Set Definite Objective

GOAL

The Bridge itself is made up of character qualities. When you possess all the character traits necessary for the journey, your success in crossing is inevitable, right? Wrong!

There is one more crucial element involved. What is this bridge crossing over? In other words, what's underneath the bridge?

Your "Bridge" Spans TIME

Time. The proverbial water is time. The things that separate you from ALL OF YOUR DREAMS are qualities of character, intrinsic in nature. Once you know where you want to go, and possess the qualities that ensure your goals' accomplishment, the only thing that remains a factor is the time which the bridge spans.

Think about this illustration for a moment. Isn't it simple, and in the same sense powerful?

You, right now, are crossing a bridge. Now, most people do not even know where the bridge leads (or could care less, yikes!). Worse, it would not occur to these same people either, that they desperately need more than just two legs and a willingness to "give it a shot" to successfully cross to the other side. They need to understand the Time concept as well.

It could be said that the Be part of the bridge is you and your intentions... your destination firmly in mind. Then, the character qualities are developed by continually looking at yourself as you begin to cross, that's the "Do" segment. Now, all that's left is dealing with the stuff underneath the bridge, time. Remember from the last chapter the importance of the "Have" part? This is the part of the trilogy that reveals your persistence!

54

See how simple it is when you look at your life as a journey? On the next page, I am going to show you the 4 bridges people are most commonly crossing. I call these bridges: LIFE CATEGORIES. This, like all of the principles in this book, is simple in nature and will make a lot of sense to you.

The Four Life Categories

1.   I don't know what I want.

Welcome to the world's largest category of people! Hard to believe, with all the options available in the free world, that so many people do not know what they want out of life, isn't it?

But, that's part of the problem. You see, with so many choices it is sometimes hard to make up our minds. How do we define exactly what we want? Remember GI Joe? (That depends on your age, I suppose.) Well, GI Joe used to say that, "Knowing is half the battle;" and he was correct! It is sometimes the WHOLE battle. When you narrow down your options, you get clarity.

Most people that are unhappy in life "Do" NOT KNOW WHAT THEY WANT. And that my friends -- is it. Don't give me this baloney about a tough childhood, chemical imbalances, and spiritual emptiness.

Think I'm wrong? Try this next time you meet someone who seems miserable, depressed, and confused... You know the type, the ones who are always talking about what they lack and about how life's not fair?

Well, next time you're around one of them, take that person swimming and then shove his or her head under water! Hold it there for a few seconds and watch how excited this person gets about living... instantaneously! Why? Well, it's not because they think they'll drown. No, it's because there is only one option, one want... one burning desire: AIR! They become focused; they put their petty problems on the back burner... and they become really focused on their newfound goal of breathing.

See? Take away options and minds become focused. Now, I know the drowning thing may be a little extreme but I think you get the point.

People who do not, no... let me rephrase that, PEOPLE WHO "Have" NOT DECIDED what they want, will *never* become happy.

The first step, which you will learn how to do with pinpoint accuracy is to decide what you want.

2.   I know what I want (but don't know how to get it).

These people know exactly what they want, but aren't quite sure about how to get there, or what it would take to cross that bridge to success. Although the evidence they need is all around them, via people who have already done what they want to do, these people still don't achieve their dreams.

They can't muster the courage to take that first step or have no idea where to begin. Sometimes, they think its luck. Or worse, they read one of my competitors' self-improvement books and believe that all they have to do is "talk to themselves in a nice way" or "use the law of detachment and let success come to them." What the *&^%!?! Sorry, gang. No touchy-feely, morphine verbiage in this book. You can create all the mental image pictures you want... You can become the Museum of Modern Art or the Louvre inside your own head, but if you don't *act on a plan*, forget it. No plan = you stay put... eternally.

3. I know how to get what I want (but for some reason... I still never get it).

You could actually call this category, "I *think* I know how to get what I want." At least these people are taking massive action! They have an idea of what they want. They have ambition. They have a plan... but, for some strange reason, they just never get their goals accomplished.

Many times, this is because these people are trying to pursue someone else's goals. Or they believe that "If I just help someone else get what they want, I'll get what I want, too." There is one motivational master who has made this his entire theme! Where I do agree that it is good to help other people reach their goals, I also know that they may attain their goals with your assistance and... say, "Thank you very much, good bye."

So, I would not build my plan around the sole purpose of helping other people get what they want. It is a BIG PART of getting what you want but, remember, there are plenty of people, organizations, and ideas that are built on the philosophy of volunteerism. The only real instances in which this mode of operation succeeds are seen in non-profit organizations. And you can donate all the time you want to those causes… once you're begun living for your own.

The other problem with this category is inherent; it is that people are following a plan that just flat-out – is not going to work for them - though someone has convinced them otherwise.

4. I know what I want; I know how to get it; I ALWAYS get it (but I still ain't happy!).

Moving up higher on the human achievement chain are these folks.

Now, I know what you are thinking: "How can a person who knows what he wants, knows how to get what he wants, goes after what he wants, and successfully gets what he wants... be considered "more higher up" on the human achievement chain than someone who has nothing but is happy?

My response to you is this: Number one... this person is not happy. They may "interview" really well. They may put on the face mask of contentment and talk the earthy rhetoric of "I am a spiritual being having a human experience." Bullcrap -- let me tell you something -- they are not happy.

It is impossible. If you do not know what you want and are not achieving anything with your life, you are a lot less happy than the person who is accomplishing much, but who forgets to smell the roses along the way.

My friend Andrew Wood said it best: "I have been broke and unhappy, and I have been wealthy and unhappy... and believe me, it's a lot better being wealthy and unhappy."

I will give you another illustration to help you to understand why the person who is achieving but is miserable is, pound for pound, in a better position to turn things around than his meditating, anti-capitalist counterpart.

I have another friend. He is a personal trainer. He's also broke. He lives from one crisis to another. There's always more month at the end of the money, and he acts as if it's no big deal... because he has his health. I've heard him say on countless occasions, "Man, I see all these high-performing, top executives who come to ME to get in shape. I wouldn't trade places with them for a million dollars!"

My friend does not have to worry; no one, poor health or well, would trade places with such an unstable person. Listen, I am in pretty good shape at the time of writing this book. And I have been in stellar condition in the past: six-pack abs, 45 beats-per-minute rest pulse, 7% body fat, etc. And let me tell you something: IT IS WAY HARDER TO DESIGN AND *LIVE* A LIFE FULL OF MEANINGFUL GOALS, THAN IT IS TO GET, AND STAY, IN SHAPE!

When you look at the two people, all the second guy has to do is get healthy, which could take weeks, months, possibly years depending how bad he "let himself go," but... The first guy has to discover all the other stuff -- AND I ALREADY KNOW THAT... THIS CAN TAKE YEARS... just to begin with.

Am I saying, "forget your health -- focus on your career?" NO! Am I saying, "forget your career, spend time with family, get a less stressful job, and try to "get by"? NO! All I am saying is don't you dare feel that you are allowed to sit on your ass and watch life go by, never knowing what you are truly capable of, and expect to be successful. Many men and women "Have" BOTH THE HEALTH & THE WEALTH!

In fact, your goal in learning these concepts is aiming at having it all! And the approach is BALANCE!

PART
TWO: BE

Being has to do with your attitude. Your attitude is the real you. Some people would have you believe that the real you goes deeper than the attitude, and that's fine. However, your attitude about life stems directly from who you really are as a person and from no other place. In this section, I will share with you the attitudes that you can use to enhance your quality of being-ness.

The Attitude of Be

"You do not get what you want... You get what you are."

~ Scott Palangi, Martial Arts Master, Author

We know that the fundamental difference between those who achieve their desires and those who wander around saying, "Boy, are they lucky"-- is attitude – or, more correctly, their state of *being-ness.*

Whatever attitude you assert the most will dictate your state of being-ness.

In this section you will learn the attitudes of great masters, high achievers, and sages. If you were to read only one part of this book and never return to it, let it be this one.

Be is the key.

Some of the attitudes I will teach you to adopt may not "fit through your mental window." That's okay. Just find something with which you can identify or believe. Then, go back and see if some of the other insights make sense or "ring true" for you.

There are 29 concepts in all that will help you adopt the mindset necessary for high achievement. Try these on. Your life will begin to change immediately. Even if you are doing the wrong stuff to achieve your goals at present, don't worry. The state of being-ness you are about to adopt is going to transport you into a different category of being.

The Universe Is Just

"You Always Get the Right Results."

Keith Hafner, Karate Master

Fortunately, I learned this one early on. Successful people know that they are always getting the right results.

Do NOT CONFUSE THIS with "they always get what they want." What it means is that these people have a clear understanding that for every action they make, there is a consequence. Further, they know and accept responsibility for their successes and their lack thereof.

They do not call it LUCK when something fortunate happens. They do not call it misfortune when something apparently UNLUCKY happens to them. If they are on a way to a big important meeting and they get a flat tire and arrive late, they do not enter the room telling about how it wasn't their fault. They simply say, "I left the house too late" because that is the truth. They know that if the meeting was THAT important they would have planned accordingly -- allowing enough time for a flat, spilled coffee on a white shirt, a car-jacking, etc. I think you get it.

They simply resist the urge to shift blame EVEN WHEN SOMETHING ISN'T THEIR FAULT!

And THAT, friends, is tough to do.

Now there is a whole group of people who would have you believe otherwise. They include: your mother (mothers never think it's their child's fault -- we'll let them slide!), your spouse (people who love us often times will make allowances for when we blow it, too), and your friends -- but not all of them. (Some of them are secretly relieved or even glad when you tell them of some misfortune.) But the A-listers of this group are the so-called experts in human psychology. They hate to let any patient think that something could be their fault.

But "Do"NT YOU be that nice to yourself. "Do"NT YOU make excuses for your shortcomings. Be tough on yourself.

63

Successful people take total responsibility for their results.

Successful people hold the opinion that their results could have taken them nowhere else but where they are now.

They love it because they know that the universe rewards action, and they know that they alone have the power to change it. Notice how this has to do with *attitude,* the Be-ing, and not actual doing.

The cool part about taking responsibility for your results is this: Most psychologists would teach you that you shouldn't blame yourself but, in actuality, by blaming yourself (and taking responsibility) for your circumstances, you are in the same breath saying that:

YOU ARE ALSO THE ONE WHO CAN CHANGE THOSE CIRCUMSTANCES.

You might want to read that sentence again! It sounds simple... but it is powerful! Consider the reverse... If you blame someone else for your circumstances, you are saying that you have no control. This means that you are forever bound by the grips of someone else or something outside of yourself...a "Destiny-er."

So, even though it may be a bitter pill to swallow, take the blame for your situations because you'll soon be taking the credit for the new set of situations that will be much more desirable.

Ever hear anybody say this, "I tried, and I tried, and I tried, but it just didn't work!" What's going on there? They are doing the wrong stuff! And worse, they are Be-ing the wrong way. Blame and self-pity are not effective ways to set the stage for the state of Be that will produce your best self!

All the results you are getting in your life are, indeed, the Right Results. They may not have been the results you were looking for, but they were the right results for the actions you took.

There Are Only TWO Types of People

"You see things; and you say, "Why?" But I dream things that never were; and I say, "Why not?"

George Bernard Shaw (1856-1950), <u>Back to Methuselah,</u>
<u>author, playwright</u>

People may come in all shapes and sizes. America may be a melting pot of different cultures. Yet, there are only two types of people, behaviorally speaking that is. Sometimes, these two types of people are not aware of their own state of being-ness. That's why you have to judge which type they are (and YOU are) based on one thing.... their actions!

Nothing into something.

Something into nothing.

All people, the ones in your life, the ones you will meet, and the ones you work with right now... are either in the habit of turning nothing into something OR something into nothing.

This can be a fun game to play with your kids (a perfect example of nothing into something!) if you have any. Drive around town and teach the concept of nothing into something. "Hey Johnny, there's a man digging a hole. He's getting ready to construct a building. What category does he fall into? Well, if he keeps at it, we will drive past here and see a building someday, right?"

"Now, look at that, Johnny. There's a person hanging out in front of a convenience store talking to his buddies, and drinking some beers. Which person is he? If HE keeps it up, we will drive past here too someday, and the store will be out of business because this dreg of the earth scared away all the customers!"

Something into nothing.

Generally speaking, we're born into the habit of turning something into nothing. We eat; we consume; we collect a pay check; and then destroy our bodies with junk food and other substances as we progress into adulthood. We put junk into our minds as well, rendering them closer to nothing as well. less than they were a month ago, a week ago.

This is what I call the parasitic model of life. Sadly, there are too many whose very existence is based on this modus operandi. Just take a look around your workplace. More often than not, big corporations are constantly in a state of hiring and firing and, of course, finding out WHO IS "Do"ING MORE OF ONE THAN THE OTHER. Want to know what Chapter 11 bankruptcy is? More people on the team turning something into nothing rather than the reverse!

Nothing into something.

The people in this category are more rare. They have the ability to take something, or nothing for that matter, and actually make it better! And, the best part is they do it with more Be than with "Do". In fact, the doing that they contribute to make things better STEMS FROM THE BeING THAT THEY ARE BeING!

You know these types, too. Often, they are the ones that no one can stand. The ones who are always trying to find a better way of doing things, always looking for ways to improve what may not even seem to be broken. Some of them may even be salaried employees... but by looking at their actions, you'd swear you own the place!

These are the people who have learned that having a high personal standard in whatever you do gives you more than just a chance for advancement; it gives you a chance to feel capable of becoming something great. The "take-nothing-turn-it-into-something" crowd, give it that little extra: they leave everything they come into contact with a little better.

What's in it for me?

In advertising, they say that everyone is tuned into WIIFM. That's an acronym for "What's in it for me?" This may be true in marketing, but doesn't work so well for becoming successful.

If people know you are tuned in to WIIFM, you would do well to change your viewpoint or to fool them into thinking you are tuned into them.

It's okay for everyone else to be tuned into that station but for you to get ahead, you must put others before you at times. Always look for ways to do a little extra while you're at work. You'll be recognized for it but, more importantly, you will give yourself recognition.

That's Not-My-Job!

The old "That's not my job" mindset is another one to watch out for. Make sure you do not have this anywhere in your vernacular if you intend on being successful. It is just not becoming of a high-achiever.

I was at a local Starbuck's grabbing a coffee during the writing of this book and started listening to a group of people. I was subtly eavesdropping on these corporate types, who were chatting away about some work-related stuff, when I heard a guy say "I told him that's not my job!" in a loud and obnoxious voice. It was right then that I resolved never to say stuff like that. It sounded so wimpy, too. Try it. Say aloud right now, "That's not my job." Doesn't it just sound like something you'd expect some oh-poor-me person to say? And your whiny, cry-baby opinion would be? You get my point.

Which category do you fall into most often?

An important question to ask yourself is, "Which person am I being right now?" Do this every so often. Stop and ask yourself, "Am I being the person who creates or takes away?"

Successful people know that they are cheating themselves out of an opportunity to grow, to Be-come better, if they do not apply themselves at every opportunity

You cheat yourself out of an opportunity to grow.

Every single moment you are awake, you are either doing something to enhance or take away from your work on Be-coming more. If you look at any "bad day" you've ever had, I promise you'll find it's because you didn't give it 100%.

And if you are to "Do" more and "Have" more, accept the fact that you must BeCOME more! Know that you do not become more by doing and having more, you become more by moving outside your natural comfort zones and your lazy tendencies.

Your Better Self

"The elevator to success is out of order. You'll have to use the stairs... one step at a time." ~ Joe Girard

Every single day of your life, you have a choice. That choice is: Will I assert my "better self" or my "usual self"? This is one of the fundamental principles of Be, Do, and Have. Your better self is cultivated during this "inner work" phase of being.

Use all of your moments to exercise your abilities to Be-come more. Instead of using the escalator or elevator, take the stairs! Stop looking for the best parking spot, too! You'll get some more exercise, strengthen your character, and feel like a winner just by taking these simple steps!

Opportunities to Be-come more are just about every where. You don't even have to look for them. In fact, most people do just the opposite. They look for opportunities to do less. Go anywhere and it won't take you long to find someone doing a little bit less. Trying to "get-by" by the skin of their teeth. You? Develop the mindset that you will take the stairs.

Most people look at their job as punishment for what they have chosen to do.

Take to your job, your career, or your business in a way that makes you more of an asset to yourself and the company. So many people think that by shirking their work, showing up late, or by sleeping on the job, that somehow they "got ahead" of the game. That's ridiculous! You're much worse off personally if you mope about on the job than if you are trying your best. The day will go by very slowly for the mopers. They will feel like saps and, when it comes time to really get it into gear, they won't have it in them because they will not be in the habit of excellence.

Ok, so I'll get a raise right?

Right about now is when someone will chime in with, "Plus, hey, you might get a raise too, right Scott?" No, wrong… idiot. The real raise is in your own self-esteem and the satisfaction you feel in knowing that you are not a sap, a taker. If the raise happens, great. If it doesn't, oh well! That's the best way to look at it.

Remember, the real reward comes not from what you "get" by applying yourself more. It is an intrinsic reward; it comes from within. It's not just that people will take notice of you. You are doing it for you. I call this putting your STAMP on it.

Leave your stamp wherever you go. It can be making the place a little tidier when you leave. It could be listening to someone a little longer even if you're praying to yourself that they'd just shut up. Just always strive to try your personal best and you will jump ahead in your life.

"I don't work hard here 'cause this isn't going to be my real job!" (Sudden discipline, yeah ok!)

Restaurant work can be some of the hardest work out there. Waiting tables is something everyone should have try at least once in their life. The experience of working for tips does something to your psyche that just sort of sets you apart from the herd. You learn that if you don't produce quality work, and create meaningful experiences for others… YOU "Do" NOT EAT!

Many of the men and women working and slaving away in restaurants today, however, have no idea how valuable this experience really is. I worked in a restaurant as a dishwasher years ago and remember some young ladies talking about how this "wasn't their real job." There is danger in BeING like that.

People who often use "this isn't my real job" and "I am not going to work so hard here, because this isn't my career" are in for a rude awakening. You see, every time you take this approach you are cheating yourself of an opportunity to Be-come more.

Do you really think that a person can work half-assed at the job they deem as "not my real career" and then make the jump to high-performance overnight when an opportunity presents itself? Puh-lease. And even if they could, wouldn't they be in a better position if, all along, they had practiced the HABIT OF EXCELLENCE?! Of course.

People who view everything they do, including their job, as an opportunity to see themselves for who they really are, will always be the ones receiving more and more opportunities for success. Meanwhile, others are calling them "lucky."

Using Your Mind To Be

"Man is what he believes."

Anton Chekhov (1860-1904), Russian writer

You may have heard this about success: It's not what you get when you accomplish your goal, it's what you become. Still, some other authors have put it in a more sentimental way: "It's not the destination that counts, but the journey." Both of these are terrific examples of why you should focus on the Be aspect. My contention, however, is that they sort of sound like afterthoughts, don't they? Like, "Hey, just in case you don't reach your destination, at least you tried!" I don't know about you but, to me, that's not too empowering at all.

I would rather tell you straight up, "The journey IS the goal!"

Seriously though, one of my mentors and a hugely successful speaker, is a gentleman by the name of Jim Rohn. Jim says, "Probably the biggest advantage of setting a goal to become a millionaire is not what you get, BUT WHAT YOU BeCOME!"

Just imagine what kind of discipline it will require to achieve that goal. Imagine the kind of thought processes you will learn to master. Just think about the type of communicator you'll need to become in order to sustain that kind of success! It's awesome!

My martial arts master pounded this philosophy into our heads, too. Whenever one of us younger students was focusing too much on the end result of getting to black belt instead of the PROCESS that MAKES someone a BLACK BELT, he would take off his own worn and tattered black belt from like 1845 and make one of us sniveling green belts *wear* it.

That's right. He would have one of us, me for example, take off my belt, put on his black belt, and say to the class, "Now then, is Scott a Black Belt?" Everyone would shout in unison, "No, Sir!"

He would say, "What do you mean, he's not a black belt? It's right there around his waist. I can see it with my own two eyes!" Then, of course, he would go into a dissertation about how just because I had the belt I STLL LACKED THE EXPERIENCE that makes the belt so revered.

Mr. Miyagi, a name which may sound familiar to you, also made quite a spectacle of the process being more important than the product. If you remember the movie, "The Karate Kid," young Daniel asks Mr. Miyagi what belt he has. Miyagi responds expressionlessly in a monotone voice, "JC Penny... $3.95."

The Lotto vs. Labor

I once had a friend who really didn't buy into this whole philosophy of "You get out what you put in." He thought that one's level of success and happiness in life came from luck, or the stars or what have you.

He felt that that if one person had won a million dollars from the lotto and another person, from hard labor -- they were essentially the same.

I couldn't wrap my mind around his way of thinking. Maybe it's because I was brought up doing the martial arts, which teach you on the physical, mental, and even on the cellular level that you Become different when you discipline yourself.

This guy really thought that, if he had a million dollars from busting his ass for say, ten years and saved his pennies, watched his spending habits, and didn't eat out so much -- And I, instead, played the lotto every day for ten years and finally won... He thought we would be the same, that we would be equals. This just does not compute.

The Power

"Whatever you focus upon – grows."

~ Unknown

There is a power that successful people have harnessed, and which they use to mold their life. The funny thing is… unsuccessful people are using the power, too. The *difference* is unsuccessful people use this power the wrong way.

When you adhere to this principle wisely, intelligently, and most of all deliberately, there can be no uncertainty as to the outcome of any endeavor; there is no limit to your possibilities.

The power we use to create our lives is often rejected by people, because they cannot see it, hear it, explain it, or touch it. Because of this stubbornness or perhaps closed-mindedness, some people dismiss this premise as self-help nonsense to be saved for the losers of life. Yet, these are the very same people who are using this power everyday! Everyone is using it. It is so simple to see - especially when you are living a life in which you don't like the results you are getting and then you change something, and Wham! Suddenly, it hits you and you never second guess yourself or this power again.

Interestingly enough, these people don't question the power of electricity, yet they believe in it, and use it everyday. I did not invent these mental laws, nor did I discover them. I merely distilled them into easy-to-understand concepts that would work for you long before you give up on them - then you believe in them for the rest of your life.

Consider man. He did not invent electricity, he discovered it. Before he discovered it, this great force was lying dormant throughout the universe. We first had to discover the law, the principle, before we put it to use for our advantage. So, it is the goal of this book that you discover the power that you have been using to create your life. Once you are aware of its existence, you will respect it. You will start to look at your life differently and the lives of people you know differently. Look at the quality of life in others around you and you'll find that the quality of each life is in direct proportion to the quality of their *thoughts*.

The best part is, once you realize this formula for success you don't need to be reminded of it. Just like when you learned math. For example, if you wanted to get the square footage of the room you now occupy, you would add up one side, add up the other side, and then multiply. That's the formula for that problem. It is the same with your goals. You follow a formula, and it works. People try to make it harder than it really needs to be. As if success was supposed to be more intricate than just following a formula. Nope. Yet some new sage comes out with innovative software, or new time-management tools, or goal setting binders that are supposed to transform us from the same lazy person we were into a… lazy person with a new leather binder. I know one millionaire who writes his To Do list on napkins and pens phone numbers on his hand! (Probably more than one of you out there is wondering, "Hmm… does he use a pen or a magic marker… a cocktail napkin or a dinner napkin.")

It seems that many "masters" of the martial arts have used this power (many unknowingly!) to create desired results in their own lives. This is one of the reasons that masters of the martial arts were revered in their villages back in the days of old. It was not for their physical prowess - but rather, for a sense of wisdom they possessed. These masters appeared to have almost magical powers that common people seemed to lack. Two powers specifically:

The ability to attract that which they desired. (The ability to manifest)

The ability to remain calm during the face of setback. (Indomitable Spirit).

I once asked one of my masters, after getting to know him pretty well, "Sir, why do they call you guys masters, anyway?" His reply was startling. After hearing his reply, I started to look at martial arts in a whole new way. He said, "The world calls me a master. And so I am, but only in the sense that I have learned how to master circumstances in my life. *I have only developed the powers that abide in all of us.*" Hmm, I wondered, and asked, "Could you explain that to me, Sir? I promise I will pay attention."

He said, "Consider the Kata (a pre-arranged set of moves practiced to improve one's skills). People say that martial arts builds confidence, personal discipline, and great self-control from its practice. Some scientist, psychologists, and therapists wonder why... It is so obvious -- and that's why people miss it. When you begin martial arts training, you come to grips with where you stand immediately. Not because you are a white belt - but because you realize that you were born into this world as a set of genetics to deal with... and a brain."

"You then discover," he continued, "that through practice, the moves are getting better. *You* are the one making the moves better. And you immediately realize that you and you alone are responsible for this improvement. But what's even more important is that you also realize that you are responsible for *all* the results in your life. And, when this happens, your whole attitude about life improves." I can tell you that your attitude will improve with regard to 4 things in particular:

- Time
- Problems
- Progress
- Results

This is why people are so amazed at how quickly training in the martial arts can improve the attitude in children as young as age five. They just start to act in better and in more joyful ways. People may think it's because the kids are learning "how to defend themselves." In essence, they are only learning how to defend themselves against the real threats we all face, such as mediocrity, apathy, no sense of mission, etc. For sure, the only reason martial arts really helps people, besides providing a great workout for body and mind, is that the practitioner is learning how to take nothing (limited flexibility, concentration, coordination, strength) and turn it into *something*! Do you see?

74

So, you may ask, "Why does karate do this better than any other activity?" Look at baseball, golf, or any other conventional sport or activity. Commonly, if you have limited skills in these activities, you go and look for a quick-fix, a special golf club or swing developer, or an electronic analysis of what's wrong with your pitch, or wear this, or take this pill to run faster, jump higher, etc. Conversely, in the martial arts, we expect you to screw up a little; in fact, we encourage it. We encourage people not to shun the hard times but, instead, to take responsibility and deliberately assume an attitude of self-reliance that transforms one's life into something of a miracle.

You may be wondering at this point, "If this is true, why don't all our wishes or thoughts miraculously appear then?" Well, many of them do but, because of our lack of awareness, because of our ignorance of universal law, they may pass unnoticed. Then again, some don't manifest at all.

A Deeper Understanding

"Any picture held firmly in mind is bound to come forth."

~ Unknown

The consciousness or a fixed picture held in mind of anything, any condition, any circumstance is the actual thing itself. What you experience through your five senses as "real" is nothing more than the mental out-picture. It is the same as the artist who puts mental image pictures upon a canvas. The artist's hand is merely the instrument through which the mind expresses itself; the artist's hand is under the guidance and direction of the mind.

I wish I were able to more clearly explain, so that you could easily understand, the process by which a picture in mind becomes objectified, but it would require hours just to make an effort in this direction, and then I might only confuse you. Fortunately, one does not need to understand the concept before they can utilize it any more than it is necessary to understand the law by which the sun's rays are transmitted to enjoy them.

Successful People Think Differently

The main difference between successful people and non-successful people is that successful people think much differently and they think much differently about a lot.

Most people think that successful people just "do different stuff" and they definitely do "do" different stuff. And they definitely enjoy a much different lifestyle, but the things they enjoy are direct results of the way they *think*.

Successful people think differently with regard to just about everything. They think differently about people. They think differently about time. They think and feel differently about money. They think and feel differently about friendships, about contribution... all of it.

Here's a funny thing to consider: if you are to ask one of your friends what they would ask Michael Jordan if they ever had a chance to have lunch with him, you would probably get the most absurd responses. I know people that would come up with some pretty ridiculous things, such as "What's your favorite brand of shoes?" or "So, do you think that Ben Affleck and J. Lo. will get married?"

What they really should be asking are things like, "What sorts of things do you think about when the going gets tough and you're down by 50 points?" Asking questions like these will give you a lot of insight into the minds of successful people.

If you ever get the chance to spend quality time with a high-achiever, be sure and make your first question, "What sort of books do you read?" Follow up with, "When everybody else is going out to party, how do you stay focused?"

When you ask questions like these, two things will happen: The first is you will actually learn something. The second thing is you may even get an invite to join them again the future!

Now, we've learned that successful people do think differently. We are also now aware that they think much differently about a few key issues than non successful people.

Let's isolate some of these key issues. Problems first:

Problems encountered by a successful person do not debilitate them. Successful people don't lose their composure. They don't lose their cool. They don't get their panties all up in a bunch, if you will. Problems are nothing more than indicators of progress to them. Why? Because, after years and years of trial and error, successful people have learned firsthand that problems are absolutely germane to success.

In fact, when no problems are present, successful people get very concerned. They think to themselves, "I hope I am still making progress, but lately there have not been any problems... perhaps I'd better get busier!"

Moving on... let's talk about money. To the successful person, money is nothing more than a "thank you" for services rendered. All high achievers know that however much money they have in their wallet, it is exactly the right amount. They know that whatever car they are driving, it's the right one.

Now, you might be think to yourself, "Sure they think they are driving the right car; they are probably driving a Cadillac!," but I'm here to tell you that even if they were driving in 1967 Dodge Dart in that special shade of avocado green, they would still think that is the right car for them. Because they know what all successful people know, and that is... YOU always get THE RIGHT results ALWAYS!

What about time? Do you think non-successful people have the same concept about time as successful people? This is probably the noticeable way to differentiate between the two.

Successful people always think in bigger blocks of time.

Non-successful people always think in SMALLER blocks of time.

You can always tell how someone feels about time by watching the way they spend it. Non-successful people don't seem to think about the fact that time really matters. They think, "Oh, there goes another day..." and isn't that unfortunate? I'd guarantee you that if you ask any homeless person what they are doing tomorrow at 1:00 PM they haven't a clue. That should tell you something. You might say that holds true for some of your friends as well, doesn't it?

If you are ever to become more than you are right now, you must THINK in bigger blocks of time! YOU must also never squander your time. If someone asks you to help them move some furniture over the weekend, you probably are not working on your goals. If you were, it probably wouldn't occur to them to ask for your assistance. They'd think, "Naw, don't ask him; he's busy working on his own stuff."

Get to work on your own stuff.

Relationships are next. Successful people do not just think to themselves, "Well, maybe this person will help me get to the next level." They think to themselves, "Wow, wouldn't it be cool to know this person five or six years from now?

Successful people look at relationships as long-term investments. Blue-chip investments, if you will. Because they are long-term focused and value their time, when a friend really could use a hand, they are their real fast to help out. Friendship to them is not just about helping one another get stuff done. It's about helping one another Be-come more.

Next, successful people make great investments. They invest in the most profitable company in America today. No, not Microsoft… "You, Incorporated" (a.k.a. "YOU, Inc.").

They routinely spend as much as 15 percent of their income on continuing education in the form of books, seminars, audiotapes, CDs, and various other forms of self-improvement. Whereas most people stopped their education soon after graduating college, these folks know better. They know that even the stuff they learned last year will be outdated a couple years from now.

They also know that money invested on continuing education will not be missed. Their take on it is: I can either pay now, or I will wind up paying later!

Now, we've watched successful people for years. We've seen what they do and we've seen what they have. But, it hasn't always occurred to us that we should observe the way they *think*.

If you want to learn from a successful person, don't wear the same clothes; don't drive the same car; don't eat the same food; and don't wear the same perfume. Instead, borrowed their "glasses" so that you may think the way that they think by seeing the world through their eyes.

If you ever get abducted by successful people, you should politely ask them, "Take me to your library."

There is the famous karate master who, not only has many, many karate schools, he is also a talented and dedicated master instructor. Other wannabe martial arts "masters" try to emulate his methods...and this master knows that everyone is trying to copy him. But it doesn't bother him. You know what he told me? He said, "Scott, they can copy me all they want... They can copy the way we wear uniforms. They can copy the color of my schools. They can copy my advertising. But they can not copy my *persistence*!

In the final analysis, the non-successful person should take the successful person out to dinner and listen to them... and then pay for their dinner.

Model their thinking not their style.

Remember the famous saying, "Give a man to fish and he can eat for a day; teach the man to fish and he will eat for a lifetime?"

There is another old saying, "Don't seek to imitate the Masters, rather, seek what they sought." You'll find on your journey that, if you truly want to model what successful people do, that in order to truly do exactly what they do, the very best way to imitate them is... to *Do your own THING*!

2 Lies of Success

"As-if principle: If you want a quality, act as if you already have it."

William James (1842-1910) American teacher, playwright, philosopher

Let's eliminate a couple of very common beliefs about success right now. I used to be a pretty big fan of Anthony Robbins. Tony says, "You need to develop your confidence if you want to achieve your goals." I disagree.

There are literally thousands of people who have achieved some pretty incredible things who are afraid of their own shadow. Many of these men and women are afraid to go out to eat at restaurants because they lack confidence. The very thought of having to manage a project, or lead people, or get up and speak in front of a crowd, will cause them to pass out!

Lie No. 1: Confidence.

Confidence comes from achievements. You don't need confidence in the beginning--you need only to take action. When you adopt this philosophy you move up one notch on the level of Be. Confidence always comes after the success. If you see someone acting confidently before they have achieved their goals, it is just that -- acting!

Lie No. 2: Charisma

You do not need charisma to make it in this world. In many cases, charisma would be nice, but it is not paramount. Some people think that Oprah Winfrey is charismatic. Opera is not charismatic; SHE IS JUST *HERSELF*! If you feel you need charisma, just be yourself all the time. Having the guts to be yourself IS CHARISMA!

Here's another example. Remember Walt Disney? He was not charismatic. He wasn't magnanimous. He wasn't even nice to people... and look what he created. Now there's always some idiot saying, "See what I mean... Who wants all that success if you have to become a crotchety, old man?" And there may be some truth to that. However, what I want you to realize here is that

80

success in any field boils down to who you "are," not necessarily how AWESOME you can make your self appear to be.

As for me, I routinely address crowds of people by the thousands, and I can tell you this -- IT NEVER GETS ANY EASIER. I remember listening to public speaking coaches telling me, "Don't worry; the fear goes away the more you do it!" Yeah right, the only the thing that goes away is your waiting for the fear to go away! Eventually, you just learn to suck it up. It just becomes a habit.

When I was 18, I met Mike Tyson in an airport. I mustered up the courage to introduce myself. Eventually we got to talking about competing. Mike Tyson told me that he's always scared when he gets into the ring! Sometimes he even cries while in the locker room just before his fights. Although it seems his career is questionable these days, what's instructive is that it is not necessary to have the innate qualities of CONFIDENCE & CHARISMA in order to succeed. It certainly cannot hurt your progress, but many people have done it without it!

You Are In Charge

"If it is to be – it's up to me."

~ Unknown

The only thing we really own is our mind. And the only things we are really in charge of are our thoughts.

You are in charge of your thoughts. Although you may not have total control or the function of your mind yet, you are still the one in charge of your thinking process. In the beginning, this will seem like a burden because, for so long, you have just let your mind run rampant. Thinking about mundane things... worrying about problems that will probably never happen... only to finish those thoughts, and then find some escape type of activity.

This is all part of Be. You learned that successful people think differently, but what you're really learning is that they think differently about THINKING.

Now there's one caveat here. ONE thing you're *not* in charge of is the results of the thoughts you think. Again, I repeat, YOU ARE NOT IN CHARGE OF THE RESULTS YOU ARE FORCED CREATE, ONLY THE THOUGHTS THEMSELVES.

Dr. Stephen Covey, author of The Seven Habits of Highly Effective People, uses the analogy of a stick to emphasize this point. He says, "Whenever you pick up one end of the stick, you always pick up the other end as well." I will amend his saying with this one comment, "You CAN pick up one end of the stick without picking up the other end, BUT you can only pick up the stick so far!"

Your Thoughts Have Consequences...

"Your life is an expression of all your thoughts."

~ Marcus Aurelius Antoninus (121-180), Roman emperor and Stoic philosopher

The Mind Rules All.

All Things Are Created Twice.

All things are created twice. This is about as metaphysical as I will ever get. No, don't worry; I have not lost my mind. But the simple facts remains that everything and anything have been created two times. First, in mind. Then, in physical reality.

The book you're holding in your hands was a mental creation first. The car you drive to work existed in someone's mind first. The table that you may be resting this book on... was also created in someone's mind first. It sounds simple, doesn't it? But ALL THINGS "Have" HAD their first creation in someone's mind...

82

deliberately. This is so very important that you will read more about it in a later chapter.

It seems so obvious. Isn't it incredible to think that all of the things around you--the buildings, the parks, the bridges, and all the items in your home, right down to the silverware, salt and pepper shakers, you name it--were mental creations first?

Right about now is when most people are saying to themselves, "Of course all things were created in mind first. How else can they be created?"

And my response is, "Do you realize that all of the bad stuff that you have in your life right now was also created in your mind first?"

The notion that you created all of your problems in your mind first, is definitely a bitter pill to swallow. But, nonetheless, it is very necessary medicine if you are ever rise above mediocrity.

People always take this personally...and they should. They say, "What do you mean I created my problems? Why would anyone in their right mind create their own problems in their mind first?"

They create their own problems because they don't pay attention to their thoughts. What makes matters worse, these are the same people who think someone else is to blame for their problems. But now, you are wiser.

People believe that, when they are thinking, it doesn't seem that they are actually doing anything--that they are not deliberately trying to create a result. And, folks, that is part of the problem. All the things you think about create a result. And, as we will discover in later chapters, your thoughts play a role in the physical results you get... AND the mental results you get.

When you adopt the attitude and accept the fact that all things are created twice, you instantly put yourself into a different category of people. You instantly become a more responsible person. I don't mean responsible in the sense that you'll start paying your bills on time or show up on time for appointments. I mean that you will start accepting total responsibility for your personal level of success.

The Mind Works In Pictures

"It is the disposition of the thought that altereth the nature of the thing."

~ John Lily (1554-1606), English prose writer, poet, playwright

The mind holds pictures.

Have you ever gone to the movies? Do you remember a time that you went to the movies and cried... like during "Old Yeller" or "Ghost."

Now, think of a time you went to the movies and laughed hysterically, like during a Jim Carrey movie. Or felt empowered while watching "Braveheart" or some other inspirational film. What was happening there? Why was it that you felt those emotions? Now, it is important to reiterate here: THE BeST STUFF IS SIMPLE; that is why it is so often overlooked. If I were to ask you why got that warm, fuzzy feeling during a romance movie, or why you cried watching "Ghost," you would look at me as if I were an imbecile and say, "Duh... it was a sad movie." And right then and there, the principle would elude you. So I again ask you: Why is it that you feel a certain way at the movies? Is it the seats? Is it the popcorn? Hey, what would happen if the movie never came on the screen? Would you sit there for two hours and then leave the theater feeling better or worse? No, of course not! It is because the mind holds *images.*

The mind operates in images. This is the important concept that many people disregard. They spend their whole lives playing the wrong movie in their heads! What's worse is that they play the same rerun day after day, year after year! Did you ever wonder why the big screen put radio shows out of business when the TV came into existence? Hollywood was the first to discover the power of the picture. On that note, why do you suppose they started playing movies in the dark? It's because when all the area around the screen is pitch black, you have no choice but to focus your attention on their creation. That's why we get so much more out of the movies; we are very focused on the images being played. And so it is with us. We go about our days oblivious to this principle - distracted by the other images in our mind.

Any picture held firmly in the mind is bound to come forth. And any picture held firmly in the mind, in any form, is bound to become reality. This is the great, unchanging Universal Law that, when we cooperate with it intelligently, makes us the absolute masters of the conditions and situations in our lives.

One surefire way to turbo-charge your ability to succeed is by taking charge of your own mental movies. It can be very challenging to succeed if you don't feel like succeeding. What many people do not realize is that they can "set the stage" of their own feelings.

Think about it again. Have you ever gone to the movies and cried? Of course. Having you ever gone to the movies and laughed? Definitely. Well, why you suppose that happens? Do they put nitrous oxide in the popcorn? We know the paying 10 bucks to go watch a movie is no laughing matter. So, what is it about movies that makes us feel the way we do?

THE PRODUCERS CONTROL OUR MENTAL PICTURES.

Again, what do you suppose would happen if you went to the movies, and the show never came on? Would you laugh or cry? No. How come? No mental picture.

The same holds true for getting yourself motivated, putting yourself in the right state of mind, and influencing how you feel about everything in your life.

What about your memories? What exactly are your memories? Are they live, physical, tangible things? No. They are mental image pictures. Nothing else. Now, all those things in your memory did really happen and were real events. But, they are events no longer. Just pictures, pictures that we sometimes use in the wrong way.

Please do not overlook this concept because it is simple. Say it out loud. "Whatever you focus upon grows." Whatever you dwell upon will eventually become physical reality. But, long before that occurs, whatever you dwell upon will create a mental state that will take you closer or farther from your goals.

This is a true success secret. Taken at face value, it may seem insignificant. Guess why? Because it is simple of course!

Non-successful people think that this concept is ridiculous. But that's OK. We'll just let them go on being the victims of their own thought processes. The simple idea of taking control, or at least having a bit of influence, over their own thought patterns seems useless to them because they regard thinking as SEEMING AS IF YOU'RE NOT ACTUALLY "Do"ING ANYTHING.

Hold fast the picture in your mind you want to create. You've already learned that you are where you are because you have done what you've done, right? Now, just take that to the next level and realize that you've done what you've done... because you have thought what you have thought.

James Allen, the author of *As a Man Thinketh*, put it best when he said, "Sow a thought, reap an action; sow an action, reap a habit; sow a habit, reap a character; sow a character, reap a destiny."

I believe that quotation captures the very essence of this entire book.

Blue Yarn.... Blue Rug. The Loom of Mind

Your mind is like a loom. Have you ever seen a loom? Looms are tools that weave fibers to create fabric. The materials of the clothes that you are wearing were once processed through a loom. If you want to create a high-quality T-shirt, you must first load cotton at the front of the loom. There is a saying in the martial arts that goes, "Blue yarn, blue rug."

It seems so very logical and simplistic. Yet, many people fail to recognize that their mind works on an identical level.

Would you be surprised if you put red yarn into a loom and created a red rug? No. Yet people carry on... day in and day out... Deliberately bitching about this and that, carrying on, having useless discussions, gossiping, standing around the water fountain, criticizing the boss, and then wonder why success always seems so far away. They begin to think that the problem must be "out there."

They act shocked when a calamity strikes.

THE QUALITY OF YOUR LIFE DEPENDS UPON THE QUALITY OF YOUR MOST DOMINANT THOUGHTS.

You are in charge of the "deliveries." Watch your thoughts. Be aware of them. Monitor them. It's okay once in a while to be around a bunch of people who are engaging in thought neglect. You just sit back and watch the show! You'll have a lot of fun with this; trust me! I used to think that this "loom principle" was so important that I had to eliminate *all* of the un-empowering thoughts from my life. To do so is near impossible. Even if you could, you'd be a very lonely person!

Instead, enjoy the fact that you know thoughts influence circumstances. When you are aware of this, you can sit in a room full of pity-partiers and have a grand ole time thinking to yourself, "These poor bastards don't even know what they are doing to themselves."

People literally wear their thoughts on their faces. Ever see a sad looking person? More sad thoughts than happy ones. Ever see an angry person? More angry thoughts than peaceful thoughts.

"Yeah, but what about when something tragic happens to us?," cries one whiner from the back of the room. "Then what am I supposed to do?" This is where Dr. Kevorkian and I see eye to eye. Some people really should think more about removing themselves from the planet... maybe it would manifest and create less traffic.

Positive Mental Attitude

"The mind is like a clock that is constantly running down and must be wound up daily with good thoughts."

~ Fulton John Sheen, Bishop (1895-1979), American religious leader, author

How long will it last?

When I talk to corporation heads and other various bigwigs in charge of think-tanks and problem-solving groups, they always ask me the same question when they give me a check, "How long will this last?" My response is, "How long will what last?" "Well, you know, the PMA... the positive mental attitude that you are going to give us?"

Even at the highest levels of leadership in some of these major corporations, they still believe that "I" am the one giving them all a boost!

They don't even realize that *they* are the ones giving themselves a boost because of a shift in their own thinking! Had they realized this, they may not need me to remind them so often. But it's sort of true, right?

You hear me say something new, or perhaps something old but in a profound way, and it causes you to act differently -- and you end up getting better results! Then, you get so psyched about it, you start doubting yourself and begin to wonder, "I wonder how long I can keep this up for?" Ahgg! And, right then and there, all that progress you worked so hard to achieve... goes right out the window! Make no mistake about it. It is TOUGH to stay motivated. But that is the best part about it!

You see if it were easy to stay motivated, it would be easy to be successful.

And if it were easy to be successful, it wouldn't be fair to those who want to work a little harder to have a little more. Or, work a lot more... which I hope is the case with you!

So here's my retort to the POSITIVE MENTAL ATTITUDE PARADOX:

How often do you take a shower? Every day right? How come THAT doesn't last? Well, because as you go about your day, you collect dirt. You get sweaty. You come into contact with the other elements in the world that are maybe a little dirtier than you are, and after a full day – IT'S TIME TO TAKE A SHOWER!

The same holds true for a positive mental attitude. Hey, I get pissed when people say that I am a "naturally" enthusiastic person! There is nothing natural about it! Just ask the people that know me really well. They'll tell you, "Oh yeah, you should've seen him a few moment ago when the IRS agents came in?" C'mon, I work hard to maintain a positive and upbeat nature all the time. And so do you! But again, as I have been saying throughout: It is a choice! A deliberate choice. You are in charge! Blue fabric -- blue rug!

Pay the price for PMA

"Change is not made without inconvenience, even from worse to better."

~ Dr. Samuel Johnson (1709-1784) English lexicographer, essayist, poet

Amended by Scott Palangi (B.1969) Martial arts master, author

Remember what I said about investing in yourself? That is part of maintaining a PMA as well. On the surface, it seems as though my thoughts are FREE... but the price I had to pay to learn how to think those thoughts was DEFINITELY NOT FREE! And quite frankly, I am glad.

The worst advice is free advice (even when it's accurate) because we don't usually take action on it! Your ability to Be-come more has a price, too. You'll have to pay the price in the sense of budgeting you time more wisely. You'll have to budget your thoughts more wisely. You'll also have to budget your money so that you can afford access to excellent information, insights, and knowledge!

PMA without ACTION is just a drug.

Never worry about sharing these insights with your competition. Here's why: Right now, you have already learned some methods of thinking that will change the way you are. You know that Be-coming aware of your pre"Do"minant thoughts gets you much closer to making deliberate, successful actions on a more consistent basis.

Many people are getting high...on many things...even mental morphine. There are many kinds of "dealers" out there. Watch out for the ones who do not advocate action.

Slant towards action: Fire, Ready, Aim.

You can take action with negative mental attitude (NMA), but will get better results with PMA.

All Things Are Created Twice

"The price of greatness is responsibility over each of your thoughts."

~ *Winston Churchill, Master Statesman, British Politician*

Think about skiing. Now, what did you have in mind? Think about working. Now, what do you have in mind? Have you ever stopped to wonder why our thoughts occur? Of course, these are rhetorical questions, right? The reason I ask you to think about them is this: Remember that the chair you're sitting in was not created in a factory first but in someone's mind first? I'll say it again: ALL THINGS ARE CREATED TWICE. First in the mind, then, in physical reality. The chair you are sitting in, the desk you are reading at, the office or room you are occupying, the building you are in, the street that building is on, and the town that street is in… all were - at one time - created in someone's mind.

All the stuff you have, all the stuff you want, whether material or immaterial, is created in the mind first. If you place a picture in your mind of what you want to achieve, eventually you will take the actions to achieve it, to draw it to yourself.

Conversely, if you do not picture in your mind what you want, you will achieve exactly that: nothing. If you look at people who are addicted to substances, people who wander around aimlessly, people who sit around waiting for their boat to come in, people who do not take deliberate action (the exact actions I will instruct you to take in later chapters), you will notice two things.

1) Their boat never comes in... and...

2) They wonder why life treats them *so* unfairly.

Before reading this book you might have felt sorry for such people, but now you know the real reason that their lives are the way they are. Intentionally or not, they did one of two things, no more, no less.

They either put the *wrong picture* of what they wanted to create in the heads - too many times. Or they put *no deliberate picture* in their minds, letting let other circumstances, people, or events dictate their picture for them. Such is the case with apathy.

This is why one's environment plays such a pivotal role in any individual's chance for success. You tend to become part of what you are around, unless you take control of the mental picture in your mind. Now, that does not mean that man cannot rise above his environment or his circumstances; he certainly can. But not until he understands how this happens. Ask anyone who has raised themselves up by their bootstraps, and they will tell you that their main challenge was holding the mental image picture of success in their minds.

You have used this principle many times, perhaps without even realizing it. Do you remember a time when you really wanted something, or were planning to go somewhere, say shopping for a particular piece of clothing or needed a good parking space when you were pressed for time... and then, W–ham! The circumstances seemed to conspire to help you, like you somehow just got lucky and found exactly what it was that you needed? You wonder if the Goddess of Parking Karma decided it was your day to receive blessings? Most people can relate to experiences such as these on at least several occasions. We often refer to them as "good days"; we wish they would happen more frequently. They CAN and WILL happen to you once you fully embrace and practice the mechanisms set forth in this book.

Your Mind

"Knowledge is not power, knowledge combined with action is power."

~ Anthony Robbins, author, motivational speaker

Powerful is the person who can take action. All action begins in the mind. All of your significant problems will be solved by learning to use your mind as a tool. Your mind is so powerful; it has the ability to create, destroy, solve problems, and take you from where you are to where you want to be. It is with the mind that you will change all of your outer circumstances. Have faith that this Principle of Mind is where all your progress lies waiting.

People often talk about the power of machines and technology. Yet, they act as if the mind is of secondary importance. The mind is more powerful than any machine, because it took that mind to make that machine.

Most people are unaware of how to use their minds to their advantage. They use their minds to simply drive their car, do their jobs, and file their taxes. There is nothing wrong with that. However, once you tap into the power that you truly possess, you will be addicted to using your mind for much more than the mundane tasks to which it has been accustomed in the past.

When I was in my mid-twenties, I had the good fortune to live with four self-made millionaires. I learned more about the mind from these people than from any other resource. Not because they were mental experts or were taught the "great secrets" of mind power, but rather from their examples. These successful people THOUGHT differently than any of my other friends. They certainly thought differently than I did at the time.

These four guys were so much alike that it was surreal. They did not have similar interests per se, but had similar thought processes about almost everything. For example, they thought differently about time. They thought differently about money. They thought differently about people. And, their biggest similarity was the way they thought about problems.

My seemingly-fortunate friends used their minds deliberately. Whereas most people go about each day merely reacting to the world, these fellows were always in control in some way.

The Two Parts of Mind

"Garbage in, garbage out."

~ Unknown

Your mind, according to top scientists and psychologists alike, is made up of two distinct components: the Conscious and the Subconscious. There have been many other groups of experts calling these two aspects of the mind by different names, such as Objective Mind and Subjective Mind, Surface Mind and Deeper Mind, etc. There may even be more than what I've mentioned here. All the experts agree on one thing, though; and that is the functions that the Two Minds serve.

For the sake of simplicity, and not to further complicate matters, I will refer to the two components as Conscious Mind and Subconscious Mind as these seems to be their most widely used applications.

The Conscious Mind

It all begins in the conscious mind. This is where you will make or break yourself...

Powerful people use this principle to their advantage. They know that the job of the conscious mind is to submit images, to place mental pictures that will bring forth change. They don't get upset at the fact that they need to take control of their conscious mind. They accept it. They welcome the responsibility.

The main role of the conscious mind is to indiscriminately send signals to the unconscious mind.

Your conscious mind is in charge of quick decisions, searching for things, noticing things and, most importantly, SELECTION.

The conscious mind acts as a filter, and is constantly on the lookout for things to occupy its time. The better you get at directing your conscious mind to focus on that which will take you closer towards your goals, the faster and easier it becomes to get what you WANT.

Challenging yourself by using your willpower will make it possible for you to slowly regain some control over your conscious thought processes. Now, I know that this is starting to seem complicated, but really it is simple. Not easy... but simple in nature.

The Subconscious Mind

"The gent who wakes up and finds himself a success hasn't been asleep."

~ Wilson Mizner (1876-1933), American Author

Unaware of its potential power, lacking awareness of its existence and the intelligence of the conscious mind, your subconscious mind will deliver whatever you submit to it. Much like the loom that creates a rug does not care what it is being fed, the subconscious mind's only job is to create. Not judge.

Indiscriminate in nature, your subconscious mind is stronger than you are. It is infinitely more intelligent than we give credit for and, this very second, is operating your blood pressure, your heart rate, the repair and re-growth of cells in your body. Most importantly, the subconscious mind is finding ways to bring to you whatever picture you hold firmly in mind.

It is predictable, AND WORKS EVERY SINGLE TIME ALL WITHOUT YOU ASKING IT.

Therefore your real full-time job is to MAKE SURE YOU ARE GIVING YOUR MIND THE RIGHT STUFF TO WORK WITH!

Think Deliberately

Stand Guard at The Door of Your Mind

The garden behind my house is one of the best examples of how you have to tend to your mind.

Weeds grow in the garden without planting any seeds. I could go on vacation for one week, come back, and the garden would be ruined. Weeds require from me no effort to grow. They do, however, require lots of effort to remove.

Daily cultivation of the garden is the only way to ensure that it survives and grows to its highest potential. You have to remove the weeds regularly or they will become entangled around – and choke the life force out of - the very plants that you are trying to nurture.

It is no different with your mind. The weeds in your mind will appear in the forms of self-doubt, skepticism, cynicism, disbelief, fatigue, and even general apathy... if we do not regularly pull them out. No one in their right mind would ever think of growing garden that never *gets* weeds. That will never happen. It's not realistic. It is the same way with your mind. You must work at the goal of avoiding or removing the so-called weeds so they do not choke out all of the beautiful things you want to create.

This is called standing guard at the door of your mind.

Become "Recession-Proof"

What do people mean when they say the economy is bad? How does the economy become bad? What they're really talking about is that your odds of winning at legitimate gambling have greatly decreased. People are still eating. People are still going places. People still need stuff! So, maybe they don't go to the movies as often now as when the gambling may have been good in the stock market. But, don't let this crap about the economy being bad prompt you into not trying your best.

You will always be compensated for the value you bring to the world. If your goal is to get a bunch of cash and stick it in a fund and sit back and allow a typical good day to be dictated by what the stock market is doing, well then, you are an idiot. Develop something of value; become the type of person who can turn nothing into something and something into more. If you do this, you will never become one of these mental midgets who bitch about the economy.

Do you want job security? If yes, then you had better invest in the most predictable stock there is: YOU Inc. I have worked in big companies. I've worked in small companies, and I can tell you: we never let people go who make it very clear that they are invaluable. Further, we'll not make that assumption based on what they say. We base our decisions on one thing: RESULTS.

Whenever I start talking like this, I always lose a few fans. Guess what? I don't care. I respect you way too much to bullshit you. If you are a janitor, and you create more value than you are being paid for -- YOU WILL NOT GET "LAID OFF."

Do you know what being laid-off really means? IT MEANS YOU'RE FIRED. Upper management use as the term laid-off so that they don't get shot by lunatics who want to keep on doing nothing and keep getting paid for it.

I'm just not ever going to believe that you get laid off because the economy is bad. You shouldn't believe it either. For the sake of argument, let's just suppose that I am wrong. Let's go ahead and say, it is beyond our control, that we have no ability to determine our future. What's wrong with pretending that you do? At the very least - if the economy is good, you'll be the first one to get a promotion. At the very worst - if you do get fired (I apologize I meant to say laid-off), at least you'll have the self-satisfaction that comes from doing the job better than "good enough" but instead a job well done!

You see, when you adopt this attitude, even if you're toll collector at a tollbooth, you instantly become *self*-employed.

I repeat: your true fortune will come from how much you invest in YOU, Inc.

Becoming More

Notice again how all it takes is a simple shift in thinking in order for you to become more. And, we haven't even gotten around to doing any doing yet! Am I talking about a change in attitude... no! A change in attitude takes a lot longer and is more difficult to accept and internalize. That's why I call this a shift in thinking.

A shift in thinking always precedes change. It is the precursor to progress. An attitude change is like a major overhaul and people love hanging onto their old attitudes as much as they like to wear their most comfortable pair of broken-in shoes.

For example, now that you have learned how the little things like "thinking the wrongs thoughts," or engaging in a "bitch session" with friends can have a negative effect on your abilities, now you get to set your sails for a different direction.

The Platinum Rule

People are the source of problems. The obstacles you face will always have people associated with them. The solution is to be able to live with all types of people so that you can be successful. Remember, no man is an island.

The golden rule of religion states, ""Do unto others as you'd have done onto you."

I will get myself into trouble if I criticize that bit of wisdom but we should ask ourselves under what context was that golden rule created?

What was its purpose? Now, if following that rule gets you into heaven, then GREAT! But, perhaps it is wise to note that there is no mention in there about what to do when the person who you have "done unto" is not schooled in the same philosophy!

Then what?

If you have been alive for even only a decade you know firsthand that you can "do unto" and get walked all over. Now, while that may get you a seat next to the Almighty someday, I should suggest that, for rest of your life, you adopt this strategy as well; use it in addition to the golden rule. I call it, "Palangi's Platinum Rule"

Be able to handle anything life dishes out to you... AND, be careful not to dish out stuff to others who don't know this rule!

You see, when you decide that you will become the kind of person who can-take-it, one who will be strong no matter what, two very interesting things start to happen

One, people treat you better. Maybe it's because they know it's hard to rattle your chain, but they just seem to bother you less.

It's like when I was a kid taking karate. I had this one bully that continually harassed me. I swore that, as soon as knew how to break a few boards with a side kick, I would kick this kid's ass. Can you guess what happened? By the time I got good enough to beat this kid up, ha had stopped bothering me *AND* I had lost the desire to kick his butt! Hindsight, I am not sure which came first the chicken or the egg. But it did seem like he miraculously stopped bothering me at the exact same time that I became more tolerant of him!

So the first part is... become tougher!

The next part will also give you a lot more happiness starting immediately. Many people are powerless. It would be nice to try to make everyone powerful, but it wouldn't be so much fun and we've all got better things to do. So here's where part two comes into play: STOP BOTHERING WITH PEOPLE WHO "Do" NOT LIVE BY THIS PRINCIPLE!

Often times, the aggravation you have now can be traced back to the way you treated someone. Or more precisely, the way someone treats you no may be because of something you said to them.

I am not suggesting that you can not or should not speak your mind because I certainly am one to do so... but I often pay for my comments if I fail to pay attention to someone's "level of toughness."

You can say whatever you want to whomever you want, but you will get along better with them in the long run if you know what they can and cannot deal with. Assess before you speak.

This is called wisdom

Don't Wish Life Was Easier... Wish You Were Better

Growth requires that you... grow. It would be ridiculous to think that you can have anything more out of life by remaining the same as a person. The irony is, when you develop this mind-set of not wishing that life was easier, it is the very instant in which you become better at life itself.

Next time you receive some bad news or someone starts giving you some drama, the first thing to do is smile (or maybe smile on the "inside" so you don't risk people thinking you're a wise-ass). I mean it, though; put a smile on your face and say out loud, "Well, here comes some change!" Many times, you'll feel less intimidated by the issues at hand, as if it's all "no big deal." Welcome all challenges. Greet all obstacles with open arms. Pretend you like it. You might as well anyway because, until you become TOUGHER than your problems, your problems never get any EASIER!

The people around you will take notice of your outlook but not because you are inspiring. Rather, they will pay attention out of sheer bewilderment. They'll be like, "How does that not bother you?" And you, having read this book, will know that the reason is because you KNOW THAT PROBLEMS MAKE PEOPLE TOUGHER and that lucky breaks make people weaker! Soon enough, they will watch you handle what would normally be viewed as stressing, or tackling challenging projects or tasks with ease. Then, you'll be able to say, "If it ain't a little bit tough, then why are we here? If it isn't a little tough, I am the wrong person for the job!"

You will be able to prove to people, once and for all, that to bitch about a problem is to want to be "on welfare" in the first place. Start thinking this way *immediately*. Whenever you hear people piss and moan over petty things, picture them on welfare, begging for a few bucks because, think about it:

WHAT GOOD DOES IT "Do" TO COMPLAIN ABOUT ANYTHING?!

If you have a teenager... does it do any good to complain? If you start a business and blow a thousand bucks on an ad... does it do any good to lament about it? Of course not! How about this one: Ever see a bunch of disgruntled people complaining about how the 'policy' isn't fair? Well, do not become a part of that group, because those people are basically saying, "Hey, I can't handle this... Could you please make it easier? Uhmm, I wanna go have some cheeseburgers... Anyone wanna join me for a cigarette?"

Losers.

Complaining is what people do after they realize they've lost their influence!

(either with someone or over something)

I'll bet you'll want to read that one... one more time.

So let's repeat it: PEOPLE COMPLAIN BeCAUSE THEY "Have" LOST INFLUENCE

Minding Your Mind

"Control Your Emotions or Your Emotions Will Control You."

~ *Chinese Proverb*

Choice and Feelings

Conscious Mind has a job to do. That job is selection. The task of selecting which thoughts our conscious mind chooses to focus upon is not a job that is to be taken lightly. For whatever we focus upon, grows. Whatever you hold in your conscious mind, the subconscious mind goes to work on.

The effects this has on your moods, emotions, and levels of enthusiasm are of paramount importance.

In the untrained state, the conscious mind will wander, letting whatever is in its environment dictate what it should dwell upon. This is the default functioning of the conscious mind. When not disciplined through the will, it is left to its own devices. Conscious mind will become ready, willing, and able to fixate on whatever comes its way... a phone call, a drop-in visitor, newspapers, gossip, idle chatter around the water cooler. When the conscious mind is in this state of apathy, you will automatically be attracted to the mundane, the trivial, what "the Joneses are doing," etc. You will be susceptible to suggestions, street solicitors, and ridiculous talk about "who won the game last night" and "who slept with whom" on a TV show.

Right now you may be thinking, "Hey, what's wrong with that stuff? I like that stuff." You like that stuff because you are used to it. Because you lack a major definite purpose, you feel no sense of urgency to choose different thoughts.

This has a huge effect on our feelings. When your untrained mind submits the ridiculous and the trivial to the subconscious mind, the subconscious mind (not having any significant work to do) goes on vacation. The next thing you know, you become bored easily, confused easily, and you live your life day in and day out telling everyone that you "want to do this and you want to do that." Because you do not control your conscious mind to focus on a particular goal, that task sits on the back burner. There it will stay until one day, by some stroke of will, you decide to act upon that goal - and then, actually accomplish it! You now sit back thinking, "Man, why didn't I do that sooner?" And if your subconscious mind could speak it would say, "You're telling me, give me some more work!"

Confucius said, "Control your emotions or your emotions will control you." A crucial part that he left out, however, was... HOW YOU "Do" IT?

Not to worry. I have some answers for you. I don't claim to have all the answers in this department, but I have enough to get you're going and keep going.

First, where do emotions come from?

Remember before when I asked you think about skiing, and where is that thought? We determined that all thoughts exist only in our minds. Do you recall what we discovered by asking that question? It was that, if the thought about skiing creates a mental image picture of the activity, than all thoughts MUST CREATE A MENTAL IMAGE PICTURE AS WELL... and THEY "Do."

Well, folks, the same holds true for emotions.

Thought always precedes emotion.

They are inseparable... you cannot feel without thinking.

When you view your emotions with this approach, it becomes imminently clear to you that you "Do" have options. Ever heard of the phrase, "waking up on the wrong side of the bed?" Well, I am here to tell you that there is no such thing. You never wake up on the wrong side of the bed. Now, you may very well be *going* to bed on the WRONG side! But, you never wake up on the wrong side of the bed.

Here's what I mean. When you wake up feeling lousy, it's because you held the improper thoughts prior to going to bed the night before. And if that's not the case, it is because, upon awakening, you are thinking about something you didn't want to do.

Some people don't like to believe this one. They enjoy saying things like, "I just don't feel good about myself" or "it's just the way I feel."

Little do they know, that they were the very *creators* of these same emotions – the emotions that they now wish would just go way. Some people will do whatever it takes... drink any liquid... take any pill... go to any doctor... to escape this pathetic existence called: their life. Sadly for these people, when they do finally manage to feel better it doesn't even occur to them that they changed their thoughts first.

If you feel lousy about anything, I challenge you to change your thoughts. After all, isn't that what taking the pills and drinking alcohol and going to see a shrink REALLY "Do"ES FOR US? IT CHANGES OUR THOUGHTS, "Do"ESN'T IT?

So, obviously, my suggestion is change your thoughts first. Change your thoughts on your own without the help of anything or anyone from the outside. You could've done this all along anyway, if you'd only realized that emotions stem from thoughts.

Yet, there will still be some people who will argue with you on this point. They will want to defend the reasons that they don't feel excited about being alive. They will say things to you like, "It's only natural to feel bad about the things that happen to you." But, you "Do" have a choice.

All of the knee-jerk reactions that we have were, at one time or another, installed. In fact, there are no knee-jerk reactions only direct or maybe trained reactions, but not knee-jerk reactions.

Let's use the example of an insult: I was once teaching these concepts to group of martial arts students and one woman said to me, "Yes, it makes sense but... if somebody calls me and idiot, or stupid, or worse, I can't help but get mad!"

Well, what if I called a deaf person an imbecile... would they become upset? Of course not. Why? Because they wouldn't hear me. I still said it. The words came out of my mouth, but consider for a moment why there would be no reaction: because, no thoughts would enter that person's mind. Not really because they couldn't hear me!

Again, it sounds simple, but don't overlook it.

What people say, the words that come out of their mouths, whether they're insult or compliments "Do" NOT make us feel good or bad. It is the thoughts that we let those words create that make us feel a certain way.

When I lived in South Korea, my friends made quite a sport of me. I couldn't speak very much Korean. And, everyone who could speak Korean fluently really got a kick out of what I'm about to tell you. There happened to be this one coffee shop that I used to go to quite regularly. Every day that I was there, there was this one young Korean kid who come up to me with a complete smile on his face and he would say, (in the Korean language) "You're a son of the bitch!"

Everyone else would laugh. Meanwhile, as I was thinking that this person was trying to make friends with me, he was extending his hand to shake my hand and call me a "son of the bitch." The whole experience has made me a bit paranoid whenever foreigners smile at me and say something I don't understand. A few weeks later, a friend of mine ho spoke Korean told me what had been going on.

My point is that the words that came out of this child's mouth, traveled across my eardrums, but I couldn't understand... therefore, no mental picture... no upset emotions.

This is probably why we love our pets. If they could speak to us with words, we might not enjoy their company as much as we do.

Here's another illustration:

As a Tae Kwon Do competitor, I once met a man who had been struck in the head and had lapsed into a coma. When he awoke, he had amnesia. Now, let me give you a little background about this person. Prior to his amnesia, he had been in some trouble with the law, had very frequent, emotionally-charged bouts with his spouse, and generally just couldn't get along with anyone.

As a result of the amnesia, he awoke with only very limited memory of his pre-teen and early childhood years. He had no memories of the past few years as life. He was completely unaware of how people felt about him. He was completely unaware of how he felt about people. He would run into people he used to know (that he slightly recognized) and, now, was polite to them. These people couldn't believe that Miguel was not acting like a jerk. Many people thought he was medicated. In fact, what simply had happened was that brand-new thought patterns were running through his mind. Old images were erased allowing new images to be installed. I still believe that this head injury was the best thing that could have happened to him!

I'm not suggesting that you bang your head against the wall... or assist someone else in perhaps a much-needed, amnesia session. What is interesting to note is the effect that our thoughts have our feelings.

Become An Early Riser

"Sleeping seems like a waste of time, doesn't it?"

Master Dae Hoon Lee

"Every morning in Africa a gazelle wakes up and knows it must outrun the fastest lion or it will die. Every morning a lion wakes up and knows it must outrun the fastest gazelle or it will starve. Either way, when the sun comes up? You'd better be running."

If you sleep past 8:00 am, you are headed for trouble. If you *want* to sleep past 8:00 am, you're headed for bigger trouble!

Statistics show that the most highly achieving men and women in this world are out of bed by 6:00 am. Some people have a really hard time with this one. But, not to worry, as always I will give you simple insights that will help you get started with this. Remember what I said about the 1-800-PERSISTENCE

HOTLINE? Well, here's another one; they should have a 1-800-GET-MY-ASS-OUT-OF-BED hotline as well. The world would have more *producers* if one existed.

Probably the surest way to get in the habit of getting out of bed by 6:00 am is to kill someone or join the Army. Either way, you will have somebody screaming at you to, "GET UP, LOSER!" Of course, I have an easier method. One that not only allows you to get up at 6:00 am, but lets you earn a fine living, too.

It's really not a method so much as it is a new way of looking at mornings. I call it Palangi's Pre-Dawn Axioms. I'll list them first, and then expound on them after. Here goes.

They work.

I have tried both methods for years on end and can tell you from experience, getting up early has everything to do with success.

Now, you may be thinking, "So what? "I am not a materialistic person... who cares... what does having a million dollars have to do with MY goals?" Well, good point. But, until they conduct a study of average people, living average lives, earning average incomes, I guess the only yardstick with which to measure success is money. Moving on...

Scientists have said that, in the mornings, our brains function at a higher level. At first, they thought that this was because subjects had an eight-hour rest the night before. They also thought initially that it was possibly due to the fact that the stomach is emptier and blood sugar levels might be more stable.

It's almost as if they were trying to find reasons that it wasn't the actual hours of the morning that were so powerful! But after further research the above factors were eliminated. It didn't matter how much rest a person had or what their levels of blood sugar were like... Morning hours simply produced higher frequency of brain waves than later hours.

Think of it logically. If you get up earlier... you have more time to do more stuff! And... if you've been reading this book, you're becoming the type of person who only does stuff to make their life a masterpiece. So if you just get going on this one, you will be on the fast track to success!

There is no such thing as a morning person.

If anyone tells you they are a morning person... they are full of it! Look, I have been getting up early for some time now. I also associate with early-risers and they all say the same thing... It sucks!

The people that say they are morning people just don't know how wonderful sleeping can be! If you have friends that tell you they are morning people, you can quickly convert them. Just get them into getting up late for a while. When they find out how easy it is to sleep later, they will fall in love with it.

The other reason people may tell you that they are morning people is that they may have a suspicion you are struggling with establishing the habit. In a surreptitious effort to undermine you, they "rub it in your face how easy it is!" I have kept a few people sleeping late by using this one myself! Now that I have this book though, I guess the secret is out.

What Are You Sleeping About

Another question to ask yourself is, "What are you sleeping about?" I developed this line of reasoning with my dear friend Tom Clifford. Tom and I observed that depressed people tend to sleep a lot more than others. If you have a friend who is depressed you may ask, "What are you depressed about?" Right? So, the question, "What are you sleeping about" was spun off the depression model. When you find yourself (or a friend) sleeping too much, just ask the question, "What are you sleeping about?" The implication of being depressed may comically prompt them into getting out of bed earlier.

The seductive siren of the mattress is very powerful. Do not overlook this because of its simplicity. You are not as powerful as your slumber. I am giving you permission right now to hate your creator for setting our default more towards unconsciousness than consciousness. We all struggle with pre-dawn habits.

Accept it. Stop the whining. Stop trying to say to yourself, "Well getting up early works for some people, but other people are night owls... and hey, what's the difference as long as I put in the same amount of time each day?" Let me tell you... There's tons of difference! In fact, I'll go as far as to say that you could actually do LESS work and get more accomplished as long as you're getting up early.

There is something about the morning hours that seems to make you more productive than the later hours.

Getting up is more important than going to bed.

Discipline yourself to Get Up not Go to Bed. Many times when you set a goal to get up earlier than normal, your brain will invent this line of reasoning that goes something like this:

YOUR BRAIN:

"Hey man, don't get up early tomorrow; It's already late at night! Besides, you'll be much more productive if you get more rest! Wake up early some other day when you have gone to bed earlier. It's already 1:00 am and you'll only get 4 ½ hours of sleep! Hey, let's see what else is on TV, since we've already agreed that you blew it tonight!"

That's exactly how it works.

I have a martial arts student named Zach Happel. He is 17 years old. He has been getting up at 4:45 in the morning for ten years now. Never missed a day! He lives on a farm with his parents and has had no choice in the matter. He's conducted his own experiments as well. Here it is in his words, "It does not matter what time you go to bed... 4:45 am always feels like 4:45 am." I knew I liked this kid as soon as he put it so bluntly!

Now, I am not saying that a good night's sleep won't make you feel better. It will. But you are fooling yourself if you think you'll ever feel more rested just by getting more sleep. Getting up is WAY MORE IMPORTANT than going to bed. Do not believe otherwise. Besides, that's why they call it getting up early? Right?

Mike Litman didn't say anything about millionaires going to bed early! In fact, most of them report NOT being able to sleep because they are so excited about their lives.

But they were excited about their lives long before they became millionaires! Remember, it's all part of "Be."

It works best to have something to do.

One problem you may run into when getting into this routine is... "Okay, Scott. Now I'm up... what do I do?"

This can be a problem because I have found that even when you have stuff to do, you still think you have no stuff to do! The reason? Here comes some more profound simplicity folks: the reason is because you have been doing all the other stuff at 9:00 am or later! Life is indeed a different world at 5:00 am! In the beginning, you feel like you are in a different land. Even your house seems like a different place during these hours. After some time, however, you'll find your routine (for more exact insights into this, see the "Tapping the Pencil" chapter in the Have section of this book.).

It never gets any easier.

For all the reasons above we come to #5. Life does become better from getting up earlier, but getting up earlier never gets better. There's no such thing as a morning person. Anyone who tells you there is -- is trying to keep you asleep.

Decisiveness

We are always making decisions. Even the least successful of us.

You have learned that we are all getting the right results based on the decisions that we've made. You know that your entire life is nothing more than a summary of all the decisions you've made in the past. YOU ALSO KNOW that your mind is constantly making decisions even when you are not aware of it.

Let me... let you in on a little-known success secret. Again, I will burn into your brain that a secret is something not "apparently obvious." A secret is something you sort of know, but don't really know -- because if you really KNEW--you would "Do".

I first heard this one from Fred Gleeck, at his seminar "How-To Write a Self-Published, Bestselling Book In 13 Days or Less Guaranteed!" (Fred, don't worry. If you don't come up with this seminar, I may put in something else like the ones that already exist i.e. self-publishing, seminar on seminars etc.) Fred is one of the quickest thinkers I've ever met. One of his operating principles is that people should develop the ability to train themselves to think faster while writing.

In fact, I'll go as far as to say that if it wasn't for attending Fred's seminar, you wouldn't be reading this book! The point being is this: During his seminar he paraphrased Napoleon Hill, the author of Think and Grow Rich!, saying: "Successful people make BIG decisions quickly, but change them slowly; non-Successful people make ANY decision slowly, BUT are quick to change those decisions.

Further, you can't "not decide." Indecision is still a choice.

Procrastination is not an *inability* to decide. It is a decision to do nothing.

PLEASE, IF YOU NEVER READ ANOTHER PAGE IN THIS BOOK... GET THIS THROUGH YOUR HEAD. EVEN BETTER, GET IT PRINTED ON LARGE PLAQUE AND HANG IT IN YOUR OFFICE...

"PROCRASTINATION IS A DECISION TO "Do" NOTHING... AND IT IS A USUALLY A PERMANENT DECISION THAT YOU WILL NOT CHANGE!"

The 7-Day Verbal Diet

"The most important conversations are the ones you have with yourself."

~ Unknown

The Seven Day Verbal Diet

Okay, so a quick recap: Thoughts lead to moods; moods lead to actions; actions lead to results. We are always getting the right results because we are the thinker of our thoughts. Results - both good and bad – are that which we are responsible for creating. Just as the water can not rise higher than its source, our results can be no better than the thoughts we are thinking. Make sense? Of course it does. Before you do, you think.

This principle tells us that it is vitally important that we influence our thoughts to the best of our ability. The trouble is that thoughts are racing through our minds at such a rate that it almost seems daunting to control. Thousands of thoughts can flash through your mind in a matter of minutes. The point is that you simply cannot gain control over all your thoughts, especially when you are new to the concept. But, you *can* get control over your tongue.

Discipline in the mind begins with discipline in your speech. The things you say to *yourself*, both aloud and in the silent chambers of your thinking, are even more important than the negative suggestions that others give you without your consent.

This is a critical point. Just as we must quietly and firmly decide to choose the kind of thought we will drop as seed into the garden of our deeper mind to grow into the desired plant, we must choose the words that speak the equivalent to those thoughts we intend to turn into habits. Frederick Bailes, in his book Basic Principles of Science of Mind, states that, "The place where progress starts is at his lips, where he checks the expression of his negative thoughts." If you put the practice of eliminating negative *speech* into effect, you will soon find that disempowering and negative thoughts come less and less frequently.

Here is the rule: Never say out loud a thing about yourself that you do not wish to see realized yourself.

Instead of saying, "Aw, I suck at painting." Replace it with, "Painting I haven't practiced enough!" I know; it sounds ridiculous, doesn't it? Nonetheless, it is actually the truth. Because whatever we practice, we get good at. So nobody sucks at painting... but many of us are under-practiced at it!

Thoughts are too fast catch. They come and go at blinding speed. With practice, you can get better at uprooting them as discussed in "The Garden" analogy but this takes a while to master. In order to "catch' your thoughts, you need to be able to notice them. The very best way to get skilled at this is by controlling your tongue first. Words are much more manageable than thoughts. Start today. Believe me: once you start to catch, interrupt, and control your words or your speech, the more aware you will become at doing the same with thinking.

Now, most self-improvement gurus will tell you that you should not say negative things about yourself because it will have a subconscious effect on your self-image. This may be true. The problem is many of these same geniuses also think that the cure for your problems is to just walk around saying affirmations like "I'm Super-awesome!" "Your Super-awesome!" "He's Super-awesome!" "She's Super-awesome!" and "LIFE IS SUPER-AWESOME!"

Here's the problem. Life isn't always super-awesome, but we can deal with it. If you try to trick yourself (or your alter ego) into thinking that life is super awesome and then find out it's not, you've set yourself up for disappointment. All I am saying is that nothing is wrong with disappointment; life is full of it. It's just less punishing when you don't dwell on it and that, my friends, is what thoughts cause us to do!

So the benefit of controlling your tongue to avoid negativity is so that you can influence and begin to train your mind to control your thoughts! Not "just because it makes you feel good." Get it?

Besides, the things you may say about yourself usually are not true. Take self-deprecating humor, for example.

Sometimes in an effort to gain acceptance with others, we will put ourselves down. This is referred to as self-deprecating humor, and there is a right time and place for it. For example if you are trying to establish the significance of exercise and you want to align yourself with your audience you might say, "If you don't exercise you may become a fat bastard like me!" People will laugh and it will most likely go over well. But do not ever say things like, "I suck at..." and, "I am not good at..." and "I just can't..."

Here's why: It isn't true.

You could argue and say, "But it is true... I am not good at getting up early." It still isn't true, because all things take more than one try in order to become proficient at them. (Wait 'til you see what an eye opener this one is in later chapters.) So, the more accurate statement would be, "I am not in the habit of getting up early yet." Or, as in the case of this assignment I am giving you: YOU COULD JUST AVOID SAYING ANYTHING NEGATIVE ABOUT YOURSELF FOR 7 DAYS!

Now in leadership scenarios you can establish a lot of credibility and demonstrate humility by admitting your weaknesses. Many times when I give presentations, I will let myself be the butt of a joke. And that's fine! But, I will not confess to that which I do not want to continue to see in my life.

Sticks And Stones Break Bones But Words Kill

Be aware also of the effect your words have on others. I touched briefly on this in the Platinum Rule chapter and, as promised, I want to expound on it here while we're on the subject of words.

Words are so powerful. Look at what people are able to do by manipulating words. Words can create mental image pictures. Words offer people kindnesses and pay compliments, and even inspire people to do great things. (Or horrible things, look at what Hitler did with his words!)

Much of your success, influence with others, and your ability to be happy, will come from how well or how poorly you choose your words.

Miguel Ruiz, author of The Four Agreements, says that every single problem that we face in this lifetime, can be traced back somewhere to words leaving your lips. I believe what he says is true. Use your words wisely.

Think of it this way: Every time you get together with someone you either leave happier -- with and about that person -- or unhappier. There is never a stagnant state of relationships. They are either moving in one direction (up) or the other (down). Those who think a relationship is simply "standing still," aren't aware that it is actually going backwards!

What causes relationships to digress? You might think it's poor communication, but many times it is just the result of poor choice of words. It would take an entire volume to illustrate examples, so I will just keep it looming in your consciousness: pay close attention to the words you select when in the company of those whom you care about (and even those you don't care about).

You may have heard a disgruntled spouse say "Actions speak louder than words," but I can tell with certainty you can get yourself into deeper trouble with words! In the final analysis, your Mother was right. "If you don't have anything nice to say, don't say it at all!"

The One Thing You Must NEVER Let Anyone Else

Say To You.

Do not ever let anyone else insult you. This does not mean that you become sensitive, but quite the opposite. If someone you are taking to says how they feel, you should listen. But insults and verbal abuse are out. Period. Here, once again, Scott Palangi cuts through the B.S. of psychobabble and amateur psychotherapy: Whereas some experts may teach you "verbal self-defense, and/or techniques of modeling, mirroring, the power handshake, how to dress to impress, and the "posture of success," I'll save you years of trial and error.

"Do" NOT STAND FOR ABUSIVE TALK FROM OTHER PEOPLE, EVER.

…even if it costs you your career, your job, or your level of acceptance at the local synagogue, mosque, or church. It is much better to be homeless and sleep outside and keep your dignity, than to be WALKED ON and later think to yourself, "I shoulda' said this or I shoulda' said that."

The Platinum Rule said that: Our objective is to become the kind of person who can deal, handle, and *endure* whatever life dishes out... Right? Yes.

You'll be pleased to know that there is another way to ensure this happens. And that is to make it *very clear* to others that you will *not* be shoved around!

Well, how's this done? Words. Yep, words are definitely the key here, friends. Here I will share a key phrase to embed in your vocabulary. It works particularly well when dealing with difficult people. Only on rare occasions has it ever had an adverse effect.

Now, there are a few different ways to say it. And, in some languages it sounds different than others. But, for the most part, when someone says something to you that is insulting, abrasive, or just plain-old "not nice" (and are clearly doing it in a way that does not include the goal of establishing a greater level of trust and communication), you can try this little number.

It goes like this, and you don't hear all too often either... I mean the phrase has changed over the years, but its perennial wisdom was poignant back in the old days just as it is today. For some reason when you say to someone, "Hey, Go-fuck-yourself," you make your point very clear. It has helped me make it a point that I am not a pushover. Also, rarely will saying that phrase cause you bodily injury, provided you are with able-bodied company and can run fast if the need arises. One caveat, however, be ready to sever the relationship.

In essence, be tolerant, but not a doormat.

There are other variations like:

"I resist that suggestion..."

"Hey, hold on; I do NOT appreciate that..."

And still, there's "Hey! Now, wait a second..."

But nonetheless.... GFY is good if you need it.

P.S. Make sure kids aren't around. Some parents aren't aware that their children already know how to use this one.

PART THREE: DO

The Discipline of "Do"

"Men are alike in all their promises. It is only in their deeds that they differ."

~ Moliere (1844-1924), French novelist, poet, critic

Without the "doing", there is no having.

Problem is, most people don't know that there ARE better ways of doing things. We do not have to "reinvent the wheel." We can simply find highly-productive people and model their methods of effectiveness. By doing this, we get to keep our goals as "our goals," but we get to learn from their methods of execution.

Sadly, many people are emotionally attached to their "ways" of doing things. They get easily offended at even the slightest suggestion that there may be a "better way."

Do not become one of these people.

Ever heard the phrase, "There's more than one way to skin a cat"?

Well, if you've forgotten my stance on that: it's bullshit.

Of course there are many ways to perform mediocrity, but when it comes to excellence – there *are* better "ways".

There are better ways of doing, better ways of *deciding* what to do, *when* to do it – and HOW to do it.

In this section you will learn how to program yourself with the actions that ensure success. Under the umbrella of "Do", we have 3 phases:

1) Discovery

2) Planning

3) Execution

In this section you will learn the best ways to do your "doing." If you already "are" the type of person who can assume that you'll

118

achieve the success you're looking for, then the doing section will take you to your destination that much faster. Many people are good at some of the doing. Your goal here is to become an expert at all of it.

From values clarification, to time management, to waking up earlier, to get more doing done... it's all here for you.

This is the only part of the book that requires you to do some writing. Feel free to write in your book; it is designed for that purpose. If you decide to do some of the exercises in a separate journal, it may not be as effective. Things can get lost, and you'll have to look back and forth between your notes and the book, etc.

Stay focused; read with a pen in one hand. Customize this book with your thoughts as they occur, and do the exercises inside the book to the best of your ability.

First... Decide What You Want

"As long as I have a want, I have a reason for living.
Satisfaction is death.

~ George Bernard Shaw (1856-1950), Irish playwright,
critic, social reformer

Before learning the technology behind effective "doing," we have to first make sure you are not in life category #1 (remember... "I don't know what I want").

Master motivator Zig Ziglar, in his book See You at the Top, likens goals to the bull's-eye on a target. Zig asks, "How do you expect to hit a target you don't even have?" This is the state most of us are mired in right when we hate the results we are getting out of life. Of course, the less-aware person would say they aren't happy with the cards life is dealing them, right? Well... we are going to discuss how "stack the deck in your favor."

The antidote for a complaining person....is a goal. It is amazing how many people do not know the simplest of these concepts.

119

Listen to your friends (or your spouses' friends -- even more fun!) and pretend that you have two mini-recorders. In the right hand, you record all the stuff they say that is conducive to what you have learned thus far. In the left hand, record all the statements that are diametrically opposed to these concepts. Unless you're like me and have labored to create a circle of friends that are well-schooled in these principles, you will find that the bad recorder will be full in less than one hour!

You will find yourself saying, time and again, "I heard you complain about what you don't want, but tell me what you do want!"

Wants are at the root of your personal growth.

This is a true success secret.

To want... is good.

Let's think about those life-categories I was telling you about back in Part One. If you'll remember, I said that the categories were:

1) I don't know what I want.

2) I know what I want - but I don't know how to get it.

3) I know how to get what I want - but I don't always get it.

4) I always get what I want - but I am still not happy.

Notice the recurring theme... "What I want."

That is what this book promises. Answers to wants.

Everything is about wants. That is the first secret. Do not overlook this principle because it is simple. Wants govern all.

Remember when you were a kid and someone (in a misguided way) taught you about the difference between wants and needs? And you somehow adopted this idea that wants might be selfish; that wants should take a backseat to needs; that (as the song goes) "You can't, always get, --what you waaant!" Now think about the words, and... the difference between the way the words make you feel... In your head, say "I need." Doesn't that sound weak, make you feel weak. Now, in your head, say "I want." Feels more powerful, right? Again, all the best stuff is simple.

For years, the issues of wants have stymied psychologists. The question of what is more important.... Needs or Wants?

Well, if you want to become successful, you had better focus on your wants!

Why? Simple. We live in a country where it doesn't take a whole lot of "improved being-ness" to get what you need! Clothing, food, shelter, most high school drop-outs with an ounce of ambition can get these things.

The real challenge of becoming super happy is not wanting what you already have (like the banana brained, self-help books tell you to do).

What the hell is all this talk about "be grateful for what you've got?" Next time someone tells you that baloney say, "If you read Scott Palangi's book, you'd realize that all the stuff you have, you got because you were grateful in the first place!"

The universe does not award you with success and then ask you to be grateful! You can be grateful and should be grateful that our God created an extravagant universe and gave us every means of accomplishing what we want.

And you can be grateful that God or whatever you like to call it, also created a universe where you have to pay first -- and play later! If it wasn't that way, everybody would be able to have what you have, without doing any of the work!

But, you do not have to feel guilty for what you've got. I am not saying that if you were "born on the 80-yard line," you should brag about how, next week, you're going to "score a touchdown." I am saying: Be leery of this "be happy with what you've got" syndrome!

And, same goes for "be content with what you have." Are they nuts?

Listen, I have compassion. Whenever I see a disabled person, I am careful not to step on crack, walk under a ladder, or stand next to trees during a thunderstorm. I am totally appreciative of the gifts God gave me. I am glad he gave me the awareness to be grateful, because we all know of those who are not grateful. They are never happy. In the same breath, let me be frank and tell you a little story about being grateful.

Don't let being "grateful" confuse you about the value of wants.

I practice Brazilian Jiu-jitsu. For those who don't know, it's an art where, if you don't cooperate, you get your arm broken! So, one day after I didn't cooperate, I was waking down the street with my friend Tom.

While nursing my broken arm (and complaining to Tom about the pain like a little baby), my good friend and I saw a guy on those really big crutches trying to navigate a busy Manhattan intersection.

As I watched this handicapped individual try to keep his balance, avoid bumping into people, and make it safely to the other side -- Tom turned to me and said, "How does your arm feel now jackass?"

I understood his point. I thought about it... and then I gave him my retort which was, "That certainly must be a tough life to live... and it does indeed put my little broken arm into perspective..."

Then I looked back at my arm, thought about it some more... then looked him straight in the eyes and said, "BUT HONESTLY, IT "Do"ES NOT MAKE MY ARM FEEL ANY BeTTER!"

You get the point. Be grateful for what you've got and be happy you can get more!

Wants Create Skills

Wants create skills. Success begins in your wants. You do not manifest success and then decide you want a 43' Bertram (a very nice boat, and a very nice want!). Can you see how each and every principle in this book is interrelated? Be, do, have -- think, do, get.

If you desire to attract a circle of successful friends... want it first.

If you desire to be skinny, do you not *want* it first? To say, "Make me skinny, so I can exercise and lose weight," would be ludicrous, right?

You have to live deliberately in order to achieve your goals. You have to place the wants there first!

Think about it for a second... Don't all the skills you now have and the knowledge you possess -- first stem from a want to get those skills or learn that knowledge?

Here's an example I learned from Master Keith Hafner.

Master Hafner says, "Imagine if you were in a building, in a room or office... and, out of nowhere, a voice comes over an intercom and says, "Excuse me everyone, but we're sorry to inform you that -- the buildings ablaze and the doors have somehow been automatically locked. Good luck." He continues with, "I got a pretty good feeling that a set of skills would magically come to our aid, skills that we didn't even know we had ... until there was a definite WANT.

I remember getting my black belt. I had no idea how you "do it." I just knew I wanted it! I thought to myself, "Man, I want that!" and then the skills sort of seemed to appear soon enough. Know that it works the same way with your success.

I had one instructor who understood this concept very well. His name was Master Lee. When Master Lee moved to the U.S. in 1978, he had nothing. He slept at the YMCA and got a job at a gas station. When he started his first karate school, the only means of marketing he could afford were flyers. His formula for success was simple. Here are his words, "Scott, I became successful because everyday that I woke up, I decided that I WOULD NOT EAT LUNCH UNTIL I MET, OR SOMEONE CALLED, WHO WANTED TO STUDY MARTIAL ARTS."

And, he held himself to that standard. Think about that: if you couldn't eat until you did something that you know you should do? How much more effective could you become? That's an example of a basic want like eating. Now, what if I were to tell you that the very same mechanism, if you will, could be used to get whatever else you want?

This is not just an "affirmation action exercise" either! I am talking about using this same process to create a clear list that will empower you to start the doing, so we can eventually have some having!

It all starts with your wants. If you recall in the chapter about rising early in the morning, I mentioned that one problem you will face if you get up at 5:00 am will be "Now, what do I do."

That's where the wants come into play.

Most People Have an Underdeveloped Set of Wants

I guarantee you that, if you walk up to anyone you know, and ask them what their wants are, they would have to think about it for a couple of minutes first. Most people just drift through life with no definite wants to speak of.

Wants are not goals.

Goals are included in your wants and are part of your wants, but wants themselves are geared towards lifestyle goals as well. Like peace of mind, for example. It's a hard thing to measure, yet absolutely necessary for success. Most people, again, cannot put lifestyle on a checklist. That's why it is a *want*. So, let's dig in right now and do some work in this area.

Let's get a clear picture of our wants and develop an appreciation for the system that takes those wants and fuels us with the ambition, clarity, and desire to fill them.

Design Your Blueprint

Where Progress is Measured, Progress is Made.

Life, like any journey, requires that you know your destination. However, a more important question to ask is, "Where are you right now?"

Take a moment and score yourself in the following areas. Your job here is not to see how "high" you can score, but to discover how well your life is "balanced."

Rate yourself from 1 (lowest) to -10 (highest)

All done? How did you score? Prior to taking this "test," most people score themselves higher in certain areas. When you see each category side by side however, it becomes a little more clear that some areas are not as well-balanced as others.

For example, before I took this test, if you asked me in an isolated scenario, "How are you doing intellectually?" I would have said about an 8 or 9. But, when I look at the intellectual area compared to the physical area (at a time when I'm going to the gym every morning), I realize that on an intellectual level -- I'm suffering.

Take this test every three months to see how you're progressing.

Create Your Dream List

Let's get to work on those wants now. Here are some rules I want you to follow coming right out of the gate:

You must put down all the things you want in each area as **QUICKLY** AS POSSIBLE! No down time. Just get the ink on paper as *fast* as you can. If ideas come to your mind too quickly to write legibly then just use a two-word description or an abbreviation to highlight the goal.

The goals must be **BIG**. No, actually I want you to make your goals **ridiculously BIG.** I'll explain later why that's important.

They must be **borderline-embarrassing**. Write down the type of goals that, if your friend got a hold of the list, you'd be mortified. (That means they had better be very ridiculous!)

Wait. Before you get going on this - get yourself situated. **Turn off your cell phones, your pagers, TV's and all other possible distractions.** This will be tough stuff! You will see how out of shape your DELIBeRATE WANTS are at the moment.

Ready? Here's the catch. I want you to **time yourself**. You get **60 seconds per category**.

Begin. Everything I've Could Want Right Now.

Done? Good. Now, here's where you're going to think I'm psychic... I would be willing to bet that during this exercise, while you were writing down your goals... You "heard" a mental voice second guessing your goals. Meaning that your goal session probably went something like this:

Places I want to go:

Take family to Hawaii (Nah, I don't really want to go to Hawaii)

Things I want to own:

A 2005 Porsche (Yeah right, I had better pay off the 1988 Honda first!)

Am I right? Maybe it was different for you. I'll still be willing to wager that your knee-jerk, almost-reflexive reaction to whatever you wrote down was not a very empowering one. That's just the way the mind works.

The great part of doing dream lists is not so much that it simply pumps you up, but also because it serves as a demonstration of how your own "inner critic" is controlling your mind!

Eventually, you'll be able to stifle this reactive part of your mind... and master it!

Most people have "Yes Wants" vs. Not "Deliberate Wants"

A second reason we work on dream lists is to exercise our Deliberate Want muscles. You see it works like this:

Deliberate Wants are -- things you decide upon.

Yes Wants are -- the things you say "yes" to.

Why do we do it... and what's the difference?

If I were to approach you and say, "Would you like this brand new, six bedroom house with a 3-car garage? It's yours for the taking!" You might say yes. Then again, you might say no...

A Deliberate Want, however, is where you tell yourself that you want it deliberately. You write out the goal in full detail, down to the year, make, model, and interior. I know. I know. It sounds simple... but wait, there's more. What you take for granted is that, since you were a baby, everything you got was usually related to "yes" wants. Your mother asked you if you wanted to eat Cheerio's and you said "yes." This went on and on for years. But our parents rarely gave us BIG choices, choices much beyond Cheerio's and milk.

To top it off, when we did ask for too much, we may have been told "no." So, as adults, it's no wonder why we sometimes have a hard time ever being able to do more than ask ourselves for something to eat and clothes to wear!

And of course the second reason we want to operate out of our deliberateness is simply because... Deliberate Wants cause you to move outside your comfort zones...and this is good, because we need to BE more in order to DO more in order to HAVE more.

Besides, it may be a long time before someone comes up to you and asks if you'd like to live in a mansion!

You can have anything in the world you want (excluding most, but not all, of the ridiculous).

This is a true success secret. You can have anything you want is the actual secret. The last part (in parentheses) is in there for a reason. See, we have been doing a lot of "talk" about achieving goals.

Let's say that me, you, and a couple of our friends decided to form a basketball team. And, let's say that our plan was to go on a barnstorming tour around the country and draw out huge crowds. Let's also say that our mission was to do this so we could raise 10 million dollars to donate to the "Starving Republicans of Texas Fund"...

Call me a pessimist, but... I don't think that could happen!

It's ridiculous.

One problem you face when starting to learn these things is that you'll go and tell a friend, "I can have everything I want!" and your friend will say, "Oh yeah, I bet you can be an astronaut!" You may wind up thinking, "Yeah, you're right. I could never be and astronaut -- this goal stuff is for the birds!" (Just don't say it out loud... remember?)

But, perhaps you don't need to want to be an astronaut! Not to achieve your dreams.

Now, notice also that is says excluding most *but not all* of the ridiculous. That part is in there because you can actually do some pretty ridiculous things with your life... probably even more than I'm giving credit for.

The Power of Choice

The Things You Like, Hold You Back From

the Things You Love.

"You can spend your life any way you want, but you can spend it only once."

When you know exactly what you want out of life, it will feel as if somebody gave you a drug. You will feel enthusiastic, energized, and excited to attack your daily action plan.

Slowly, however, other parts of your life will factor in. It's a funny thing about success in that you cannot compartmentalize achievement. This means that, when you are focused on a goal, the other activities you engage in will affect how well you do in the really important ones.

The things you like will distract you from the things you love. You will have to make some decisions. The things you like not only distract you from the things you love, they will kill every chance you have at attaining them. Just what are the things you like? Well it's different for everybody, but one thing is the same for everyone:

THE THINGS YOU LIKE "Do" NOT CAUSE YOU TO MOVE OUTSIDE YOUR COMFORT ZONE.

The things you like may include reading magazines, watching sitcoms, hanging out at the bar, watching sports on television, and pretty much everything else that doesn't have anything to do with your dream list.

You may be thinking, "What's the big deal, when I am not at work, I want to relax... I want to unwind... I deserve to watch a few episodes of "Friends." That's fine. However, those little activities that do not sharpen your mind do take time. In many cases, valuable thinking time is lost.

For example, I am a musician. Most people don't even know it. I play the drums. For several years, I was really into it. So much so that, whenever I heard a radio, I would get hypnotized and start "air-drumming." I'd listen to jazz stations to see if I could "pick up" new beats or new fills. It was fun. It was healthy. And, for the most part, the "drummer crowd" is a pretty clean bunch stereotypically speaking. I had a drum teacher. I used to drive 54 miles just to take a one-hour lesson once or twice a week.

One day, it occurred to me that this hobby was... just that, a hobby - it held about the same importance as my dork friends watching football all weekend long.

So, I quit. Cold turkey. Now, let me tell you something; you don't just "quit" being a musician! It's practically impossible. Everywhere you go you see your friends, some very successful, too. But, I knew that if I was to excel in other areas, I had to shift my focus.

Drumming, I liked.... but teaching the martial arts, I LOVED... and I still do.

Now, would I have been able to achieve and enjoy the success that I enjoy now if I didn't give it up?

Maybe.

But I can say with veracity that, when I replaced the drumming with stuff that caused me to stretch i.e. public speaking, writing, learning marketing, reading great literature, spending quality time with the most important people in my life, I started achieving goals like magic.

It was like it all came together. The things you like will usually not be bad for you... and that's the part that fools most people! It's not a matter of the Good vs. the Bad...

It's a matter of the GOOD vs. the GREAT!

I could have very well argued with my "smarter self" that it was "good for the soul... great friendships... great stress-release," and so on. But the fact was -- I didn't need it. I wanted it, but could see how it was taking lots of other time in my "schedule". I had to prioritize.

When I quit my drum teacher was like, "I thought you loved it! Why'd you quit?" I did love it. Yet, it did not cause me to stretch; it was more of a social thing; I had more room to Be-come more without it.

It's probably fine to have these kinds of things if, at the same time, you have "important goals" to their regard. However, my goal was to have a martial arts program that would afford me the opportunity to learn more arts while really creating something meaningful. I am still working on it.

On the surface it seems as though, if we just block-off specific times for specific activities, that we could -- do it all. I am here to tell you that this is impossible.

This is the reason we have all fallen short of achieving our goals. As you know we are always making decisions, choices.

Think about it... A man wants to spend more quality time with his family, but he works all week. His only day off is Sunday. His favorite team is playing and, at the same time, a family member has some issue that needs to be tackled. He wants to watch the game... He can turn a blind eye to his daughter's problem and participate in 'pretend listening,' but he can't do both.

Or say: a housewife wants to complete her associates' degree. Her kids are old enough now. She has the time to do it. But she has this routine with the 'girls'. They get together every Tuesday and Thursday and do pretty much nothing, but it's important to her. She bonds with her friends. She feels her friends need her and she needs them. She's comfortable. So comfortable, in fact, that the "tentative plans" with the girls for next Tuesday take precedence over the "could-be-plans" to find out the schedule for her would-be-degree.

Hanging out with the girls seems "harmless." After all, its not like she's going out and getting drunk, but it takes valuable time.

Accept this right now... All things that will set your life on fire are going to be developed in "down time." I just haven't found it to be otherwise.

Everyone Is Achieving Goals... But Not Their Own

You will meet some people who do not believe in goal setting. These people are not just indifferent to goal setting, they actually think that it doesn't work. They fail to realize that they are already achieving goals.... Probably goals for someone else WHO "Do"ES BeLIEVE in goal setting!

We are all working on some kind of goal, whether it's for a company, a person, a friend, an organization... we're all doing it. So since you're already setting and achieving goals (or achieving goals others have set for you), you might as well set your own too - or at the very least, get better at it.

You Can Have Everything In The World You Want... (Excluding most, but not all, of the ridiculous!)

Think In Bigger Blocks Of Time

"Do you love life? Then do not squander time for time is the stuff life is made of."

~ Plato, philosopher

The way you think about time is revealed in the way you spend it. People who know what they want, think differently about time. Successful people think differently about time. They also think about the way time unfolds a lot.

If you want to accomplish anything meaningful in your life, you must value time wisely. I do not know of any achievement, not even sleeping, that does not count the cost of time. Ever hear the saying "time is money"? Well, that's B.S., too! Time is not money. Time is TIME. Once it is gone, it is gone forever.

My instructor used to say to his class, "For the next hour, you will be making a decision. You will be deciding how important it is for you to earn a black belt. If time is money, will someone please show me where to buy more?"

He knew the value of time. Everyone says there aren't enough hours in the day. But, we all have the same amount of time. We have 24 hours. 17 hours if you really think about it. But really, some of us, based on the way we spend time, really do need more of it.

In martial arts, they say that 10 minutes of meditation is like an hour of sleeping. Most of us would say that 10 hours of sleeping feels like one hour of sleeping! What they are saying is that you can leverage time. Here's how:

If you look at time, you'll notice there are three ways to spend it: Productively, Neutrally, and Unproductively.

Let's take a unit of time -- say one hour. For the sake of simplicity lets give the 1-Productive Hour a nice even, round number... the unit of ten (10)

Now, let's give the 1-Nuetral hour the number of zero (It's only fair right? If the time is spent not doing good stuff but not doing bad stuff, we'll give it zero.)

The 1-Unproductive Hour we will give minus ten (-10).

With this model you can see that, if you are conscious for 16 hours per day, the highest score you can possibly get is 160.

Here's the problem: if you spend 9 hours doing something totally productive and only 7 hours unproductive, you are only at a score of 20!

See how time is leveraged? You cannot afford to fool around with your time, even if it seems like you have nothing to do. Doing nothing costs you! And doing something unproductive totally kills the whole ratio.

If I were to tally up the way you spend your free time, what would your score reflect?

Now, here is the best part. There are very high-leverage activities you can do that will make that score of 10 as good as a 30 or even 40!

Take reading for example. Exercising. Going for a walk with your kids. Listening to your spouse. The problem is not that there is not enough time – it's that there is not enough good time being spent!

I know of people who manage to run a household, raise children, meet a payroll, visit relatives, increase their knowledge, take martial arts classes, get law degrees… all at the same time. How? Do they have superhuman powers? No. they have a superhuman understanding of time!

If you were to go and ask them to hang out and shoot the breeze they would say, "I'm sorry but I won't be joining you... I hope you invite me next time!" They have been bitten by the time bug and know how to say no to the time bandit!

What about you?

Have you ever noticed that when you have nothing to-do, and your friend has nothing to-do... The two of you wind up helping each other do nothing together?!?!?!?

When I lived in Florida, I got a little caught up in trying to help the homeless for a while. Looking back, it was not a great investment in time. Not really a high-leverage activity. But I learned something very valuable from being around these people: THEY "Have" NO CONCEPT OF TIME.

They aren't thinking past noon tomorrow.

How about kids? If you ask a five year old, "Would you rather have a dime right now or a dollar tomorrow -- what are they going to say?

They have no concept of time.

People try to purchase time management tools. I've spent hundreds of dollars on these systems. Let me tell you which one works best. None of them. You do not manage time! Time just unfolds! You can only manage *yourself*. And last I checked, they don't make people management tools.

Here's the only secret I can really share with you about time and how to spend it. Pretend you have deadlines on EVERYTHING. This is especially tough for self-employed people because there is no one checking up on you that you can "fool" about your level of productivity!

I often drive by Blue Hill (a popular office building in Rockland County, New York) and I ask myself, "I wonder how many people up there are holding themselves to a personal deadline." Forget a project deadline; those are easy.

You've got to pretend there are deadlines on stuff, even when you aren't working. Just resist the temptation to fall into Haagen-Dazs syndrome, even if you've had a tough day at work. You'll find that you get more stuff done, faster! When you do finally get the time to sleep, you'll do it soundly because your mind wont be wondering WHAT YOU'VE BeEN SLACKING OFF ABOUT!

Use this deadline stuff with your family, too. If your son is home from college, pretend you have a deadline... Hold yourself to a challenging, personal standard and get in good quality time. The kind of time that, years from now, will make him say, "Hey, Dad. Remember that time when I came home from college and we did this, that, and the other thing?

Why? Because you do have a deadline! Why do you think they don't call it a life line. 'Cause were all gonna' die! Yet, by the way some people spend their time, you'd think they were going to live forever.

Am I suggesting you start honking your horn while you're behind some daydreamer in traffic? No. Simply manage yourself better.

If you ever go to a construction site, you can tell how high they plan to erect a building by the way they build the foundation. Likewise, you can tell who is serious about life by the way they spend their time.

No Plan "B"

Some of the lessons we received from attending institutions of conventional education can create some very subtle, self-limiting habits. We are told to get such-and-such knowledge to guarantee this or that type of job or career. For example, have you ever heard someone say, "Well if this thing doesn't work out, I can always fall back on my degree, my this job, or my that thing."

Rest assured, if you have a plan "B," you'll need it!

How do you think it is that people like my instructors can come here from places like Brazil, and South Korea and after ten years -- achieve the American Dream that many of us are still struggling to attain? I believe it's because they have no plan "B."

They have nothing to fall back on and, as a result, succeed incredibly well!

If you come from a background of limited resources or relatively low assistance, do not despise this. All of the greatness that has ever been achieved had this sort of challenge fueling it. Do you think you'd be motivated if you found out that you had a secret uncle who was leaving you millions of dollars. No way. You'd be taking it easy.

I am suspicious of people who are taking it too easy. They are either secretly wealthy or openly lazy. The curse of family wealth will rear its ugly head in all your affairs. Do not envy people who are born with millions and then create more millions. That's what Doctor Phil calls being "born on third base and then running around talking about how you hit a triple!"

Pretend that if you don't succeed, you'll be executed! My good friend Andrew Wood taught me this when I was like 22 years old. It applied then and it still applies today. Andrew wrote the book, Making It Big In America. He arrived in the United States from England with $300 dollars in his pocket and a set of golf clubs!

He then went on to create two ultra-successful companies in less than a decade!

When I asked him what his secret was, he took his hand out of his pocket, made the shape of a gun, put it to my head and said, "If I was your boss... and I told you that I was going to put a bullet in your head by 5:00 pm if you didn't make something happen... Could you make something happen, Scott?"

He then said that this is the main problem with Americans who bitch about what he calls "the lack of..." Mr. Wood said that people who don't pretend that this is the way they have to look at success are only fooling themselves. "Scott, most people just don't assume enough responsibility to be successful."

And then, if you do manage to amass a fortune, keep it a secret from your kids!

The movie "Knock Around Guys" illustrates this concept beautifully. I went to go see it twice just to hear these few lines so I could use them for this book. Don't worry. I won't give up the movie in the process. There is a mob boss who has a spoiled son. His son has a Cadillac, all the cash a guy in his mid-twenties could want, respect from his peers, etc. It appears he has it all, but he feels this emptiness inside, and wants to break into his father's business by taking on a job.

When he approaches his father (dressed in his leather jacket, Bally shoes, and Cartier watch, of course) he says, "Dad, I wanna do something... I can do this. Give me a shot. I won't let you down... I swear it!" His father reclines back in his 'chair and says, "Son, its been my experience that a man only does what a man has to do... if a man has a need. And, as I look at you, I gotta ask my self one question, son... what do you really need?"

Ready, Set ...Wait!

If You Wait around to Decide What You Want to Do -- You've Done It.

I first heard this bit of wisdom from Master Robert Brown. I don't know Mr. Brown personally... yet, but I know I would like him! He said, "If you wait around to find out what you want to do... Eventually you'll discover you did it!"

Now, when I first heard this, it was on an audio CD. I had to rewind it like a thousand time to really get it. Do you get it?

I think it sounds a bit esoteric and rhetorical when you first hear it but here's what he's saying. When you say to yourself, "I have to think about it..." what you're really saying is "I don't want to think about it." In fact, you're also saying "I want *not* to have to think about it." This means what you're really saying is, "I want to procrastinate."

You don't wait around to decide what you want to do, because you actually want to decide.... you wait around to decide what to do because you do not like to decide!!

Remember indecision still has the word decision within it. You show your true decisions by your actions, not your words.

Make Procrastination Your Friend

Procrastination is the sworn enemy of achievement. Most of the things you have accomplished in your life probably still had some degree of procrastination associated with them. Ever found yourself finally doing something you're proud of, only to beat yourself over the head thinking, "That wasn't so difficult. Why did it take me so long to get moving on it?" It's funny right?

Yet, it happens all too often. If you think about it, procrastination is really only about just waiting until you absolutely must do something. Now, take a look at all the things you haven't accomplished, but know you should... How come that stuff isn't getting done? I mean, right now, you've probably got some things that you damn well have the time to do...

And, that's just the things we know we should be doing. Here's the problem...

All the stuff that will lead up to, and add up to, getting your dream list accomplished, are usually not the things you *should* be doing... but rather, the things you *could* be doing!

Isn't that true?

So, what's this procrastination stuff all about? I mean, you already know the stuff you should be doing: exercising, learning, fixing things around the house, working a little more, maybe working a little less even... These are all things you're going to have to do.

So what's the problem? Isn't finishing some half-done, incomplete project that you know you'll be glad you finally got out of the way worth much more than any of the procrastination time you gain?

And, all the time that you're delaying... all that time you think you are actually focusing on other important things? I guarantee you that you can't recall what you were doing.

It's like this. Let's say that you have this dream of writing a screenplay. And let's also say that you have other stuff that needs your attention... If I come to see you a year from now, you should be able to tell me, "Oh yeah - that's 99% complete, and we've got a friend working on getting it produced"

But, instead, what will you tell me? Whatever the answer, will you be telling me about the other thing with the same amount of fervor as the screenplay...had that project been accomplished? Probably not. Do you think you'd say, "Uhm, well the screenplay is on the backburner right now, but my shrubs look great!" Or, "Well, we're on page two. It's not my fault...see, my friend who was helping me flaked out. But, I got a lot of extra sleep accomplished!" Sounds ridiculous, but isn't that what usually happens?

Now you can begin to see where the extra time is leaking away. Remember, those little things -- those extracurricular, small things that do not seem to take up a lot of time... are taking up more time than you think.

You should be dying to know how to conquer your procrastination by now. From my experience, I can tell you that procrastination is never conquered. You see, procrastination is not really your enemy. It is only the enemy of achievement. You have the procrastination mechanism in you for a reason. Just start procrastinating *the right way*.

For example, I have been procrastinating with a few things. While getting this book written, I procrastinated by going to the beach on my vacation. I procrastinated by having a few beers with the fellas'. I procrastinated by finding out who's competing in the upcoming Jiu-Jitsu tournament. My point is: you're supposed to procrastinate *now* with regard to the things you could be doing after your goal is accomplished. Do not procrastinate on what you could be doing to accomplish your goal!

Now, we already discussed sleeping. So there's an extra couple of hours there! So, why wait? The choice is yours.

It is not possible to "not decide". Instead, you're deciding to waste time or you're not. It may not seem like it, but that's the truth.

Waiting For All The Green Lights

"Whatever you think you can do or dream you can do... Begin it. Boldness has magic, power, and genius in it."

~ Goethe (1749-1832)

Have you ever found yourself in the "getting ready" phase of achieving your goals? You look; you search; you re-search; you get the facts straight; you tell yourself, "All right... now I'm *really* ready to get going." But then you just keep waiting until "Things "Are Perfect."

I have been there so many times that I can now sense when I'm doing it. I learned this valuable lesson from my friend Chris Esposito. We all have our strong points and this happens to be one of his.

Some people will take very calculated action steps... only to analyze them later again, and again, and once again! It's called paralysis of analysis.

Chris, on the other hand, sees a good idea, takes action on it, and then does any necessary research as he goes along. And I noticed something about this: he always comes out on top *because* he kind of just figures it out along the way!

We opened a kickboxing gym together in November (historically the worst the month to start a business, that is, besides December!) His philosophy, (or should I say "action philosophy," because he never really verbalized it; he just did it.) was that "all the lights will never be green."

If you were leaving the house to go shopping, would you look down the street first to see if all the lights were green before heading out?

You say, "Of course not." Yet, when it comes to something bigger than shopping, we sometimes find ourselves waiting for 'something else' to happen first. As if there is some perfect time to begin! Do you have any idea how many people.... under the guise of "It's not the right time yet" will sit on their asses forever? Only to find that when it finally is the right time, they are now distracted by something else!

Trust me. If you are going to fail (which we will take a deeper look at later on), you are going to learn what you needed to know much faster if you go for it now than if you wait for the right time to begin. Fortunes have been made by people who just began.

Boating offers another great example of this strategy… of taking action first, getting information later. One of my colleagues has a huge boat, the kind where you have to climb up the tower to navigate. He told me that on foggy nights, in order to steer, you have to walk out to the bow (the front of the boat) first, just so that you can see what you need to see in order to drive the boat. Now, the lesson there is that sometimes to find out what step 6, 7, and 8 are, you simply have to take steps 1, 2, and 3 first! Put the horse before the cart instead of vice versa.

Often the only real thing you need to know in order to take action is that you need to take action to know it!

Can't "Just Do It?"... Then "Just Lean."

"The journey of a thousand miles begins with the first step."

Confucius

What Confucius overlooked was that, sometimes, taking that very first step is the tough part.

Here's the deal. We have learned a lot thus far.

You've worked on the Be: You've thought about your goals. You've done the inner work to discover what achieving those goals would mean to you. You've realized that the truest merit of achieving those goals will actually be found in the type of person you'll become in the process in the process... which kind of makes it seem all the more worthwhile, doesn't it?

In addition, you've identified a few weak spots within yourself that need a bit of attention. You discovered that the skills you need to accomplish your goals will be a natural product from the things you want. When you *choose* to 'want,' you will find the skills that you need to achieve. Remember that old adage: "Where there's a will, there's a way."

You also learned that your decision to want – things, skills, goals - actually serves as a mechanism for creating even *more* desire. We simply are not born with enough natural desire... at least not enough natural desire to rise well above mediocrity.

And, to top it all off... You've made some decisions about putting ALL THE STUFF YOU 'LIKE' aside so you can focus on all the stuff YOU <u>LOVE</u> which... inevitably... will make you happier.

So now, how do you get the courage to take that first step?

The answer? Nike would say "Just do it" but **I** say, if you can't muster the courage to just do it...

Then just "<u>lean</u>."

In the martial arts, we learn that in order to execute a technique successfully, you must first view a particular movement as being each of the "steps" involved. Then, once having broken the movement into steps... you dissect the steps even more... right , down to the obvious...no matter how sublime.

I'll give you an example: If I were to teach you a front kick (one of the most basic martial arts techniques) and I were a relatively new instructor, I would first say, "Go like this." And you may, or may not, be able to learn it.

But if I were a more experienced teacher, I might say "Okay, first, pick up your knee and hold it like so -- *Now*, go like this!"

But, if I were a *Master* Instructor... "I would say FIRST... shift all your weight onto your left foot. Now, pick up you right knee and hold it like so... *Now, go like this!*" Do you see the difference?

Let's apply this concept metaphorically to taking a step. That's right... the way you leave your bedroom in the morning, go to your mailbox, walk to work... How do you actually walk forward? Do you just pick up your leg, move it ahead, and place it on the ground in front of you? No. Whenever you take a step... You first lean forward, and then, in almost a "faith-like manner," you throw your foot out to firmly and then catch your balance so that you can continue walking.

Sounds simple, right? So simple... that something like walking is something we practically taken for granted! If you think about it though, we always lean forward... and *then* we take a step. Picture it! Can you imagine how ridiculous walking would be if we stepped forward before leaning?

The lesson here is that success requires us to *lean first*. Sometimes we don't succeed, and only because we don't realize that taking the first step is simply a matter of leaning forward... lean into it!

Look at your own life. What plans do you have that contain a series of steps that you know are necessary that could be, well... "leaned into?"

Right now, while it's fresh in your mind: identify what actions would constitute *leaning into your own success*!

Sometimes just leaning will give you the momentum to keep on your path towards progress!

When I was a white belt in Brazilian Jiu-Jitsu, I did not particularly enjoy going to class. Once I was there, however, I was just fine.

After learning about "leaning into success," I identified that leaning (in regards to taking a jiu-jitsu lesson) was as simple as folding up my uniform and getting it ready for the next practice.

As it turns out, once I started taking action on preparing my uniform, I was halfway there!

I encourage you to dissect your "leaning." Would it be as simple making a phone call? Picking up a pen? Getting in your car? Shaking someone's hand? And <u>now</u> the NIKE: Just do it!

Begin With No Guarantees

Achievements of great worth will always involve some form of risk. My friend Andy Cooperman once told me this with regard to investments. "Low risk -- low return. High risk - (higher rate of failure) higher return." Thank Andy who also mentioned one other critical factor. He said that if you invest in your <u>own</u> company, "…at least you know what 's going on!"

It was then that a huge lightbulb went off in my head: "You never lose when you invest in YOU, Inc." …<u>but</u> you must begin investing without attachment to any guarantees!

With the stock market, or any other type of investment, you are not in control of production. You *can* pull your money out whenever you like (usually with a penalty), but you can not go into the workings of the company you've invested in AND SHAKE THINGS UP!

THAT IS THE PROBLEM! And trust me... no one can shake things up at a corporation better than the shareholders!

Am I saying yank all your money out of the NYSE? Well… just about. Investing in anything where you have little or no control over sales and/or production is always... a losing proposition. Create something yourself. Go out on a limb. When you have 'No Plan B', you'll get pretty damn' ambitious!

Investing in yourself does not GUARANTEE your investment, but if you want to achieve your goals, you shouldn't want it any other way. The universe consistently rewards action that creates <u>value</u>. Not action for the sake of action. Not value standing alone. The universe will reward you when you put your money where your mouth is, by either:

144

Starting your own business;

Taking a different job;

Changing your career;

Embarking on some new and unfamiliar challenge;

You percentage of success is a 1000% higher if you do this than if you don't -- but do not look for a guarantee!

Remember Andy? Your return will not usually be greater than the distance you venture out onto that limb!

When you hear a "great idea" about some new venture, resist the temptation of asking, "What guarantee do I have?" I sat this for a couple of reasons:

a) You'll look naïve.

b) There's never are true guarantees... not if the venture is worth your time.

The greatest success you'll ever experience will stem from opportunities where you can *not* see around the next corner. I am not saying throw the dice and put it all "on red," but do not be emotionally attached to "guarantees." Anything guaranteed either isn't of much value or is just plain-old BS!

Board Breaking. Think out of the box. Gotta do it first, just try... You can talk til' your blue in the face, but the "See, Amanda can do it" will not work for YOU.

Once you take the chance, the template is created.

Aiming High is the best way to increase your own chances of success!

Reaching Past

You must set your goals <u>past</u> your own expectations if you want to achieve them!. Aim <u>higher</u> than what you want to achieve. At first, this may sound like you're setting yourself up for certain disappointment. But really... you unknowingly already use this method to achieve many of your goals anyway. In the martial arts, we have a teaching metaphor that captures this point beautifully. It's called "reaching past." The analogy we use involves taking a look at the seemingly simple task of picking up a glass of water.

Every time you try to pick up a glass of water... in order to actually "grasp it," you first have to reach *beyond* the glass. Only then can you close your hand around it and take hold. It makes total sense and, once again, seems so obvious right? I mean, just imagine what would happen if you were to only "reach toward" the glass in order to grab it. You would, at best, only bump into it with the tip of your fingers - possibly knocking it over, too.

In order to actually pick up the glass -- you have to extend your hand beyond the glass… "reach past" the space the glass occupies, so that you can firmly get your hand around it. Makes sense, right?

Take a look around and you'll find many other things that conform to the philosophy of "reaching past."

Academic performance offers us another perfect example. When you were in school, you can probably recall using the approach of trying to get an A so you'd at least get a B. The idea is to aim a little higher than is comfortable to ensure that, at the very least -- you'll scratch the surface of success. Imagine trying to get a C in academics... If your lucky, you'll get a D right? So you must aim a little higher. You must "reach past."

Success Is Simple But Not Easy

Success is simple, but not simplistic. Fred Gleeck, a prominent guru in the field of Information Products says, "If you can brush your teeth, you can become successful."

Reaching high levels of achievement in any field requires mastering the execution of simple but powerful tasks. It is always the easy tasks that are repeated over and over which grant our achievement. The tasks don't usually involve a long drawn out process. Just like brushing your teeth.

Running a marathon requires that you put your body through the punishment of 26.2 grueling miles in one day. But finishing the marathon is not accomplished solely on the day of that marathon in Boston or New York. It is *accomplished* in the hundreds of days around your block, hundreds of miles in your neighborhood.

The actual activities of success are easy, but getting them done consistently - everyday - is tough.

We often do not persist at these simple tasks – the ones that lead up to success - because we are not sold on the idea that they will work. Instead, we look for "some other solution." If you study the most successful person in any field, you will find that he or she managed to get themselves to perform the necessary, little easy tasks... over and over again.

I love the movie "Forrest Gump" for this reason. How did he do it? Ho did he become so successful? Did he have superior intelligence? Not really. Did he have a great idea? Sort of, but nothing new. He simply had the sense to take action once... AND THEN KEEP ON TAKING ACTION!

Take learning for example. Did you know that just by reading 15 minutes per day, you can earn the equivalent of a Master's degree over the course of 18 months!

Success is never found outside of ourselves. We do not need any programs to follow per se. We do not need any outside information. We need only to *do* the stuff we know we need to do to make huge strides in achievement.

So why don't we do this if it involves only simple steps? Because it's hard! But wait, I thought it was simple.

Here's what makes it hard: what makes something hard to do is that it is... easy not to do!

We have all heard the phrase "An apple a day keeps the doctor away." So why don't we do it; why don't we just eat that apple every day? Because it's also easy not to do.

The things that will set you apart from the masses are always the tasks that are simple to do, but easy not to do.

Define Your Base Hits

In baseball, success is most often achieved by a series of base-hits. The problem is -- base hits don't make the front page of the newspaper! Home runs, on the other hand, lead to fame and fortune -- or do they?

We are a generation of home-run hitters. The guy who holds the home-run record becomes a household name. The person with the most runs batted in is never remembered. Yet, the team that makes it to the World Series is always the team that can hit singles. And... hit them <u>consistently</u>!

The best salespeople, the best managers, the best businesspeople focus on getting base hits. They know that the power of repetition is too strong for success to resist. Look at all the top producers in any field and I promise you'll find -- they focus on hitting singles.

I have a friend who earns millions of dollars as a financial planner. He said that while everyone is walking around trying to "land the big fish," he is taking care of a bunch of little accounts. He takes such <u>good</u> care of these so-called, little accounts that, often times, his clients give him keys to their homes. The trust level is high.

Now, let's do the math. I don't mean to turn this into a tirade about business, but it provides a great example because dollars are measurable. Who will get more referrals -- the big fish hunter or the guy who takes good care of everyone?

When you focus on base hits, you are forced to develop integrity. You simply cannot fake taking care of a bunch of people. On the other hand, when you hit a homer, you can quickly slip into the mistake of resting on your laurels.

There's one other crucial factor that comes into play... Do you know how exhausting it can be waiting to hit a home run? It is stressful; you become anxious. And, when you do manage to "land one," you're so nervous that the next one will be a long time in coming that you feel like taking a rest... because you "worked so hard."

This is no way to run your life. Nor is it any way to run a company or any other entity that requires growth and longevity.

Much like the saying "success is simple, but not easy," single hits represent those simple things. Those very important simple things.

Find your single hits. Hit them. Hit them all the time. Keep hitting them. The single hits in life are always easier to hit, will occur more frequently when you focus on them, are more affordable, are easier to manage, and ultimately... will provide more success and long-term happiness.

Working Harder IS Working Smarter!

One of the biggest stumbling blocks of success is the phrase, "Work Smarter, Not Harder." Have you ever known someone who is always looking for a way to do something faster or better?

It's like these people could have discovered the wheel just yesterday... And today, they are already trying to figure out how to attach a motor to it.

Work smarter, not harder? What the hell are they talking about? Working harder is working smarter.

Guess why? BeCAUSE EVERYONE IS TRYING TO HIT HOME RUNS!

Just work hard. You can't go wrong working harder. It feels better, and you'll develop confidence and determination. The efficiency will come as you get more skilled at doing the hard work. It will continue to become more efficient, more easy. *Then*, you will have worked smarter.

Hey, don't get me wrong. I am one of the first people to say "God Bless America" when I discovered the mail-merge feature! What I'm talking about is the allure of quicker, faster, and easier... in the name of finished, done, and accomplished. Working harder is working smarter.

My friend Ivan taught me a very valuable lesson with regard to this principle. I was working for an organization that was growing very rapidly. I came on board their team with lots of energy and enthusiasm. I was quick to introduce some time-saving strategies to the boss.

The plans worked. But, the boss wanted to know more. He became addicted to shortcuts under the guise of let's work smarter not harder. After a couple of months, the boss' lack of follow- through on the tasks that were already proven to be successful in the field - - began to rear its ugly head. So... we decided to have a meeting. Everyone gave their two cents... With the exception of, you guessed it: Ivan.

The boss couldn't take it any longer. So he singled out Ivan. Now, Ivan was well-schooled in sales... He knew that there were no shortcuts. Having been involved with the company for a decade, he knew damn well what the problem was. Ivan sat there looking at us like we were drunk... oblivious to the "real" problem.

So the boss said, "Well Ivan... what do you have to say? Everyone else is contributing... What gives? Don't you have input?" Ivan paused, (I could feel it coming) and he said "I think we should just stop trying to outsmart ourselves and focus on doing what we already know works." Ivan then scanned the room and made eye contact for a brief moment to let everyone know that he absolutely "knew the real deal." There was total silence. We all knew -- even the boss -- that he was right. He then folded up his planner, excused himself, and went back to his desk.

It's the only thing I ever heard him say that stuck with me. Ivan knew that working smarter actually meant working harder.

Understand, there's a difference between *staying in the Dark Ages* and *working harder*. Those folks who are so busy trying to find an easier or a faster way? Do they ever get anything done? This is a trap. There are countless numbers of individuals who are always trying to look for a better, easier, or faster way to do something that simply requires… work.

Failing To Plan Is... Planning To Fail

Skill in any area requires that you set aside time, to do what you have to do. As it stands, any project, goal, or undertaking involves planning. What people fail to realize is that *planning* must be planned as well.

Planning is the one single activity that requires discipline in and of itself. Yes, carrying out plans is the only way anything get done... But planning *what* to do can be very challenging.

Weddings offer a great example for observing otherwise-organizational-slobs develop this sudden penchant for planning. Seemingly overnight, individuals who are normally "all over the place mentally" grow this wild hair to be organized. It can be pretty entertaining to watch, too! You almost can't resist poking fun at someone who is suddenly becoming "organized."

Think about how much people actually accomplish when they plan weddings. Imagine where you could be if you approached other events in your life with the same focus and structure!

With the scenario of a wedding, you know that failing to plan is surely planning to fail. Remember the principle of "You can't not decide?" Here is a perfect example of that! You can't *not* plan! You are always planning.

Ultimately, when you finally do to see things beginning to happen in a big way, it will always have stemmed from planning. So, why not become an expert at it now? Follow my four-step system for planning, and you'll always be working on tasks that will take you to your higher self.

Plan deliberately.

Pioneers Return Home "Full of Arrows"

Action is the only true cause of achievement. You've learned that every result you obtain in your life has had a specific action that preceded it.

More importantly, you've discovered that the *simple* actions -- the "easy-to-do/hard-to-stick-to" actions -- are what will lead to future successes. Conversely, you've had it drilled into you throughout this book, that the "easy-to-do/hard-to-quit" actions are also what have caused most, if not all, of your current disappointments.

The question now is... what do I *do*? What plan should I follow? Whose advice should I listen to? What specific actions should I take?

Simply by asking these questions, you promote yourself to a higher level of existence.

One great idea that you can use right away is derived from the law of modeling. Modeling offers a fast shortcut. Modeling is "Do"ING THE EXACT SAME STEPS... IN THE EXACT SAME ORDER as someone else who's already attained the exact same result you're hoping to achieve!

Right about at this point, when I'm giving these talks to groups... is when some Macintosh user who is hell-bent on creativity, and/or "being original", will raise a hand and say, "Excuse me Scott, but isn't that just copying someone else? What about originality?"

I used to launch into this whole dissertation, breaking down the pros and cons of modeling. However, after years of trying to persuade people who are stubborn about something that works, I now just answer that question by saying, "Uhm, yes... That is just copying them. And no, it is not really original... Does anyone have any more questions?"

Remember, skeptics are the folks always playing defense. They rarely get much done. That, and the fact that, everyone else who works with them wants to kill them… So, don't worry about it. It is an effort in futility to try to influence a stubborn person. Stubborn people are easier to deal with when they are either sick or sleeping, so don't try to engage one otherwise. Let them stay on the porch while we move on to better things.

Modeling is based loosely around the principle of "pioneers return home full of arrows." Spawned also off the maxim of "do not try to reinvent the wheel," modeling will give you some solid results! Now, I am not knocking creativity. Innovation is awesome! Without it, we'd still be living by candlelight. But, try to invent your "own wheel" in your spare time -- the time you have left over after a day of accomplishing what you *know* will work!

Remember: many of the so-called "wheels" of today are really just the improved-upon "wheels" of yesterday anyway.

Pioneers prove a particular method will work again and again to create a consistent result. To get that same result for yourself, one fast way is to find the persons "to-do list" and then, do what they did. But this is only the starting point.

Modeling does have its drawbacks. Can you guess what they are? They focus first on "Do," instead of the "Be." Nonetheless, I highly recommend modeling if you currently lack a plan. The best plans to model are the ones in which your successful models' "Do"-ing sort of gels with or compliments your Be-ing. Then, you've found a turbo-charged success plan!

Remember, success leaves clues. Act like a detective. Search for the underlying principle that makes something or someone successful.

Mentors – The Fastest Shortcut

Masters have masters and mentors have mentors. If you look at the most influential people of our time, it won't take long to discover: they all had one thing in common besides the fruits of success. They all had access to wisdom coming from people who have "done it" or "made it" it before they did.

In the beginning of our journeys, we usually focus of the modeling part of success. We re-create the action steps of those who have traversed the lonely road of achievement so as to "save time" and to avoid the frustration associated with trial and error.

The fastest shortcut, however, is not just to model what they do... but rather model what they *think* and how they *feel*. Included in this are the elements of attitude, outlook, and a general sense of underlying philosophy in all that they do. If you want to model someone successfully, model their being-ness first and doing-ness second.

On the surface, this may sound like I'm saying "try to be something you're not." But let's take a look at that, too. If you are not getting a result that you desire in your life... or, if you are getting results that you do not desire -- the problem lies not in what you do but what you *are*. Further, you may find that by adopting, borrowing, or even "trying on for size" someone else's attitude -- YOU MAY DISCOVER YOU ACTUALLY LIKE IT! What's more is you may discover IT ALSO WORKS.

Model attitude... the rest will follow.

Jack LaLaine is one of the healthiest men alive. If you wanted to be just half as healthy as he is, it would benefit you to find out how he thinks, feels, and philosophizes about fitness.

If you wanted to be an all-star basketball player, you wouldn't just buy the same sneakers as Michael Jordan, or shoot hoops for the same amount of time that he does... You would instead say to yourself during practice, "I wonder what Michael Jordan thinks about when he feels like quitting?" If we can borrow "an experienced brain" during the difficult periods of life, we will always come out on top. Always!

Here's an example of how I used modeling to succeed:

I wanted to own and run my own karate school. I was a State Karate Champion, so I figured, "Hey, everyone will want to train with me!" I was wrong. Everyone wanted to train with this other gentleman. So... I went to see what he did. Fortunately, the man I approached was willing and even eager to help me. He gave me his plan. I followed it... And it worked. Everyone soon wanted to train with me. Well, at first anyway...

After a while, I got bored. I had to keep doing the things he was doing, but I couldn't maintain my excitement about doing them! I loved the lifestyle of being a great karate teacher, but didn't truly appreciate what I had created. So I returned to my new-found "guide". This is when my model became my *mentor*. My mentor taught me how to think about people, how to think about problems, and how to think about learning.

And you know what? I no longer needed to copy his *actions*. I was able to create my own based on his attitude and philosophy. It worked effectively. In addition, the attitude I learned to adopt about one thing from him began to carry forward into many other areas.

This is important to note. We already have mentors whether we acknowledge them as mentors or not. But, one huge problem is that our default mentors are usually underperforming or underachieving. I know it sounds disrespectful to say, but many of the philosophies we adhere to were embedded by people who just didn't know any better. It doesn't make them bad people... but it makes them horrible mentors.

Do you remember my philosophy about "you can't not decide?" It means that you are always deciding. Well, you can't not have a mentor. If you don't actually have one, that means your only mentor is you... and you never want to be your own mentor.

Don't Seek To Imitate The Masters... Rather, Seek What They Sought.

The above phrase comes from martial arts philosophy. I wish I had learned this one a little earlier. It might have saved me some time.

Here's the literal translation. I believe it is very germane to what were discussing here. If you "seek what they sought," then you are truly modeling your mentors. You will not live an identical life-pattern as them but a pretty-much-identical lifestyle.

I learned this one from a mentor of mine named Fred Mertens. At one time in my life, I really admired (and still do) the philosophy of a very famous, very highly-skilled, and very successful master. His name is Tiger Schulmann. Now, I was not the only one trying to model Master Schulmann, practically my whole industry wanted to know what he was doing.

In an effort to help me, Fred, my mentor at the time, gave me some of the most valuable advice I have ever received. He said, "Scott, it appears to me that Master Schulmann did his own thing... So, if you really want to enjoy his results -- do your own thing! Then, you'll really be modeling him!"

Years later, Master Schulmann and I became friends. Not really friends though, more of a periodic teacher-student relationship. The kind where I just sort of check in; he asks questions; and I listen and learn... a lot.

One time during one of these visits, we got to talking about how so many people copy his style, or methodology. Master Schulmann said something in passing that I'm sure he had no idea would stick with me forever. He said, "They'll always be able to copy my actions... but never my character. They cannot copy my persistence."

What will you pay your mentor?

There is always a price for success. Subsequently, mentors are never usually free... not the good ones anyway.

Be ready to compensate your mentor. However, money is only a part of this. Many mentors will not keep you as a student unless you're *progressing*. After all, your success is a reflection on them! Be ready to receive assignments and to be accountable for your own results as well.

You also better be able to give them something back in the form of philosophical progress as well. Whenever you learn or discover something, make a note of it. Then add your perspective and tell

156

your mentor about it. Together, you will both refine and isolate certain principles of achievement. Remember, mentors usually do not need the money – you pay them by becoming more than what you currently are.

Paying for your mentoring assures the best advice anyone can get. When you pay for something, you respect it. The reason free advice is the worst (even if the actual advice is identical) is because it usually will not be acted upon! Thus, it becomes useless advice... because it was not used. Paying also shows you're serious. Unfortunately, until you get to know someone in this country, the only way you know if someone is serious is when they put-up or shut-up. My advice is do-both. Pay your dues financially and metaphorically, and then listen twice as much as you talk.

Remember, the "poor man should take the rich man out to dinner... listen to him, and then pick up the tab!"

A Sure Fire Way to Find and Be Accepted by a Mentor:

Be up!

You must be enthusiastic. Act upbeat. Put some pep in your step.

Show up!

Often times, I have found out where a mentor usually will be and just shown up. Unannounced. Be careful with this one. Use your judgment. While it shows you're a go getter, you don't want to come off like a weirdo. My experience is, at first, they think you're a weirdo... unless you are a person of substance - then you will have their attention.

Be real!

Do not brag, act like you know it all, be pretentious, or be overly confident. You'd better have manners too; and no, this is not advice geared towards recent college graduates. Plenty of people in their late 50's are rude and have been so for so long that they don't even realize it. If you are not regularly complimented about your manners, you probably lack some.

Ask!

Acquiring a mentor is much like getting a job or making a sales call. You have to apply and/or ask for the sale. Do not wait for them to say, "Wow, I'd love to have you as my personal pain in the ass, can I please be your success coach?" Just politely and sincerely say, "I firmly believe I can learn from your experiences. I have an idea how it might be beneficial for you to take me on as a student. Would you be willing to coach me on a trial basis?"

If they accept, follow up with, "Thank you." Then, without hesitation, take out your checkbook and say, "I know that your knowledge is worth more than I can probably afford, but what do I need to give you as a retainer to get started?"

Pay your mentor now or pay later from mistakes you could've avoided. No, not everyone has a mentor. Then again, not everyone is successful either.

Monkey See, Monkey Don't

Choosing someone to model or appointing someone as your mentor can be deceiving. Not that they are dishonest, although it's a possibility, but things are not always what they seem.

Look past the leased vehicles! Plenty of morons have fancy cars and homes, but don't have a dollar to their name. Avoid younger mentors if they do not have a proven track record.

Your mentors' age is not important in comparison to yours. Many men and women choose mentors for certain areas of their life that are ten years younger than they are. Remember, we are going after a particular result in their lifestyle. Don't hold it against your mentors if they are single and you are looking for real estate advice. They may not teach you about love, but you will love what they can teach you about finding properties.

More Problems With Modeling

When you focus solely on what someone is doing without considering the "Be"ING element, you run into a few other problems.

"Do" is considered 2nd generation. You are focusing on the hand, not the brain that makes the hand move. In this way, you are forcing the "Do" habits onto yourself. Michael Jordan doesn't have to force himself to be like Michael Jordan! He only has to be *himself*, which is focusing on his own being-ness.

There is a universal truth called "As a man thinks – so he is." Liars... lie. Crooks... steal. Nice people... do nice things. Force a crook to get a job and he'll get sick, go crazy, or jump out of a window. If you feel skeptical about this, just imagine if you were forced to rob banks. How would you feel?

Could you merely copy the actions of a bank robber and consider yourself a true-blue bank robber? Probably not. You may enjoy the cash – but, we all know that bank robbers enjoy the robbing too. Putting this idea into a ridiculous hypothetical scenario makes it simple to buy into the need for "Be." Bank robbers are still bank robbers, even when they're not out robbing banks!

Putting Be and "Do" together is the key!

Focusing on Be allows you to see the way the world works from another's point of view. In this case… the model.

When you see the world the way they see it, you can figure out what parts make up the doing. How, you ask? Because you are borrowing their eyes.

For example: I collect seashells. If you wanted to become as skilled as I am in seashell collecting, you have some options.

You could go to Google and do a search for seashells. You could join a seashell collectors association. You could buy a set of videos entitled, "How To Become an Expert Seashell Collector In Just 14-Days". You could even follow me around and capture the essence of the master doing his craft.

Then, we could seashell hunt together. And, guess what would happen? I would come home with 50 and you with 5. Why? You're only copying the "Do," and I'm *being* the be, *doing* the do, and *having* the have!

As you and I walk the shoreline side by side, you are looking for seashells. But I am not looking for sea shells. I am looking for a little white thing that pokes up through the sand when the water breaks on the beach.

For all intents and purposes, we are both hunting sea shells – BUT, WE ARE NOT LOOKING FOR THE SAME THING!

Planning... The Pen Is Mightier Than The Sword

If you want to quickly achieve more and more goals than you ever thought possible, you should have a pen with you at all times.

Writing out your plans is one of the only sure-fire ways you will ever actually "Do" your "Do"-ing. Take vacations for instance. The day before you go away on vacation, you probably find yourself getting a lot of things accomplished. For a moment, you think to yourself, "Imagine if I worked like this everyday of my life!" -- and that's good; You should think about it that way.

Writing down the things you need to get done the "night before" triples your ability to get "at it.' I know it sounds simple, but many of us do not do this on a regular basis. Most people only do it when they "have to," and that is not the way to operate.

Writing imprints upon the brain

Always write down the stuff that you think you can remember. Chances are you'll forget, plus... writing imprints upon the brain. When you write something down, you send a signal to your subconscious mind to "go after it." When I teach goal setting to people and I follow up on them months or weeks later, usually 100% of them tell me that "strange things" began to happen that helped them achieve those goals.

It sounds so simple, too. Let me highlight how powerful this practice really is, and then I'll give you some scientific proof just to back it up.

In the practice of goal setting, there is something known as a *"quick-list"*. A quicklist is where you take a sheet of paper and a pen and you write out a list of goals as quickly as you can. The only rule of thumb is, you are not allowed to think about it -- you just have to do it. Well, I once wrote out a "quick-list." I was instructed to do this by a man who became incredibly successful at a very young age. His confidence in the method impressed me enough to "give it a shot." Now, one thing you should know here... I wrote down stuff just as a joke. I wrote down things just to appease him, things that, at the time, had zero possibility of happening.

He said, "Write down some things you would love to do if you knew they were guaranteed to happen... if you only took the first step." I was 18 at the time. So I wrote out two huge goals... Goals that transcended money. Goals that money couldn't buy.

One: Get accepted to train at, and actually go to Seoul, South Korea.

Two: Win a State Championship Gold Medal.

Doesn't sound so big right? Well, at the time I wrote that stuff down, it was so far from ever becoming a reality that I can't even explain it. I knew no one in Korea, didn't even have a job at the time, couldn't speak Korean, and I had - what appeared to be - nothing to even ensure my means of getting there.

Next, I had never won a competition in my life. I was the guy with talent that couldn't get it together in a competitive arena. I had lost 9 straight tournaments over a two-year period. I had become so accustomed to losing that I could taste it.

Yet, when you take an idea and then put pen to paper, it's as if your telling your mind, "give it to me."

Never let a good idea go by without writing it down.

Did you ever get a great idea and then you let it slip out from under you? Another brilliant idea that just... slips through the cracks and disappears? One more great reason to write something down is to memorialize it. All day long, your mind is thinking and processing thoughts. Many times, you will come up with a great idea, and think to yourself, "Wow, this is great, I should write this down." But you don't. And then, six months later, you get that idea again and you're like, "Man, I should have written that down a long time ago." Or worse, later on you see someone else running with your idea... because they thought of it and took *action* on it!

This is known as "Respecting The Genesis of the Thought." I first learned this from Anthony Zacharakis. "Mr. Z." was a successful real estate owner and he firmly believed in writing things down and then reviewing them at a later time after "sleeping on it." Most of us already know this is powerful if used on a regular basis, but how many of us actually do it? Mr. Z. knew it was important. He always had a pen in his hand and a small pad to write on.

Another great example of this is the world famous copywriter Bob Bly. Mr. Bly is renowned for his creativity. He has produced more broadcasted copy than any other advertising creator in the history of advertising. If you've ever watched a late night infomercial or listened to a radio commercial, there's a 100% chance you have heard words that, at one time, entered Bob Bly's mind, were written down, and then entered your ear.

I had the good fortune of meeting Mr. Bly. While we were talking, he got an idea out of thin air and quickly pulled out a tiny spiral notebook. Nothing fancy, just your typical dime store notepad, and wrote down the idea. It hit me right then and there that Mr. Bly is probably not as creative as we all might think -- he just takes massive action when a creative idea strikes his consciousness!

Writing things down gives your brain the signal to give you more!

When you write something down, you tell your brain with total authority that you are respecting the genesis of all thoughts. Your brain then acknowledges that, although you may not follow through on all the great ideas it gives, you are, at least, taking the first steps. It is afterwards that it becomes evident just how great the power of this really is. Your brain feels like it has been given a promotion... and then will start showing up everywhere you go. You will be in the shower and it will give you an award- winning idea. You'll be at a movie theater watching a film that has nothing at all to do with your goals... and "Pow" -- your brain will give you to the solution to a pressing problem.

Car trouble or an epiphany?

Give your brain permission to assist you... But, when you do respect, watch out -- make have a pen handy everywhere. I have developed the habit of actually pulling over in my car and writing something down. And it happens all the time. You know, I always wondered why you see someone pulled over that seems to be just sitting in their car... They're probably solving the troubles of the world for all we know. He either has car trouble or has just had an epiphany... and he's writing it down!

However, the reverse is true when you get an idea and *dismiss* it. When you do that -- you're sending a signal to your brain that says, "No thanks, I don't need that. I already know everything. Don't bother me with that stuff right now. I'm going to watch "General Hospital" now. Get back to me later!" And your brain, because it always does what you tell it... goes into hibernation mode.

Keep a pen and pad within arm's reach. Be with that pen like the paranoid person who keeps a gun everywhere... You will become paranoid that your brain will attack you at any given moment.

Using highlighters is a waste of time.

You should read books with a little pad of paper next to you ... pen out and ready to go. Someone once said to me (a typical know-it-all), "Well I don't like to carry around extra stuff; so usually when I read, I just use a highlighter. Yeah, ok... sure. Look, I know that trick, too. And don't tell me "Well, some things work good for some people and some work good for others." Baloney. You and both know what happens when you use a highlighter.

Two things:

You end up highlighting things you either already know or things you have already heard! When I teach this one to groups, there's always like ten or twenty people that burst out laughing. It's so true isn't it. I mean occasionally we highlight a good idea. But, more often than not, we read something that's a good idea,. but is usually something we already know... and it's kind of like we want to highlight how smart we already are!

Here's the real reason highlighting is a waste of time. What is the general mindset when highlighting anyway? Sure, I know. You're going to go back later on and study what you highlighted. Gimme' a break. Oh, how about this one. I'm going to go back and transfer all the stuff I highlighted into a special notebook. Lies.

Smart people know that they don't have the discipline to go back and review what they highlighted. They realize that it not only saves time, but will actually get done if they simply read with a pen in their hand and a pad nearby.

Writing things down burns ideas into your memory. My friend Chris understands this principle better than anyone. Chris knows his memory is limited. Yet, if you ever hear him speak about a subject like personal development, or nutrition, you'd think he had a PhD. I learned Chris' secret. We lived in California together as a couple of bachelors in the mid-90's. When I would go out and party on Friday nights, Chris would listen to audio programs.

When I would return, he would have like 12 pages of notes on a legal pad. And here's the kicker... He never had to go back and study the stuff again! He could repeat it verbatim, even years later. To this day, I don't think he's even aware of the impact this had, but I saw it first hand. His hand burned it into his memory by just taking notes. He does it with books, too. It seemed so effective that I started trying it myself. It makes reading more of a job but, hey... don't get me wrong -- it works.

Scientists know why it works!

When you write something down, YOU LITERALLY MAGNETIZE THE IDEA TO YOUR CONSCIOUSNESS.

There is a part of the brain known as the Reticular Activation System, a.k.a. RAS. The function of the RAS is to filter out, analyze, and detect important things from non-important things. Now, one point in particular you need to be grateful for is that you can CHOOSE what the RAS deems essential or non-essential.

Here's an example of what the RAS does. You go to a coffee shop. It's packed full of people. You can barely hear yourself think, let alone concentrate enough to read a magazine article. But, through the babbling and background noise, you hear your name. It's faint but suddenly, like a squirrel who hears someone step on a twig from 200 yards away, this person has capture your rapt attention. You develop super-human hearing powers that, until moments ago, lay dormant - asleep.

That was your RAS letting you know that you might want to snap out of it. Here's another one. Ever notice that once you start driving a new (fill in the name of your car here), you suddenly start spotting them EVERYWHERE?

Or... let's say you plan a vacation to go to Arizona. You call a travel agent to get prices - but nothing else... it's just an idea (or is it?). Now, later that same day you go shopping and what do you see out of the blue? An Arizona license plate on the car in front of you! You start thinking, "Wow, it's a sign." Then, as you're driving back home, and you round the next corner, you see an Arizona Iced Tea Truck making a delivery! Now, you are convinced that your Creator wants to send you on a mission to Arizona!

But really... it's not a sign. God could care less if you go to Arizona or go to the beach. There *are* no coincidences. It's selective perception – you became more aware of "Arizona." You are just another idiot who doesn't know that the RAS works around the clock to help you... if you'd only pay attention to it! Until now.

Here's how this applies to writing down your goals. Putting the pen to a goal is like planning a trip to Arizona. You command your brain to let you in on what you need to know, do, or watch out for. The car with the Arizona license plate has always been in the neighborhood. The Arizona Iced Tea truck has always made deliveries, and you have always driven past it.

Likewise, all the things you need to be, do, and have to get more out of life... are all around you -- RIGHT NOW... waiting for you to step up to the plate -- or the pad of paper, I should say!

The RAS is probably responsible for the old martial arts adage: "When the student is ready, the teacher will appear."

Living On Paper

You will commonly find yourself in one of two categories when you're trying to carry out your plans. You could say that people generally fall into one or the other when it comes to planning.

The Challenge of Planning

Long Range Visionaries-

These people have a clear vision of where it is they would like to go. They know what they want to do, and they have a pretty good understanding of how they want to live the life of their dreams. The trouble they have is: after they invent this grand plan, they can't get the rubber to meet the road - so to speak. In other words, they don't really see, or know what the next few action steps will be necessary in order to attain their dreams.

A young man wants to be an actor. He's not sure what genre of the big screen he'll specialize in... He's not clear as to how to go about getting connections... He may not even have a role model or acting coach to guide him in his next dozen steps. All he knows is, "I wanna' act!"

A man works in a cubical for a major corporation. He's got ten more years of what is now incessant misery until retirement. His passion is... food. He's a great cook. He's got friends who are chefs who have great ideas about prep-work, seasoning, broiling, etc. In his heart, he knows he was built for the kitchen, for the hospitality world, and for service... However, he's also a talented engineer. He makes too much money doing this to feasibly do anything else... He's not quite sure how he can safely leave his job and start his restaurant.

Short Range Expeditors –

Give this person a to-do list and consider it done! She can write down 14 things to do... add to the list -- handle a crisis -- and *still*

166

get it all done with finesse. Her colleagues know that if you want to get something done, she's the man for the job... figuratively speaking.

She has her Wednesday all mapped out by Monday afternoon. She's allowed time in her schedule for heavy traffic, flat tires, unannounced building inspectors, trips to the ladies room for that bladder problem, and even has a back-up babysitter in case the regular sitter flakes-out... again!

By 8:30 p.m., the kids are asleep; the tasks are done; email is deleted; tomorrow's lunch is packed... And now, she enjoys a glass of red wine while sitting in the tub with her favorite novel. The day has been conquered... and, once again, she has done it stress-free! People are amazed at how well she can juggle life... fall in mud... and come out spotless.

Yet, she feels this emptiness inside. She doesn't have a bigger picture of what her dreams could be. She's gotten so skilled at "Do"ING that she never stopped to think about where she's *going*. The kids will be teens soon. Then, they'll move out of the house. How will she spend the rest of her days? Forget dying with her music still in her -- she's not even sure if she likes Beethoven or Bach!

Now, sometimes we find ourselves floating back and forth between the two types. But, if we only had a more comprehensive, or more complete, map we'd be just fine. Often times, we will excel at one end of the spectrum, but can't quite grasp the bridge to the other.

Why people hate planning and to-do lists

One reason you'll hate planning and working from a to-do list is because, in the beginning, it often seems like you're going nowhere... fast.

The list seems too structured, and you get so frustrated from having to constantly look at it that, before you know it, you're sick of the very thing that is supposed to help!

One reason for this reaction might be that sticking to a list doesn't provide for spontaneous living. But, that's not really the deal. Not by a long shot.

The fact of the matter is, when you first start working from a to-do list, you're always working on things that you should've done a along time ago!

In the beginning, you are digging yourself out of hole - as opposed to building a foundation for your future. So, each time you look down at your list... you're just reminded of how much you still have left to do. And that sucks!

Soon, you start thinking to yourself, "This is why I am not successful in the first place - I am just a bad planner!" But don't think like that! Planning, just like riding a bike, takes time. Not really the planning so much but the execution... THAT IS THE TOUGHT PART. Remember, great plans happen -- implementation is the obstacle.

But, once you are started... Look out! You'll become a force to be reckoned with. What's more is, once you're halfway out of the "hole" -- you will have already built up enough momentum to keep going! Then, it won't seem like you're just trying to play "catch-up."

This part of the "Do"-ing always takes a little getting used to. Just accept the fact that, for the first few days, you'll really need to force yourself to get things done. Even if the rewards are big, your self-discipline will be tested to its maximum. So, suck it up!

Success will never act on you

Eventually, we all TAKE ACTION towards our goals. It's just that, many times... we are five or six years behind the 8-ball. It's not because of lack of talent but rather -- lack of ATTENTION, WILL, and ACTION!

Too many times we wait until life acts on us to react. This is why we don't really get good at paying our parking tickets. That is until we've paid hundreds of dollars in late fees up until we have reached our forties!

Listen, you will, sooner or later, act on your goals. All I'm saying is "Do" IT NOW -- GET MOVING!

When you do-it-now... you are taking steps towards dreams out of proactive-ness (you attack) vs. reactive-ness (you react). The difference is tremendous! Many people think that the only thing lost is time. NOT SO.

When you move towards your dreams proactively - taking steps to ensure your outcomes are deliberate - you marshal a power 1000 times greater than waiting for opportunity to knock! You're using your will to improve your circumstances.

By waiting until you need-to or have-to, it is often too late, too depressing, and too unfulfilling to lift even a finger! Your action muscles have become so atrophied and you can't stop beating yourself over the head thinking, "Why didn't I do this sooner?" When life knocks on your door, you are often caught in your proverbial underwear; the house (or one-bedroom apartment) is a mess; you haven't taken a shower; and just the thought of changing your lifestyle sucks!

But when YOU rap on the door to life (by writing out your goals), you catch life in its underwear... And unlike you, life is glad you knocked first - and is at your beck and call!

Life will always cooperate when you grab it by the throat. It has to. It will always open the door unto which you've knocked!

Learn To Say, "That Emotion Is Bad."

Picture this, you're trying to achieve a daily goal, task, or some other routine that requires deliberate scheduling and execution, i.e. reading, studying, etc. Granted, you already know that these things have to be acted upon; they require action. And, you also know that many times they are NOT FUN BUT NECCESSARY, right?

169

Well, isn't it funny how, when you try to get some of these things done, the most tempting distractions will suddenly scream your name?

When you make a declaration to seize the day... The day will test you. Not to worry. though. I have a foolproof plan that you can follow! I know it sounds simple, but we already know that the best stuff is simple.

The first step is to recognize when it's coming (the distraction). Whenever you start to plan to do one thing, you think about it first. A mental image picture created in your mind attracts you to the thing you want. This in turn CREATES EMOTIONS. In previous lessons, you learned that thought always precedes emotion. But emotion is what continues to draw us closer and closer to the thought held in mind. Sounds like a catch-22 right? Well, hang in there.

The way to stay on track is to simply tell yourself, "That emotion is bad."

You see, when you go to the gym, you create an emotion that supports this, draws you closer to it. But, on your way to the gym, you drive past a Honda dealership. You see that car you've been thinking about getting. Now, you're ready to act on this new and unexpected thought. And a problem now emerges.

You're brain kicks in... "Gee, I guess I have a couple of extra minutes -- I'll just stop in and take a look. Besides, at this time, the gym's always packed anyway."

And, what happens? Your "quick stop" turns into a one-hour ordeal. You end up not going to the gym *or* buying the car!

The field of attention

We have what is called a field of attention. Picture a target. In the center, lies the bull's-eye or your goal (going to the gym). The outer circles, visible but not in your direct focus of intention, are your interests - or better put... your distractions, i.e. the Honda dealership). Every goal you have, big or small, will have these outer circles - lovingly called "interests" - associated with them.

Your ability to succeed depends on how well you can deal with these distractions and say (aloud if necessary) "That emotion is bad."

Some people will suggest, "Just take a different route to the gym" (remove the distractions). This is often the viewpoint taken by drug addicts. They believe that if they could just get out of this town, they'd be fine. You already know how ridiculous that is. We do not want to pray, hope, or wish for... our distractions to go away -- instead you should want to develop the wisdom to recognize when they are about to take hold of you -- AND THEN BeCOME STRONG ENOUGH TO RESIST THEM!

The real problem is not the distraction, though. It is the feeling or the emotion triggered by the distraction!

Simple in principle, but powerful in understanding isn't it?

It's not the distraction... Distractions will always be present to do what they do best -- distract. It's the *emotion* that we let take hold of us that turns a distraction into a new or different goal! The emotion created by entertaining the thought of the distraction is the real culprit.

When you focus and accept the viewpoint that the emotion created by the distraction is the problem, not the distraction itself, you begin to co-exist more effectively with your distractions.

Here's yet another reason we want to focus on distraction management opposed to removal. Remember the target analogy? The center represents the current or immediate goal. The outer rings represent what could possibly be in your "field of attention." Because it is very possible to have other goals in your field of attention, you do not want to simply "put on your blinders" in pursuit of the present goal. You see, distractions, as well as other goals, make up the outer rings on the bulls-eye. Learn how to recognize the distractions, the other goals, and every thing else in the outer rings as potential emotion-triggers. When you feel them getting the best of you, say to yourself, "this emotion is bad."

This strategy will also save you tons of money and enable you to become more disciplined with your cash. Take shopping, for instance! Ever go shopping for something specific, yet leave with other items... items you had no intention of getting? Sometimes, we even fail to get the very thing we went shopping for specifically. I suggest that EVEN IF YOU SEE A SALE THAT IS A STEAL... Develop the habit of saying, "This emotion is bad" and do not buy the item. Even if you know you will absolutely need it... someday.

Even if you know you will never see the item at that price -- ever again -- do not get it on impulse. If you do, you'll rob yourself of an outstanding opportunity to develop your focus muscles. Say, "that emotion is bad." Walk away; go to lunch; think about it some more, ... and THEN go back to get the item if need be. Become the kind of person who does not collapse unto impulses... even with the things you love.

There are literally millions of people who think that the distractions must be removed. To adopt this perspective is to give away your personal power. Remember the Platinum Rule: "Be able to experience anything..."

Surround your goal.

If you are to become successful, you must recognize your field of attention for what it is... permanent, but manageable. You must develop the ability to sense when your field of attention is creeping in on your goal. Ignore this important skill and you will always be behind in your goals, plans, and desires.

The Power Of The Week... The Perfect Unit of Time

The week is the perfect unit of time in which to achieve the short-term goals that will eventually add up to your long-term goals. This block of time gives you the urgent, do-it-today action opportunities, as well as room for the smaller building blocks which can lead to your huge accomplishments. The week allows for the all-important flexibility necessary to address unpredictable occurrences, such as family crises, a health issue, or even a screw-up on the part of someone else.

You can't go wrong by using the week as your platform. Typically, when the "Long-range Visionary types" attempt to act on their dreams, they tend to think that the week is too short. They instead resort to "hoping within the month" as opposed to the subtle, yet "urgent pressure of the week." They overlook the power of the week as a significant chunk of time, because they fail to break their BIG DREAMS into semi-large, but manageable bites. Bites that can easily be consumed over 7 consecutive days.

At the other end of the spectrum, we have the 9 to 5'er. This day-to-day model so often used by the "Short-Range Expediter types" is great for getting things done, but lacks the power of the week. They do not realize that a week is not a ¼ of a month - it is only seven short, but high-leverage days -- if you let it be so.

These micro-managers become uptight when a particular task cannot be accomplished within the 8-12 hour workaday routine. And when this happens to them -- watch out. They will be miserable to be around and will always upset at the end of the day... A day that would actually, and truthfully, be considered productive by all standards when using the "week model." These type-A's often forget what day it is because of all the stress. And when its the weekend, they can only remember what wasn't done "last Friday" and will be ready to warn everyone on Monday how this week had better be different.

The solution for all is the week. You must master the week in order to Be, Do, and Have your life's desires... especially if those desires include a family life, peace of mind, and co-workers that are glad to see you on Monday!

It allows for the unpredictable.

Another reason is... the week is believable! Both to you and those with whom you've made commitments. This is a very simple principle, another one of my "Wow, I never thought of it like that" principles. First, let's talk about you. If you were to tell yourself today that you're going to get the car detailed tomorrow, you know damn well it ain't gonna' happen. In the same breath, if you tell your spouse you're going to take the kids to the library next month, that too… ain't gonna' happen. But, all of these things can be managed within a week. And the best part of the week is this: If you really can't get a particular important undertaking done inside of a week you always have ... NEXT WEEK!

Next week is always more acceptable to other people and more believable to one's psyche than tomorrow or next month. If you are accountable to someone and cannot get something done within a deadline and you need an extension... ask for another day and you're considered inexperienced -- ask for another month and you're fired. But ask for another week, and you'll be thought of as reasonable.

The tools to plan for a week

First, purchase a planner that allows you to view one week at a glance. For years, I have used the same kind of planner you'd find at a hair salon. You know the one. It is one of the only planners that has a twelve-hour day. Most planners end at 7 or even 5 p.m.! (Who finishes work at 5 p.m., huh?). It is also broken down into 15-minute subsegments. I FEEL THIS IS CRUCIAL. A lot can happen in one hour... and a lot can NOT HAPPEN in one hour.

When you "schedule" your tasks (as well as your appointments), you truly step into the next generation of self-management. And after all, isn't that what we're doing? You cannot manage time! Time is not manageable. You cannot control it! We do not *manage* time, (Hell, who are we kidding? We can't even manage people!)… BUT, WE CAN MANAGE OURSELVES! Further, the wisdom behind planning your tasks is truly amazing. Instead of having your to-do list, your list of calls to make, and your list of actual appointments, you schedule everything in small 15-minute increments. This is a much more effective method than anything I've ever used… and it gets RESULTS!

Now, I know for a fact that there are some of you who love electronics... Do not be fooled! Your handhelds (a.k.a. PDA's) are great... that is until they breakdown when you absolutely need them the most. Also, they do not give you the larger scope that the paper, one-week, produced by At-a-Glance planner does. Sure, the electronics are great for thirty-thousand phone numbers, and great for doing re-schedules (because you don't have to re-enter data), and so on. My contention is this... Why do you need that many numbers at your fingertips when you're away from your desk? And, if you have that many reschedules, you had better look at the effectiveness of your appointment-making (that is unless you're the one always breaking them!).

Next, you should buy a stack of three by five cards. Do not overlook the simplicity of 3 x 5 cards. For years, I procrastinated about living out my goals because I could not see the difference between a small notebook and 3 x 5 index cards. I know you have raised an eyebrow at this, but bear with me. I first heard about 3 x 5 cards from Harvey McKay, author of <u>What They Still Don't Teach You at Harvard Business School</u>. Harvey tells the story of the famous dean of a university, a man known largely for his ability to turn his ideas into action! He says this man walks around with 20 or 30 of those 3x5 cards... and whenever he gets an idea, a thought, a plan for a task, or hears something that makes him go "hmm" -- he stops what he's doing and quickly jots down the idea. Later, he returns to the item, and then asks himself, "Should I schedule it, file it, or act on it?"

One of my mentors, Fred Gleeck, swears by this method. Fred wouldn't even take me seriously until I started using the cards. He was like, "How do I know you'll be able to keep track of all the million-dollar ideas I'm going to give you? I know what happens to notes... They end up in that place where all the other notes are!" The very first day I tried it, I wanted to kick my self in the ass for not following through on years earlier!

I have found this system to work wonders for me. There is a huge difference between keeping good ideas in a notebook or a computer file, and 3x5 cards. Notebooks do not give you the flexibility to move the ideas around. You cannot make piles or shuffle ideas using a notebook without tearing the pages out of the book. Another, and more important reason to use 3 x 5 cards is that you can file them into categories quickly and easily. And, as far as a computer goes? Forget it! I have struggled with the paper problem for year. I love technology too, but there is no way you get to "go over" (let alone compare) the files stored on a PC as well as you can with real cards. Once the information goes into a computer, even though it does save space and eliminates excess paper, that information remains out of sight for a long, long, time. And you know what they say, "out of sight, out of mind!" The 3x5 card method is awesome. They stick around... You get to thumb through them fast, too -- much faster than opening and closing files on a PC... and cards don't "crash."

In fact, I'll let you in on another secret... The book you are reading right now... WAS FIRST CREATED ON 3 X 5 CARDS! Yep, it started by "modeling" all the concepts that had stirred around in my brain for months. The 3x5 cards serve as a handy catch-all for your mind.

With these two items: A one-week At-a-Glance appointment book that has a 7-day, 12-hour/day format, and a stack of 3x5 cards, I've made a lot of stuff happen.

How to plan for the week

Okay, you've got the one-week planner. You have an idea of what things you'd like to accomplish this week, as well as a definite must-do list of things you need to accomplish this week.

First:

Get set. Do this: On Sunday afternoon, or some other day towards the end of the week, sit down in a quiet, comfortable place. No phones, no TV's, no interruptions. You may even find that it's necessary to schedule your scheduling! The goal here is to be able to carve out an hour or so of quiet so you can really hold a picture in your mind of how you want your week to unfold.

Second:

Discover. Do this: I call this the discovery phase. Again, I amaze myself with my intelligence... First, ask yourself two questions. These two questions will do you a world of good in all areas of your life. These questions are usually asked by people only when their lives are either in dire straits or after they've achieved most of their significant goals. Ask yourself these questions and you'll rarely find yourself in the first category, but instead heading towards the second category -- almost always.

Here goes. *First*. Recognize the 3 areas of your life that exist no matter what you are doing. If you have ever done any type of time-management work, study, or seminars you've probably heard a very long-winded, esoteric, intricate version of this concept. I will spare you that type of diatribe due to my penchant for simplicity. We will not delve into the roles and goals, or the "true happiness" principles that will serve as mental morphine. Rather, let's just all agree that these three areas do indeed exist regardless of your opinion of them.

Work: This category covers all things related to what you do for a living.

This includes people, places, things, study, goals, and anything else that is associated with it. If you are retired, this includes contribution, legacy, volunteering, teaching, and anything under that heading. If you are looking for work it includes all the skills, knowledge, contacts, actions, and whatever it takes to begin your dreams.

More simply put, the Work category encompasses the first 12 hours of your day.

Home: This category includes family, household, relationships, events, vacations... anything not career-related.

This area is always tougher to work on. It requires a lot of deliberateness. Whereas work has continual deadlines and other external prompters, home requires more care, more intention, and more inquiry. "Do" not - NOT SPEND TIME HERE. You can not neglect "Home." If you are happy at work, but not happy at home - you are not happy.

Self: The most neglected - BUT MOST Important area.

You know, whenever you tell someone that the "Self" is the most important area of his or her life, you always get some moron saying, "But what about the children?" or "But what about my sick and dying grandmother?" Listen up: If you've got nothing to live for except your kids or a sick relative, you do indeed have some problems on your hands. What in the world will you do when your kids grow up or your Grandma croaks? Huh? Then what? I'll tell ya what... You'll become more neurotic than you may be already, and then you'll find something else to be neurotic about.

Here it is in plain English: YOU ARE MORE IMPORTANT TO YOURSELF, whether you want to accept it or not. If you are not happy and healthy, you will be of no use to anybody else... end of story, period. You are the one that has to live with *you* 24/7, so let's cut the crap. People put the company, the kids, the friends, the neighbors, and the church ahead of themselves and render themselves useless in the process.

Think your children are more important than your own personal exercise regimen? Well, won't that be nice when, after all the years of sacrifice you've made for them so they can have a better life than you've had, your health takes a stand and -- comes to bite you in the ass... And, what then? What happens when (because you haven't established exercise as habit) you are unhealthy, need constant care, and are forced to impose on your children's lifestyles when *they* are adults... because they have to come take care of you. Only because you neglected to take care of YOU. Won't that be a nice present? I'll bet they'll appreciate having to wheel you around, instead of enjoying their weekends. Now, that could just be one opinion, right?

Well, let's see what else falls under the umbrella of *Self* to determine why it's the foundation for everything else. Finances, Health, Peace of Mind, Knowledge, Confidence, Inner Strength, Spirituality... should I go on? Get lax in any one of these areas and your whole life will be turned upside down. Conversely, focus on these areas alone... and you could lose it all in the home and work areas and still be Okay. You'll be miserable if you lost it all in the work and home area, but a lot *less* miserable than if you lose any element of the self area.

Two questions to ask yourself now -

Work:

What is one single action I have been procrastinating about that must get done._____?

What one thing could I do this week to put me ahead of the game in this area of my life. _____?

Do this for all three categories: work, home, and self. Then, record your answers on your index cards. You'll find yourself writing down things as small as "floss my teeth" to things as important as "write out my will" (under the personal category); from, "send a thank-you note to a long-time client" to "learn how to use Microsoft Front Page to create a website for client updates" (under the work category); from, "fix the seat on my daughters tricycle" to "open a saving account for our vacation next year" (under the home category).

The answers to these questions will and should have both long- and short-term elements, and also include things you should've done along time ago and things you will need to do a long time from now!

Becoming consciously aware of these answers will put you in a state of mind that is very well-balanced. You'll be able to see the forest from the trees, as well as the forest and the trees - isolated.

You now have 6 things. Two each... of: personal, professional, and home-oriented tasks.

Now, you'll sometimes have action items that overlap and that's okay, i.e. get the oil changed could fall under either -- if not all -- of the home, personal, and professional categories; because if you don't have a working automobile, you can't do a lot of things. Also, the things you've been procrastinating about and the things on which you could take some action that would catapult you in a better direction will, often times, be the same things!

In a very real sense, you'll discover that the answers to the questions are not nearly as important as routinely asking them of yourself.

Notice how, when you first start to learn the power of these questions, the first thing you think of is how much SOMEBODY ELSE should be doing them. When I first learned about these powerful planning tools, I was always accusing other people in my life of needing to ask them. Word Of Caution: Clean up your own back yard first. It's much more rewarding.

Plan: Schedule the 6 things.

Deposit the Action Items into your one-week planner. Try to put them in during the beginning of the day. Accomplishing these things early in the day will boost your confidence and keep you more focused for the remainder of the day. Each day, try to get something done before 9 a.m. It is when you get your world jump-started while the rest of the world is still sipping their first coffee of the day – that you become a shaker and a mover. Your schedule could look something like this.

INSERT GRAPHIC HERE OF PLANNER WITH PLANS

Spontaneity Lies In Discipline

The rationale I hear for "not being disciplined with time" is really quite ridiculous. Typically, when people make excuses for not purposefully using a planner or engaging in planning itself, you'll hear comments such as, "Who wants to be a slave to a leather binder?" or "I don't want to hold myself to such rigidity." Then there's the "I want some spice in my life. What about leaving some openness for random acts of fun?" and the "Hey, I want to have a little spontaneity in my life from time to time. How are ya going to do that if you're always trying to control your day?"

Please, read all those comments again. They truly are the hallmark statements made by people who "Do" NOT and, unless they pick up this book ,WILL NOT achieve very much.

In fact, they have a life of spontaneity all right. Once in a while, they'll get a surprise phone call from a creditor. Or maybe an unannounced firing from their job. Or, hey, if you don't want any structure in your life, there's always the good ole' "sudden death brought on by coronary" because of the "I don't wanna' have to force myself to exercise" attitude.

Listen up and listen good. This may be one of the only times I've written those words (listen up and listen well) in my life....

Failing to plan is planning to fail. If you think, for a second, that by not: writing down tasks, budgeting your time, disciplining your whims, and forcing yourself to stick to a plan... that you are actually LIVING SPONTANEOUSLY -- YOU ARE AN IDIOT.

If this tough talk offends you... please, stop reading my book right now! Put it down; walk away; don't tell anyone you read it. If someone ever asks you, "Have you ever read Scott Palangi's book?" Say "No, I haven't. Ya wanna' go bowling?" Change the subject and opt-out of my online newsletter!

Trust me on this one, gang. I have tried it both ways! I have been the moron who went to South Korea, shaved his head, and lived in a Buddhist temple. Now, there's nothing wrong with that... it's just not a great way to accomplish anything except for... nothing. Even if you want to renounce the materialistic world and achieve enlightenment... YOU'LL NEED A CHECKLIST, A PLANNER, AND SOME DISCIPLINE!

Be one of the individuals who is tough on themselves about time. Being disciplined is a *virtue*... you never "just get it;" you always strive for it. I know because I am still inclined to sleep late, talk about the Joneses, bitch about the Democrats and the Republicans... I am distracted by the smell of hotdogs, and my car still finds ways to go to Home Depot instead of going to the gym!

In the words of my friend and colleague Thomas Clifford: "If you think that not holding yourself to a disciplined routine gives you spontaneity, here's what'll happen for sure...You'll become a prisoner of your own freedom."

Once you get too used to "no goals, no structure"... Hey, its tough to snap out of it. I mean, even if you realize consciously that you need to change things -- you won't... because your body is too used to apathy and your mind will resist change even more!

In my relationships, I need to schedule my spontaneity. Don't laugh; it works. Who's more spontaneous... The person who never plans, and then finds themselves having to take their loved ones out to dinner to make up for lost time (a day late and a dollar short) or the person who deliberately schedules spontaneity into his or her life and comes home and says "Hey gang, guess where were going for dinner tonight! (twice a month like clockwork)."

Discipline Makes The Difference!

The Timer Method.

One of the best ways to get a sense of how well you use time is to use a simple wristwatch with a stopwatch-countdown timer. You will be amazed at how time seems to "slip through your fingers."

Try this for an entire day: Set your watch to "go off" every 15 minutes. When the timer goes off, ask yourself, "Is what I am doing right now taking me closer or further away from my short- or long-term goals." You could even write what you're doing on a piece of paper or put in your planner/journal. Believe me, you will get a shock when you see yourself writing down such ridiculousness as, "thinking about lunch; talking to a friend about nothing; complaining; trying to waste time; driving; arguing; thinking about someone at work," etc.

Using the timer method is not a drill where your goal is to time yourself in all of your activities. We do not want to try to rush ourselves through life to beat the clock. Instead, the goal is to learn through observation that we 1) waste far too much time, and 2) that there is, in fact, more time in the day than we give credit for. The timer lets you become much more aware of how you spend your time.

Your views about time and the ways in which you value it will become magnified when you begin using the timer method. You'll respect your own time and the time of others in a whole new way. Here's something to think about regarding time:

A successful life is made up of successful years;

Successful years are broken down into successful months;

Successful months into successful weeks;

Successful weeks into days;

Days into hours;

And hours... into minutes.

Successful years are had most by those who tend to the minutes.

Successful People Are Never Surprised

Successful people are often referred to as being lucky by non-successful people. But, successful people will tell you like it is: luck, they'll say, had nothing to do with it.

This is why I say that successful people are never surprised. If you played and won the lottery, you'd be surprised. Why? Because you didn't expect it. You'd be surprised to win because you know that you did nothing except spend a few lousy dollars to make a few million.

Successful people, on the other hand, take deliberate steps years in advance to make their fortune. And, when they look in the bank account one day and see a fortune... They do not jump up and down screaming for joy about the fortune that "miraculously" appeared. Fact is, they knew it was coming. They know that deliberate, consistent, and hard work lead to good fortune... not luck. The difference between the two is tremendous.

This point is not to suggest that successful people do not gamble -- they do. They make and take calculated risks quite frequently. But successful people do not call their success luck. They know that specific actions lead to specific results.

On the other end of the spectrum, the successful are not shocked when lousy results happen to them, either. Oddly, if you look at the non-successful people, you'll often find that are just as surprised at the bad results that life seems to hand them as they are the good luck.

Successful people are not surprised when they create good fortune because they anticipated it's arrival. And, when the results aren't so great -- well, they retrace their steps to find the error in their ways.

This is the main reason you may sometimes hear the non-successful people in a moment of jealousy say of the successful people, "They have no hearts; they are emotionless... they don't care."

Nothing could be farther from the truth. The main reason you do not see the drama so commonly displayed by the losers in life as with the winners is because the winners... are never surprised.

While everyone at work is gathering around the cafeteria table, talking about "Can you believe they laid-off John Doe?," the successful person seems to be emotionless because he responds with, "No, not really. Could you pass the salt, please?"

Lose The "To-Do" List; Focus On The "To-Done" List

We've talked a lot about a to-do list in this section. Now, I want to turn you on to something truly revolutionary in the "Do"-ing department -- The Journal.

More than just a diary, a journal is a record of your life. Your journal will contain all your victories, defeats, desires, dreams, goals, and also... your life-lessons. Journals are those empty books that are more expensive than the typical "books with words" that you may be used to purchasing. In fact, though, when your journals are used-up or all filled in, they will become priceless.

Perhaps the biggest impact of journaling is what I call the "What Little I Did." You see, unlike a to-do list which contains all of your intentions, plans, and not-yet accomplished to-do's, the journal painfully shows you what little you actually *did* get done. You will get a smack in the face at how much you squander your time.

It is painfully motivating to sit down after an 18-hour day and stare at your journal while thinking, "Wow, I didn't do anything significant today! Where did the time go?" More powerful than a to-do list, discovering "Wow, I didn't do squat today" can be much more life-changing than "Hey, look at all this stuff I still have left to do."

Even if you don't keep, have, or utilize a to-do list... You always have a to-done list, so to speak. You always have something to put in the journal. Your to-do list can be completely empty, but you will always have something to "journal-in" even if it is only to write, "Today I was a loser. I did nothing."

Look at your journal as the "to-done" list. Notice the disparity between all the objectives you planned in your daily to-do lists compared to what you've jotted down in your journal. It can be very motivating.

Memorializing Life's Lessons

Every one of us has a story to tell. One of the reasons I love meeting with all sorts of different people is to hear their stories. Sadly, many of us never record the moments that make up our lives -- moments that will be great to remember to tell later on in life. And... moments that are hard to forget that we'll want to use to teach others.

Have you ever learned your lesson... but then you forgot? That's painful isn't it? Another great benefit of keeping a journal is to be able to use it to reflect on your day, week, month, and so on. I find it very invigorating to journal after an eventful day. Getting into this habit will allow you to release frustrations as well. For years, modern psychologists have recommended journaling as a method for isolating issues. It's a way of allowing yourself to look at your problems from an objective standpoint, rather than just the typical ranting that our brains will force us to go through if we don't command them to be still. Journaling *creates* stillness. It's just you and the empty page. At first, you will sit in front of your journal feeling a little empty... Not to worry, just start tapping the pencil or pen - and a thought that needs isolation will enter your mind.

All of the great thinkers of our time believed in journaling. Goethe, Rembrandt, and Picasso were all known for walking around with a small journal in hand. Goethe in particular was quoted as saying, "While traveling in this world, to lose my passport would be an inconvenience -- but to lose my journal? …THAT would be a tragedy."

Walk The Edge

Progressing towards your goals requires you to live outside of your comfort zone on a regular basis. How regular? I say at least once a week. You should deliberately schedule time to "push-beyond" what is comfortable in the mental, social, physical, and spiritual areas of your life. At first, you will just write down your intentions but not act on them. That's okay. Keep on writing down your activities that will demand more of you. Eventually, you will act on them. At the very least, writing these things down will imprint your brain and tell it, "Hey, I need to do this!"

Do not think for a second that writing it down and not acting on it will lower your belief in yourself. Quite the contrary! Remember, your subconscious mind cannot distinguish between what you want to do, and what you've done. When your conscious mind is exposed to goals like, "Attend a public speaking class; donate time to the church; commit to mastering a computer program; learn to speak another language; take a surfing class; go shopping for Ferrari's; go to confession" -- or whatever, it tells the subconscious mind to act on it.

It doesn't matter what the goals are as long as they are ones that make you a little intimidated. They should make you feel alive. I'm reminded of the movie "Braveheart," with Mel Gibson. I rented it on VHS. I am not a Mel Gibson fan by a long shot, but the box of the video tape caught my attention. It said "Everyone dies... But few people truly live." Wow! Make that your motto.

If you are not living with your "heart in your throat" at least once a week, you have *impotent* goals. Decide on Sunday what you will choose as your "edge goal" for the week! Remember, just because you are writing it down, does not mean you are committing to it. It simply means that if the opportunity presents itself and the courage is there -- you intend to act on it!

What is a Template for Success?

History, it is said, repeats itself. The question is, what part of history do *you* want to constantly repeat? The great or the lousy? Well, then you'd better work on developing a template for success. A template, by definition, is a like a map. We use templates to save time, frustration, and also to eliminate the much-hated trial and error of success.

When you are using a template to create something, in this case a goal or task, you are calling on a previous "successful model" to guide you along the way. Template usage builds confidence and predicts a more reliable result than a non-template method. For example, if you were to bake cookies, you might use a cookie-cutter – this, in its purest form, is a template.

But what about you? Wouldn't it be great to have a template for success that you could use to accomplish any goal of your dreams? Great news! You already have them. And you've got plenty. The trick is... finding them.

Difficulties can be quickly overcome if you have a prior template for success. When you begin to hit an obstacle, you simply call upon the memory or "template," and then apply the same attitude that you used to create the past success. The best way to do this is to master small tasks and eventually make them into more elaborate tasks.

Have you ever been so good at something that someone said to you, "Wow, you make that look so easy!" Like figure skating... An expert figure skater can do a triple axle jump without even thinking. But, there was a time when that task was very difficult. After years of mastering smaller moves, however, the figure skater finally develops this thing called a triple axle, and now can do it almost effortlessly.

The figure skater, when confronted with a similarly difficult task later in life, can use the template of the "triple axle" for future success. The skater remembers what kind of thinking it takes to grow the small tasks into greater and more difficult maneuvers. Drawing upon past successes, no matter how small they may seem, gives you a template for future successes.

Developing a template for success is *crucial*.

Thinking can either make you or break you when you are trying to achieve goals. Thoughts, often times negative, can creep up on you and rob you of your belief in yourself. After a while you might begin to think to yourself, "Maybe I don't really want this goal." This is often the attitude we adopt when we can't see the light at the end of the tunnel. And this is *especially* when you need to remember your past successes and use them to foster and solidify your belief in your ability to accomplish the task at hand.

A template allows you to put your mind on autopilot and refer back to that previous achievement. This will give you the perseverance to stay on track until a new and more recent template for success is developed.

Right now, in your journal, write down some things that could serve as a template for success if you let them.

The Power of Individual Activities

Strength of character is what will dictate how much success you will enjoy as an individual. By becoming highly skilled at sports or activities that are individual in nature, you will have a better chance at developing some of the latent qualities that are essential for success. Whereas cooperation is an attribute that team activities can instill -- confidence is not. Usually confidence is tested - not built. What's more is this: You can be performing miserably and the team can be doing great... And that teaches you "I am a winner." While the truth in fact may be, "I am a sap!"

Conversely, if you succeed as an individual on the team that loses, your reflex may be to blame or accuse others for not pulling their own weight. Dependence on team success lends itself to, "It's not my fault - I DID MY part."

You may have heard the saying there is no "I" in team. What you may not have heard is that a team is no better than the quality of its members. After all, what do they do when a team underperforms? First, they blame the coach. Then, they change the training. Finally, they trade players. *Your* goal is to become an excellent individual at <u>all</u> times. If you are not at your best, you should not expect, nor want, the team to pull your slack.

When you accomplish something as a team, you're not sure 100% if you can do it alone. This is why many music bands have members that leave and "go solo." They are not sure if they can do it on their own. Deprived of the personal challenge to get great at something, they feel this longing… to stake their own claim in the world. A better, wiser entertainer would first become all he or she could be on one's own, and then seek to be surrounded with other like minded talent. It's no wonder that a four-person band often has the productivity of only two people -- all four members are living up to half of their potential!

Partake in individualistic activities to develop these qualities. The person who can stand on their own two feet, and knows it deep inside... is always more valuable to the team anyway.

The Gas & The Brake

Achieving success is, many times, not so much a matter of "stepping on the gas" as much as it is "not putting your foot on the brake." You will often find yourself progressing just fine without having to force yourself to be more, and do more. What holds us back is not that we are failing to do more but rather, that we are avoiding the restraints of success. If we can just decide on our goals, set them, and begin -- were set! Then we can sit back and allow success to happen to us.

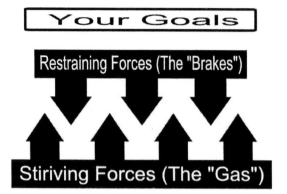

The all-too-common scenario is to step on the brake and not even be aware of it! You start to achieve some goal and, at the same time, you're engaging in all the behaviors that will take you away from the goal just as fast as you can excel towards it. "One step forward, two steps back" will then seem to be the story that fits yours best. Meanwhile, somebody else, someone less talented, less skilled, and less gifted... beats you by a mile while traveling at what seems to be a snails pace. Why? Simple! They just never stepped on the brake.

What brakes are you currently stepping on while trying to achieve a worthy goal? Once again, a journal will be of great help. I think you can see how all of these principles are interrelated.

Stepping on the gas and the brake at the same time is like running on the treadmill and then going to McDonalds after (One of my "brake issues.") Hey, for all you single people, what about dating? Isn't a successful date often a matter of not saying anything stupid rather than saying all the right stuff?

In sales this applies, too. Sometimes customers are ready to buy. They are already accelerating in the right direction. But an unknowing sales person will try to step on the gas... when it's not even necessary. Look around for other examples of where achieving success is simply a matter of not "stepping on the brake.

PART FOUR: HAVE

The Persistence of "Have"

"Nothing can take the place of persistence... Talent cannot... the world is full of wasted talent; Genius cannot... unrewarded genius is almost a proverb... Education cannot... the world is full of educated derelicts. Persistence and persistence alone is omnipotent."

~ Calvin Coolidge, U.S. President

While on the bridge to achievement, you will find yourself face to face with the very qualities you'll need in order to cross this "great divide."

Okay, so let's review. You've learned that, in order to be able to "do" what it takes to achieve your goals, you first need to "be" the kind of person that can perform the necessary tasks. You've also learned that focusing solely on the "being" without any doing... will get you nowhere. In addition, you learned that merely "having" doesn't do *anything*.... It doesn't allow you to be; it doesn't allow you to do. Now, folks, you no belong to the crowd that believes that simply having "money" or "resources" or any other external factor, will allow you to "do" or "be."

Be always precedes do; and do always precedes have. But there's one missing element:

If you recall, I mentioned that there is a **bridge** to achievement. You, and your state of being-ness (whether conducive or incompetent) are on one side of the bridge. Your goals are on the other side. And the steps on the bridge involve your character traits and qualities. These qualities alone are what will get you over the bridge. They are intangibles. You cannot *buy* these qualities. They are earned and learned... while you are working on "be" and "do," respectively. The proverbial water that this bridge to achievements spans is made up of <u>time</u>.

The time that the bridge to achievement spans is very significant. You cannot look at this time as *typical* time, per se. It is not like

193

the time spent at the movies... Time spent playing sports... Or any other time that just seems to disappear while you are doing things that are "fun" or "easy."

The time spent on the bridge to success seems longer, more testing, and more difficult to "manage" than any other sort of time. It is the kind of time that feels like it takes forever. Like staring at a clock.

There is only one thing stopping you now... Perseverance and persistence. The <u>bridge</u> of the bridge between "do" and "have".

If you can persist now -- you're "home free."

Before studying the principles of be, do, and have, you may have wasted some valuable persistence time. You may have persisted in doing something that was never on your list of dreams. You may have persisted in a relationship that was not one becoming of you. When those things happen, it can be very easy to become skeptical about the power of persistence. You also may have used persistence while you were being the type of person that can't possibly engage in the type of "do"ing that wins success. You may have persisted being something for so long already, that it seems tough to believe in the power of persistence.

But this time, it will be different. You are doing the inner work of "be" and adding the external acts of "do". In short, you are doing all of the right stuff. Now, the only thing missing is… have.

Persistence will get you there. If you can apply the power of persistence, the "have" is sure and soon to come.

We will examine the insights surrounding the development of the attitude, the faith, and the determination that will take you across the rest of this bridge to the "Promised Land."

No Problems Are a Huge Problem.

"He knows not his own strength that hath not met adversity."
~Ben Johnson (1573-1637), English Playwright and poet

Life is… a series of problems to solve.

The chair you sit upon to read this book solves the problem of "needing a place that is comfortable enough to read." The lamp solves the problem of lighting the room so that you may read. Cars solve the problem of transportation. Tables solve the problem of having to bend down too far to pick things up. Televisions solve the problem of having nothing to do. Everything in life is about solving problems. One reason our country is so magnificent is that we solve problems better than any other. We take the car which solves the problem of transportation and find ways to make it solve other problems at the same time (make it luxurious enough to drive just for fun, spacious enough to go shopping and tote children, stylish enough to feed the ego, etc.)

You often hear people these days talking about their problems. They speak of life as if all they need to do is solve the next problem and then everything will be fine. They say, "If only problems A, B, and C were solved… then there would be no problems." This is a sign of immaturity. Problems, and the pursuit of solving them, is what has taken us out of the Stone Age and into incredible areas of existence.

Failure has been called the "fertilizer for success." With that philosophy in mind, one can sense that problems are absolutely necessary in our lives. If you look a little deeper you will discover that man, or any other life form in this universe, seems to love problems. A problem is more important than freedom. Problems keep up interest. When a man has a problem and can't solve it, he really has few too problems. He needs more.

The insanity among the idle is a matter of problem scarcity.

You may have heard it said that, "It's not the achievement of a goal that has significance - but what you become from achieving the goal." That statement suggests that it is the "act" or the busy-ness of solving a problem that makes us excel!

More than likely, the "Problem" responsible for many peoples' unhappiness is that they are solving the wrong problems, someone else's problems, a problem that exists only in their head, or a problem that is just not big enough!

If everything you put your hand to was a breeze… if everything you wanted to own was a snap, you would become dulled to apathy and, then, be among the truly miserable.

The funny thing is, the number one reason for failure, or lack of a happiness? It's root cause is that people say they're not achieving an effect that they want to achieve… so they quit. Then, there is no problem.

It is important to understand this point if you are to be successful in life. As long as you are having problems while *trying to succeed* - you are indeed succeeding!

If people adopt the attitude that problems are, in fact, assignments... a sort of growth tonic, and if they develop the attitude that problems do not define a person but, instead, reveal a person... there would be no failure.

At the very least, problems are the antidote for boredom.

Deciding How To Look At Obstacles

The only people who do not have to face obstacles on a daily basis are those who dwell in cemeteries. If you are living on the edge and pushing yourself beyond your comfort zone, you will hit obstacles. It's just a fact of life.

The people who say "yeah, yeah" in response to the simplicity of that statement are usually the same ones who say, "Darn it, why is it always so difficult?" You should accept the fact that obstacles are inevitable... and, instead of resisting them, just accept them -- in fact, welcome them!

Obstacles are nothing more than proof that you are trying to achieve something.

If you're doing something that doesn't take you face to face with an obstacle, you are probably not working on a goal. Goals that do not make an achiever encounter obstacles are not really goals - they are pastimes.

Of all the obstacles you will encounter, usually the toughest ones are not people, places, resources, or things... No way. Usually the most daunting obstacles have more to do with our inner nature; self-confidence, ambition, perseverance, positive thinking, faith, vision, and hope.

These are the elements that will be tested when you are executing your plans. And the best part about it is... these qualities become stronger each and every time you use them to work through obstacles.

Obstacles themselves are not as difficult as is managing our attitude with regard to them.

Successful People Use More Self-Discipline Than Others

Discipline is one of the most misunderstood principles in the achievement of goals. Do you believe that some people actually have more discipline than others? I do not. The difference between those who accomplish their goals and those who don't has little to do with the amount of discipline people have... but more so, the amount they choose to use.

The main difference between the successful people and non-successful people (and there are many differences) is that successful people choose to do the tasks that the non-successful people would rather put-off for a while… if not, indefinitely.

People of high achievement recognize that most of the tasks before them are "sucky" -- but they choose to do them anyway. And when they do, they not only get the things done that need to get done, and not only do they strengthen their levels of self-discipline, but they actually start to "override" the perceived suckiness factor. The "sucky" task becomes "not so bad." And now, they can use this model as a template to achieve all future goals as well.

You can even make a game out of using your self-discipline. Rarely will you ever just wake up and feel like using more self-discipline, but the opportunities are everywhere. I'll give you some examples.

Have you ever had to take an elevator to like the third or fourth floor? Of course… and what do we usually do? We wait, sometimes for a minute or two, for the elevator to arrive. You *know* that the stairs offer more benefits. Obviously, they're faster; plus you'll get exercise. But the real power behind taking the stairs is not what is does "for you"… but what it does "to you!" By doing something as simple as taking the stairs instead of an elevator, you increase your self-discipline.

Here's another one. This one I am sure you've experienced. It involves putting things back where they belong. Have you ever stayed overnight somewhere, say at a hotel? Can you remember leaving your shampoo or other toiletries behind? Now, here's how that usually happens. You're in the shower and you use your own shampoo. Just as you are done with it and go to put the cap back on the bottle, it occurs to you: if you put the bottle down while still inside the shower, you may forget to go back and pack it up with the rest of your belongings. So, you play out the scenario in your head… "If I get out of the shower right now, I'll drip water all over the place; I'll get cold," and so on. Consequently, you decide to wait until you're done showering… *then* you'll put the shampoo with the rest of your stuff. At this moment, you realize that, in the past, you've left things behind plenty of times while staying at hotels. You come up with a solution! You start repeating to yourself over and over while still in the shower, "Don't forget the shampoo... Don't forget the shampoo." What happens? You forget the shampoo!

I ask you, what would the person who decides to use more self-discipline do? They would get out of the shower and put the shampoo with their bag as soon as they are finished using it! They know themselves too well. They know the odds of remembering it later, after styling their hair and putting on socks -- are pretty slim.

As you move through your day, try to find opportunities to say, "How can I improve my personal level of self-discipline?" Typically, household chores provide us with tons of chances to exercise our will power and self-discipline.

Love Is A Verb... Not An Adjective

You Don't Have To Like It

Labor of Love. Ever heard that one? It implies that there are occupations, careers, and opportunities for success that you can actually love to do. Wow, imagine that? Imagine waking up everyday - *totally enthusiastic* and dying to "get to work" or, to "your labor of love."

This is a fallacy. Do not fall for it. Having a job that you totally love to do, and one that is non-stop fun from 9 a.m. to 9 p.m. (you do work 9 to 9 right?) is something that is talked about by people who hate their jobs. I mean it. Usually, it's the people who do not particularly care for their occupation or job duties that are always searching, looking, and wanting this illusive job of pure joy.

I am not trying to be a killjoy, or a negative person.... Nor am I trying to say I'm just "being realistic!" I am simply saying that work is work.

I know guys who love fishing. If they fished for a living, they would still enjoy it more when they are not "working."

I am a martial arts teacher. I love the martial arts. I love to practice the martial arts. I even love to teach the arts. But it's still work!

I love my job, but I still love it when it's over for the day, too.

So if you are thinking to yourself, "Hey, at least you love your job - I hate mine." I say to you this:

Change your attitude about what work means to you.

You show me any type of occupation and I'll show you people who like it and people who hate it ... who do the same "type" of work! The difference is this: One person will get promoted because of the attitude they choose to adopt and the other - left behind!

Searching for the "perfect job" will quickly drive you crazy. You will fall into the trap of going to "meetings" to try to start your own business with little or no money down, or little or no work involved, but... guess what the #1 hook is in "job opportunity scams." Make money doing what you love.

Don't believe me? Guess what author Steven King says? "Writing sucks." That's a direct quote.

I promise you that even Mother Theresa said, "I love helping the homeless, but it's a real pain in the ass" and that Walt Disney said "I can't stand kids" on more than one occasion.

Now, obviously these people did not hate their occupations. But, they do understand that work is work... no matter how you slice it.

I have a friend who is always looking for the "best job." He has had more failed, home-based businesses than anyone I've ever known and has purchased program after program of get-rich-quick-schemes. The funny thing is... the job he does right now is one that most people would kill to have! Yet he is always looking... elsewhere.

The solution to finding a "labor of love" is to first "love the labor" you're doing.

All work is work. Do you love animals? Yeah? So much that you'd like to "work with animals" for a living? Guess what? It isn't fun. It is fulfilling – but, it is far from fun.

How about being a teacher? Many times you hear bright young people declare that they "turned down" higher-paying careers because those other careers wouldn't make them feel as fulfilled as would the contribution of helping others learn. Well, go ask them if they "love teaching" they will say yes usually - because they would look like idiots otherwise. But, they will also say "teaching has its drawbacks." Hmmm, sounds like.... Yep, you guessed it -- WORK!

Go to whatever job you have, and act like you love it! After a while, you *will* love it a little more.

If you think that money alone makes the "highly-paid" love their work, then go ask some high-paid neurosurgeon if I'm wrong. Walk up to one and say, "Excuse me... but, if you had the choice between sleeping late or performing a brain surgery -- which would you pick?"

Jack LaLaine was the person who really proved this principle to me. Jack is "the person" who made American realize that exercise something you "must do" – not something you have a choice about doing. His point? You don't have to *like* doing it, you just have *to* do it.

I remember one interview in particular when Jack was asked, "...Now Jack, *you* of course love exercise... But what advice can you give to the folks at home who "just hate exercising"... what sort of inspiration or hope could you give to the rest of us?" The interviewer was definitely not expecting the response that was about to come. Jack looked her straight in the eye and said, "Are you nuts? What are you talking about... love this stuff? Do you honestly think I love this stuff? I HATE IT! In fact, I hate it more than any of the folks at home, because I been doing it a lot longer... so I should know how much it stinks!"

Despising your work is nothing to be ashamed of. If you want to change careers ever in you life -- do it! But do not do it simply because the grass looks greener. Work is still work. Anyone who tells you that they *always* love what they're doing is either trying to impress you, "green" to the profession, or just plain medicated!

A Lesson From The Masters

Martial arts masters have a theory about persistence.

It was well known throughout the East, that if you want to find someone to help you accomplish something very difficult... Just get your local martial arts master to assist you. They will have cracking up at even the most insurmountable of obstacles, when you hit the most difficult spots. Many stories exist about martial arts masters actually laughing while performing thousands and thousands of repetitions. In almost a slap-happy type of fashion... you won't be able to distinguish whether these fellows are laughing because they are tired and ready to give up, laughing because the task at hand is easy, or laughing because they are entertained at how much their mind is telling them to quit. One things for sure though -- they laugh and actually *enjoy* difficult tasks. When I first observed this, I was wondering if it was just an act. Like, are they laughing to impress us? Or, are they actually enjoying what is going on.

I now know the answer.

All martial artists who have been trained properly subscribe to what is known as "The 100 Times Theory." Again, we learn more from their love of simplicity. The "100 Times Theory" says that you make a very simple resolve to attempt something 100 times before giving up. Period. No trying to find a "better way." No searching for a shortcut. No second guessing yourself. If you are trying to learn how to hammer a nail. That's it. You decide to try, attempt, or practice, if you will... 100 straight tries. You begin to use this theory in everything that you do as well.

It is amazing how many people start to actually become thirsty for opportunities to test their "mental mettle," find excuses for fortitude. You'll be searching for things that will make you want to give up when you begin to discover the power of the 100 Times Theory.

Most people quit after 3 or 4 tries

Laypeople take quite a different approach. They say, "100 times? Are you crazy?" Their thinking is, "Well, I think it would be better to find something I am good at." What a shame, right? It's as if they think that the purpose of life is to simply go around until they find something they're naturally good at. And, guess what folks? I am here to tell you that all the stuff you are naturally good at -- NEVER MAKES YOU BeTTER! Do you get it? Finding whatever you are already good at is -- nothing other than a discovery of something you do not need to do.

How come this is not understood by more people? Well, it probably starts with the way our society as a whole regards even the most fundamental aspects of education. Take aptitude tests for example. What are they for? To find out how hard you do NOT have to try at something! Now, I'm not saying that if someone is 4' 1" tall, it would be valuable to set a goal of playing in the NBA! No.

What I am saying is that, if you take a look at your life and reflect upon all of the things you've already accomplished that are meaningful to you, you will always find a little bit of the 100 times theory at work. Reflect on this for a moment. Think back to a time when you totally felt alive while doing something. It was probably something that required you to *persist*.

The great thing is you can put the 100 Times Theory to work for you whenever you want. You don't have to study martial arts to "live" like a martial artist. Whenever people persist, they are -- in a sense, practicing martial arts. They are employing the 100 Times Theory.

Use this theory when you hit sticking points

Physical examples provide the best and fastest opportunities to discover the power of the 100 Times Theory. I like using physical examples because they are very objective. You can count amount of repetitions, attempts, minutes elapsed. You can even measure and record your data, so you have a yardstick with which to see the evidence: that "persistence" is the absolute facilitator in goal achievement.

While doing whatever thing that will take you closer to your goal, simply resolve to do it in blocks of 100. If it is mailing out letters - - set a goal of 100. If it is push-ups, make it 100 (you may not be able to do 100 in one sitting, but you can break it up over a period of several minutes and surely accomplish 100). If your goal is 100 minutes of study -- do it, 100 minutes.

You will notice that, somewhere around the number 30 or 40... your mind will start to make deals with you. It's just a funny thing about the mind. It must be like some sort of a survival mechanism or something; the mind will always beg you to you find a way to conserve your energy. So, I suggest you do this: Play a mental recording of "one more, one more, one more" in your head until you can quiet that voice that says, "Hey, you already did 15... Why don't we chill now and come back to this later.

Now, what starts to happen here is - you begin to "habitual-ize" exercising your level of perseverance, stretching your persistence muscles. In the meantime, you get some solid work done. The best benefit has yet to come though!

The deeper value of this theory

Transforming your thoughts into goals, your goals into actions, and your actions into persistence that will lead to the achievement of those goals is only a side benefit, however. The real value in sticking something out for a minimum of 100 tries is, in fact, that the student will become the teacher -- the teacher of self.

You see, when you try to attempt something 100 times and you reach that point that I mentioned when "the mind plays tricks on you," you will be tempted to get outside help. Help -- in the form of instruction, more information, or consulting. Now, what do you find after you've enlisted this "assistance?" All you'll find out in the end -- is the something you already knew from the beginning! And that is: there are no shortcuts! You still have to "put in the effort" or the sweat.

Resolve to attempt whatever you have to do with the attitude of the "100 Times Theory." Resist the temptation to "seek help" as a shortcut to avoid this 100 times principle.

You've Already Been There and Done That

All you need to know -- you already know. Well, sort of...

Often times, we're constantly looking for that "missing link" that keeps us from attaining our dreams. Truth be told: the missing link is *persistence*. It is still the opinion of many that there must be some other "knowledge" that we lack... that, if we only had this certain knowledge, we'd be successful. It seems to make sense initially, too. After all, if we haven't achieved our goals, it must be because of something we do not know - right? Well, this is only partially true.

All of us... down to each and every last soul on Earth - have learned enough "things" to achieve their hearts' desires. We have all been on the right track to success, but often we lose sight of the goal. Why? Because the goal takes time. The only missing link to our success is our own understanding that we are, indeed, many times.... perfectly on track.

The fact is, we've all been millionaires -- at least in the form of "Be" and "Do." We have all established the habits, and lifestyle -- even if only for a day or two -- that will lead us to the exact destination we desire. It's just the "Have" part... the part that requires persistence that trips us up.

Remember, the process of be, do, and have is the cycle for all accomplishments. Unknowingly, we start the be, and the do, and then... because we are not aware of the amazing power of something so simple, such as "not quitting".... the "have" part totally eludes us. We think we must be missing some key component or something.

The thing that messes us up is the "time" that it takes in between the Do and the Have. You lack follow-through, not new ideas, if you haven't yet reached your dreams.

When you begin to grasp this concept -- the power of persistence -- your self-esteem should rise. That happens when it becomes clear that we all can actually assume the necessary states of "be" and "do" that would readily give us the rewards of attaining the likes of a millionaire, a Harvard Graduate, an Olympic athlete, etc.

"Wow, This Works! Now, Let's Change It.

Why is it that we always try to change things when they are going along just fine?

We think about something for months on end. We develop the courage to make a plan. We act on the plan. We see some solid evidence that success is "right around the corner"... only to change things just for the sake of changing them.

I've witnessed this occur many times, especially in situations where fantastic progress is being made. It's because we forget what it's like to not be getting any good results. When finally achieving some decent results, we get into this state of euphoria that makes us feel exempt from good follow-through skills. In one sense, you could call it resting on our laurels. We think that somehow all our "hard work" is paying off -- not because of our small but necessary persistent actions -- but rather, because we are just "working hard." So, we think that if we change something, it won't have any impact on our current good results. Soon, we leave out something in place of something else... Take our eye off the ball, so to speak... And, before long, we end up getting a different result.

Do not change what works. "If it ain't broke, don't fix it." Keep a journal of what you are doing everyday, so that you can really drill into your head exactly what it was that brought you towards this new success. Also, keep in mind what it is like to get lousy results.

This will serve as a good "bad memory," so that you remember which certain actions led to the good results as well those that led to the bad. This way, you won't ascribe your new good results to "luck" or "happenstance." You'll also then resist the temptations to "change" things when they are going well.

Next time you're at work or leading a team through a project -- watch how quickly people are ready and willing to change, add, or subtract vitally important steps to certain tasks or objectives. Tony Robbins, a famous self-help guru who you've probably seen doing late-night infomercials for his "30 Days to Personal Power," calls this "self-sabotage." He says that it's almost as if somewhere deep inside, we actually "like" to struggle. When things are going well, we'll conjure up some other cockamamie scheme to make it even better (in the name of "improvement"), but really it's our habitual pattern of mis-thinking... of being so used to not getting the results we want.

I've seen this happen in every field and career. I once had a friend who was a successful real estate agent. He was so successful that he would often give his own seminars on prospecting (a not-so-fun headache part of real estate sales). My friend was the first one to admit that he should take his own advice. He would say we work so hard all year long to put certain systems in place... systems that require little amounts of daily discipline... And then, right when we begin to reap some terrific results, we take our eye off the ball -- and start some new "habits"... End result? We're left wondering "What the hell happened? Things were 'so good' last month."

All along, things were *fine*! But there goes that "human" flaw... that impulse to change things when they are working perfectly well.

It will always be there, too -- the temptation to stop doing or change what you are doing when the results you are getting are just fine, if not excellent.

If You Can Brush Your Teeth, You Can Achieve Your Dreams

"Chip away" at success

What do brushing your teeth, chopping down a tree, starting an exercise program, growing a plant, and Chinese water torture treatment all have in common? They result in success through small, repetitive actions... actions so seemingly insignificant -- you might wonder while executing them if you weren't just wasting your time.

One of my mentors Fred Gleeck said, "If you can brush your teeth, you can be successful." Now, when I first heard this, I was in a room full of people. I looked around to see if anyone else would grasp "the big idea" from that little statement. Only about two or three other people "got it." Everyone else had this look on their face like "Yeah... so?" And that's how it is sometimes... We miss out on success because of its *subtlety* (I know that this seems to be a recurring theme of this book but, trust me -- you haven't heard it enough).

Let's take a closer look at the brushing teeth metaphor. Fred could have used some other example besides "brushing your teeth." I believe Fred picked that one specifically for four reasons. Think about it...

Brushing is simple. Brushing your teeth is something you learned to do when you were young. It is easy to do. It takes no "talent," but it is the only way to achieve good oral hygiene. You simply have to put in the little... annoying... petty actions -- of brushing daily, in order to get the desired result!

Brushing isn't fun. And, if you'll remember, brushing is not something you cared to do as a kid (or even as an adult) either. It wasn't -- and still isn't -- fun! No one really likes brushing... Why do you think they come up with all the different types of toothpastes and brushes for kids. To make it fun, of course. But, now that I am an adult, I don't really mind brushing two or three times a day. I enjoy the benefits of what brushing does -- more than the actions of doing it -- to the point where I actually like doing it!

There is no substitute for brushing. This is why brushing is such a great metaphor... The old saying, "There is more than one way to skin a cat" does not apply here, does it?! Imagine *not* brushing -- only to let the dentist "pick up the pieces?" Would that work? No. At best, the dentist could clean your teeth, give you some fillings, and maybe even a root canal... a much more severe price to pay, both figuratively and literally! There is no substitute for this method of oral hygiene, nor can you hire someone to do it for you!

Brushing has to become a habit in order for it to "work." Now, how about "part-time brushing?" How well will that work? Could you ignore brushing for 2 minutes, 3 times a day -- a total of 6 minutes... For a whole month? Well, of course you could. But then, could you brush on the 31st day for 180 minutes straight to make up for lost time? (That's 6 minutes a day for 30 days, in case you missed it.) Hey, how much fun would 3 hours of brushing be...? More importantly, how effective would it be? It would NOT be fun and it would NOT be *effective*.

The steps necessary for achievement of your goals and aspirations very closely resemble the characteristics of the brushing example. Success, so it seems, follows a similar structure...

There are things -- little things -- that must be done on a daily basis to ensure that you will achieve your goals. In fact, if any of your big goals do not require at least some type of daily attention, chances are they are unrealistic goals or are goals that will not be achieved. Examine your daily short-term goals. Do they have "daily disciplines" attached to them? They should!

Just like brushing, there is no shortcut or substitute. Any attempt to find a shortcut will only lead you down a path that will distract you... more so than the things that normally distract you when you are focused. It's challenging enough to block-out distractions when you are "in the zone", let alone adding the distraction of trying to find a different way.

The tasks that warrant success are also not usually a lot of fun. Not that they are complex, it's just that they are usually mundane. They are easy tasks to do if you do them, but they are also easy tasks to forget or fall behind on as well.

Dr. Steven Covey calls this the "Law of the Farm." His observation is that all things -- especially those things that will be long-lasting -- are subject to "natural principles." In his example, "the farm," you have to give a plant or crop consistent care in order for it to flourish. Dr. Covey asks, "Can you fake 50 push-ups?" The answer is obviously "no", but how many times do we act in the exact opposite manner of Dr. Covey's Law of the Farm? We miss a few days of watering the proverbial plant... In hopes that we can give it "an extra dose" later to make up for lost time.

Exercise provides a simple example of this premise. Can you remember a time when you didn't exercise for three months or so (or ever!) and then hit it like gangbusters! You went to the gym six days a week, for an hour or two at a pop... only to quit, many weeks later. And then repeat the cycle all over again later that same year?

Meanwhile, all the other gym-goers (who have an established routine) seem to be getting all these great results... An interesting thing about them is that it seems like, when they workout, they don't even appear to be trying! That's because they know the only real effort involved with getting great results from exercise is the *consistency* part. They are simply pacing themselves because they understand and apply this Law of the Farm principle.

How about savings? How well would you do if you managed to save 10% of your gross income each month, but then, slacked off for three months? Would it be easy to forfeit 30% on the fourth month to make up for it? Of course not!

I mean, we've all heard the saying, "Rome wasn't built in day," even though we think to ourselves, "Well, that's because they didn't have the modern tools we have today." The phrase implies that no matter how much we try to speed up the process -- we still gotta' put the time in.

After identifying your "High Payoff" areas, set a plan to stick to those daily deposits. Imagine if you walked over a small bridge everyday... and your objective was to create a dam. Well, if you put one rock in place every single day, your dam would be built in no time. Best of all, it would seem effortless in the process. In contrast, imagine neglecting it for two weeks! Now, you've got to hump 14 rocks in one shot just to "make up for it." I am telling you... most of our unhappiness stems from this yo-yo type of behavior -- behavior we all engage in when we aren't paying attention to what our little actions add up to -- whether neglected or focused upon. If you focus a little bit on something negative everyday, the results will be astonishing (but in a bad way). Conversely, when you focus a little bit everyday on a *positive* thing the results will also be astonishing (but in a positive way).

It sounds simple... But people tend to make huge efforts in order to institute a positive behavior and eliminate negative behaviors.

We decide to start eating healthy. So, we gather all the information; buy all the books; shop for all the food; tell our friends about the benefits of "healthy eating." And what happens... Not much... and it's right back to where you were!

The same holds true for getting rid of bad behaviors... We decide that a certain person is "bad for us." And, instead of applying the "have" principles of "little by little," we try to go cold turkey. We start avoiding the person's phone calls, we find ways to sidestep seeing them, and we tell everyone, "I am not hanging around with so-and-so any longer." Then, so-and-so shows up and we say, "Hey, long time no see... How ya' been? Let's do lunch!"

Find ways to work the Brushing Your Teeth principle into your long-term goals. I promise you -- after only a few months of dedication, people will say you suddenly became a success. But you will know the difference!

Keep Your Eyes Fixed On The Destination

You're Always Closer To The Beginning Than The End

Optimistic people are usually despised by underachievers because, even during the most turbulent of times, they keep their "eyes on the prize."

My own ability to remain resolute has cost me the friendship of more than a few "realistic thinkers." The realists, who seem to get "bummed out" easily when things don't go their way, will often say, "So, what are you positive about -- can't you see we are in a crisis?"

When you hear that comment, you might be tempted to try to persuade them towards "positive thinking" and attempt to teach them the concept of "if you expect the negative, you'll keep getting the negative," but you'll largely be wasting your time. Here's why:

You see, people who create, act-on, and achieve worthy goals have surrendered to the fact that we are "always closer to the end than to the beginning." The reason for this is that, as you accomplish your goals, you replace them with new ones. Sometimes you do this even before your current goals are finished.

By constantly taking steps towards new goals and replacing achieved goals with new, more challenging goals, you begin to keep your eyes focused on your destination. This "Goal Replacement" outlook ensures that you'll maintain a proper perspective of the time it takes to finish goals. You'll become a person of amazing strength by accepting that, as long as your goals are potent... You're always closer to the beginning than the end.

On the outside, you appear to be optimistic... because you won't be the one to fret over the inevitable setbacks that seem to accompany achievement. But, really, you're not optimistic at all. You are the one who is being a realist! You have realistically accepted the fact that the bridge between "do" and "have" is a continual bridge.

Discipline Gets You Going...
Perseverance Keeps You Going

The difference between Discipline and Perseverance

Success begins to come more easily when you know exactly when to apply the right mind-set to the certain situation. Usually, it is felt that people "of high self-discipline" are the ones who achieve their goals. This isn't really true at all. The most difficult part of any task is always at the beginning. Once you've started, you've already applied "self-discipline." The key *now* is to use <u>perseverance</u>.

Often times, so many people do not take that first step towards their dreams because they do not think they are disciplined people. Such a pity! The fact is, you only need an ounce or two of discipline -- the rest of success lies in *perseverance*.

Self-Discipline is the ability to do what you're supposed to do -- whether you like or not, right? It is the prioritization, the selecting of the great vs. the mediocre, and then taking that initial step to start across the 'bridge.'

Perseverance involves a totally different deal! Once begun – once that first step has been taken -- it is crucial that you "lock-in" on your target... Hold the picture of your desired result in your mind... And not get sidetracked. That does not require discipline, but perseverance! For example, say I start walking to the store, I am using discipline to decide to get up... and even to decide to put one foot in front of the other. I am busy doing one thing now. My self-discipline "muscles" now go into coast-mode... Now, perseverance takes over.

Yes, the two are inseparable. But… you should consider self-discipline and perseverance separately. Use them as tools to help you through the different stages of accomplishment.

Using Persistence And Self-Discipline At The Right Time

Timing the application of the right amount of self-discipline to the proper goal and then following up with the right attitude of perseverance is *crucial* for the attainment of your goal. All results from the goals you've accomplished in the past stemmed from the proper sprinkling of a combination of these two mindsets. If you apply the "stress" associated with self-discipline -- when really your goal is more dependent on the more "happy, sure, and calm demeanor" associated with perseverance, you may not get your goal. But, you will get a great deal of frustration.

Here's a fine example. It's like when a guy like Lance Armstrong is competing in the Tour de France. When he goes uphill (a new goal), he applies a lot of self-discipline... He talks to himself in a different way. This is when he kicks himself in the behind and becomes tough, critical, even abusive towards himself. He is focused on the next *revolution* (the 100 Times Theory again) of the bike pedals... jus to get a little further up the next hill. Still, when he reaches the crest of the hill, you may see a slight smile break on his face... separating his lips slightly... Trust me, he is definitely thinking about something different now. He is not resting by any means, but rather applying a more persevering attitude... He is now thinking about the finish line, or the next goal... or the next hill! What's important is that he is no longer beating himself up like he was on that hill... His mind is already focused on conquering the next obstacle that might block his path to success!

Now, if you look at the amateurs, or say the less-veteran of competitors in this event, you'll surely see that even if they do happen to talk themselves through a difficult hill... They tend to burn out on the flats -- because they are still in a the "struggle mode". Meanwhile, Lance is mentally congratulating himself and pacing himself and progressing. Soon, he passes the less-experienced competition on the plains! How did he do it? Simply put: with his attitude... to power of his mind.

Self-Discipline And Perseverance Create Different Moods

Anxiousness makes your goal seem a zillion miles away. Using anxiousness at the beginning of a goal will serve to fuel and can help to sustain your ambition levels until your perseverance needs to kick in. Yet, it you let yourself get anxious while trying to cross the proverbial finish line -- you will only meet with frustration and disappointment.

You can actually feel what it might be like to have these two powerful emotions – self discipline and perseverance -- in conflict with one another. For example, consider a particular role you have had to fulfill in your life? Let's say you're in the role of project manager on deadline… leading a construction team to complete the last two stories of a 12-story building. Now, you know that the team already has completed similar tasks at least ten times over already... The only things to really be wary of are the distractions, i.e. shoddy work due to too much rushing, and perhaps some safety issues as well.

The emotional states you'd be smart to instill in order to get your team to effectively finish the job are probably quite different than the emotions you had to support in the beginning. Those initial emotions were probably more along the lines of "C'mon, let's get this foundation laid!" or "Where's the delivery of the lumber?" or "I thought you promised you'd have this done by 12 noon!"

Now, guess what happens when it is necessary to have to shift gears like that? You sometimes end up staying in one gear too long! The results can be devastating -- not only to your desired results -- but to your relationships as well! Have you ever been in "work mode" so much so that you then go home and take it out – unleash your stress on someone? Yes? If so, that was a result of not being conscious of the difference between the discipline and perseverance mind-sets.

215

Applying These Mindsets At The Right Time To The Right Degree

Charismatic people are not really charismatic -- they just seem to know exactly when to apply these mental tools to their advantage. Their peers think they always have the right answer to the right problem... but, what's actually going on is that, they know exactly where they stand while on the road to "have." They manage somehow to magically know when to push and when to let up.

They are not trying to please other people in the process of accomplishing their goals or even their team's goals... but, they sure are a heck of a lot more fun to be around! It seems as if they know something other people don't. It seems like the calm, cool attitude they display is because they have a crystal ball or something. And in a way -- they do have a crystal ball. They know that you apply the attitude of Self-Discipline in the *beginning* of a journey -- not the entire journey -- and perseverance for the remainder of the journey.

Off Track – But On Target

Journeys rarely follow a straight and narrow path. Similarly, the paths, journeys, and various missions that you will encounter or endure are quite similar to the path that an airplane takes while going on a trip from New York to Miami. Now, you're probably aware that airplanes have a built-in mechanism called auto-pilot. The auto-pilot serves as a guide so that each plane arrives at its intended destination, regardless of -- for the most part -- the skill of the pilot. What you may *not* know, however, is that airplanes fly *off-track* 99% of the journey! Again, this has little to do with the skill of the pilot.

The path that an airplane travels is never direct. It weaves back and forth... sometimes proceeding for miles and miles... off track, while somehow always remaining on target. As the plane flies, it may meander a little to the east, a little bit to the west, but eventually -- it gets to Miami. What's instructive here is that your journey towards your goals follows a very similar *flight plan*. Like the airplane, you will be *off-track at times but still on-target!*

Do you think that the pilot gets upset or anxious when the plane is off-track? Of course not. Why? Well, one reason is because the pilot (or the system that operates the plane) takes into consideration *how long the journey will take... including and considering the off-track part of the journey!*

Sometimes, we achievers get flustered while we're in the *end-zone*. It may seem like we are always flying off-track. And, we may be! But, that's okay. It's okay because, as you get more and more skilled at accomplishing your goals, the more and more you consider the *off-track* segment of the journey as ...part of the journey. Do not get all bent out of shape while you're 30,000 feet in the air... so to speak! Keep your eyes on your destination. Realize that, whether you're at the start, the halfway point, or at the end... you're sure to be off track on part of the journey. Remember Alice in Wonderland... where the Cheshire Cat says, "it doesn't matter if you're sure where you are going (right now). If you walk long enough, you're sure to get there?" Persistence! Do not let any off-tracked-ness cause you to abort your mission!

Your Journey is Never Straight

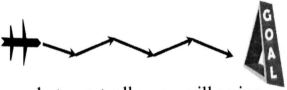

... but eventually, you will arrive.

Here are a couple of other insights with regard to this airplane metaphor that I think you should consider if you're going after big-game goals. The first of which is: Do you know how many times a typical pilot has made that flight to Miami? Probably hundreds of times depending on the experience of that pilot. What is instructive here is that, no matter *how many times* a pilot has flown that route, they are still always off-track 99% of the time! Yes, I know. You'd think that after a few thousand times, they'd finally get *better* at it, right? Well, they don't. It still takes just as much fuel each and every flight. It still requires just as much *correction* from the pilot to compensate for the auto-pilot mechanism as well.

Now, if you ever get a chance to meet a pilot, or better yet - a fighter pilot - you should ask if they use a checklist. I once asked a pilot about all of the complex controls that are in the cockpit. I said, "How do you know what's what in there?" His reply revealed a lot about how something as simple as a *plane ride* to Miami has in common with goal achievement. He said that even the most repetitively flown sojourn requires a checklist! He also said, "No matter how many times I've flown to a certain destination, or how *familiar* I think I am with the flight pattern, I always use a checklist!"

Can you image using a checklist for stuff as simple as *"turn on the lights?"* It sounds a bit tedious and perhaps redundant to apply to your daily routine, but imagine if some of your habits could be as automatic as brushing your teeth. Wouldn't that be a useful and valuable skill to have?

Pilots have more to worry about than just their trip's destination… their very lives are at stake… in addition to the lives of their passengers. What you may not realize though is that, if you do not treat your life as an important journey, it is at stake, too! What is the difference between losing your life in a plane crash compared to letting your years slip solely due to lack of planning, focus, and intentional steering?

You are the pilot of your life. No one else can steer your plane. However, if you do not *take command of the controls,* you can bet that someone else, sure as heck, will try to make you a passenger on *their* plane!

Make your flight plan, make allowances for being "off-track," and use a checklist even for what seems "obvious." The final destination may sometimes seem a million miles away. Keep putting in the efforts that will inevitably lead to success... stick it out! Even when the people in your crew are ready to pack it in – inspire them to *persevere*. Teach them the lesson of the airplane.

The Power of Habits

Nothing will assist you – or hinder you -- in persevering more than your own habits. Your habits are sort of like a double-edged sword. On one hand, once established, your habits will carry you closer to your goals, regardless of how you feel about the actual actions that comprise those habits. On the other hand, however, you also have habits that are taking you *away* from your goals... just as fast as you are moving toward them! This is a problem.

You are not as strong as your habits. Meaning that the "best" of your *great intentions* are not nearly as powerful as your "smallest" worst actions! This is why it's vitally important to be mindful of your small actions! All actions – when repeated over time – become habits! You must learn to use this to your advantage.

Now, I will freely admit that I, too, feel we should all be rewarded (at least a little bit) simply for deciding on some goals, planning our days and weeks around our goals, and taking some action towards achieving them. But the truth is, it is all just an "ante" until you *habitual-ize* your *most important actions*... enough so that the world finally tosses up their hands and says, "Okay, take it – its yours!"

Let's examine habits a little more closely. You now know that you need to "be" in order to effectively "do." If you didn't know and believe that, you wouldn't have read this far, correct? So, it must make sense that to make "do" turn into "have,' it's going to take some repeated "doing."

You've also learned that you "Don't have to like it," right? Well, this is where you should be glad that humans are called creatures of habit. It's awesome that we're creatures of habit! It means that if a particular part of goal-achievement "really sucks," all we have

219

to do is make that thing into a habit... *Something you don't even realize you're doing...*

Rest assured that, whatever you need to do *that you don't like doing,* only has to become a habit in order for you to reap the benefits of its drudgery!

Habits Do Not Discriminate

Habits are the DNA of achievement. You can have all the desire in the world... the best plans... the best coaching... the best attitude – all of it! But, until you instill the necessary habits that glue your desires to your outcomes – forget it, it isn't going to happen. Ever heard, "The road to hell was paved with good intentions?" There's a reason for that: intentions without actions produce nothing.

Amazing things are being accomplished all around us -- right now – this very second -- by people who have less of an IQ, less talent, and fewer resources than you and I. And the things they manifest are happening because they have deliberately created the habits that will take them there!

Really, success is not as mystical as many of us make it out to be. I have a friend who lives a pretty wholesome life. He has great manners, lots of ambition, and he is also above-average in the intelligence department. Pretty much... he's an all-around great guy. He even goes to church and helps people who are struggling with spiritual issues. Yet, he is mystified that some people... people of less "goodness" and/or "ethics," are experiencing so much success!

His rationale is that, "It's God's plan." He thinks that, "They are getting what they want out of life because they have selected their goals to the sacrifice of something else." It's almost as if he thinks he could reach his goals if he "sold-out" and became a "less-godly" person. Now, I do not get into spiritual discussions. Frankly, I think it's an effort in futility. But, it's an interesting thing to me that some people think they deserve a better lot in life because they are...all-in-all... "*good.*"

Why doesn't it occur to these people that, all a "bad person" has to do to be successful is to acquire "good habits" that will help them reach their goals? This is beyond me. Please, never do yourself the injustice of judging whether or not someone deserves their success based on how "nice" or how "moral" they are. I know lots of quote-unquote "nice people" who have no idea what they want, no idea how to get it, and no idea or nor comprehension of the simple fact that the universe rewards action.

Now, I ask you… Are they getting what they deserve out of life? Is it fair? Is it "justice" that the nicest people in the world sometimes die of health problems at young age, or worse yet… *live their entire lives without accomplishing their goals?* You bet it is!

Now, before you throw this book in the garbage, calling me a "bad person supporter," please realize this: It is *less fair* that the universe does not give up its gifts to those who <u>work *for them*</u>... than it is for those who *sit on their asses* to get a *freebie* just because "they are polite." Heck, what if I want to be a great person *and* a high achiever? Shouldn't I get more and greater results than both of those people? Of course! And, if you take charge of your own habits, you will accomplish the goals you set out to achieve.

One of the great things about recognizing that habits are the master skills of success is that you will learn to respect the success of others. too. Whenever I see people who have attained a high level in their field, I have a deep respect for them, because I know that they have found this principle to be true and applied it.

I don't care where you've gone to school. I don't care who you know. I don't care how much you *think* you know. Your success will always be based on your ability to create great habits and recognize (and then, *dis-create*) lousy ones.

Perhaps the greatest part about this universe is that "the world" rewards habits. And, it rewards them handsomely.

Habits Have Powerful Pull

Did you know that when a rocket, or a space shuttle, or even an airplane leaves the ground to pursue flight, it will burn a disproportionately large amount of its fuel just getting to the proper altitude?

The space shuttle, for example, has fuel tanks that hold somewhere between 1 and 2 million gallons of rocket fuel. It is said that the shuttle typically burns about 500,000 gallons just to reach a little beyond the earth's atmosphere! But, once in orbit... it will then conservatively burn the rest of its fuel and be able to travel 4 times that initial distance. There is wisdom to be found in this fact.

Your habits have incredible gravitational pull. To create a new habit, it will require a similar effort: A concentrated period of resolve, where every single obstacle both logical and illogical, may stand in your path. But, you must be resolute and remember the space shuttle. Once you have applied sufficient mental tenacity and willpower, your new habit will be relatively easy to sustain. But, there will always be this initial period of resistance to change.

Imagine if you'd been aware of this principle the last time you quit too early after making a resolution to form a new habit. You would have welcomed the problems (or resistance) and thought to yourself, "This is to be expected and will soon pass. In fact, it is *good* that it is happening, because this means we are "in flight," so to speak, and will eventually arrive at our destination." Again, please do not overlook this concept just because it is simple.

Decide That Challenges Are Fun

Challenges are indeed fun! It all depends on how you look at them. In order to gel your "doing" with your "having," it will be helpful to decide that challenges are fun. Now, I do not mean that the actions of overcoming the challenges are fun. No... I mean that you can make a game out of watching your *being-ness* change as your actions start to override your "lack of like" for the habit you're trying to establish.

Have you ever seen all-star athletes begin to smile when the pressures is on? I have… and I have actually implemented this "mental skill" as a martial arts competitor myself. Some people who witness an athlete using this skill may think that the reason the athlete is smiling is because they *like* being in the position of "high-stakes pressure." I assure you, they would prefer a *shutout* to a *sudden-death win* any day of the week! However, high-level athletes *do* understand that *the way they think* about challenges affects their performance during those challenges.

By forcing yourself to smile, be it on the outside or the inside, you instantly gain access to all the benefits of teaching your mind and body to enjoy the "work" that is occurring. And, guess what happens? You accelerate the rate at which your nervous system tells your mind to make a new habit of this so-called difficult situation.

It Doesn't Get Easier

One huge reason that people of "great potential," "high intelligence," and "natural talent" never get anywhere is because they are waiting for their habits to become "*fun*."

If this is starting to sound like a mantra… good! That means I am doing my job. If you are waiting for the habits to become a party, you'll be very let down if I do not tell you straight up: it won't get any easier. So-called "gifted" people have a really hard time with this, too. For them, because things often come easily or naturally, they'll tend to give up long before their actions have become habits. In a sense, you could say that their giftedness can be a curse, because they never learn to stick with things as well or as long as their "ungifted" counterparts.

Accept that the feeling of "fun" will not usually accompany the actions of hard work. However, the enjoyment you'll receive as a result of those "un-fun" efforts… far outweighs any price you have to pay to get through them.

It is a sign of genuine maturity and self-leadership to acknowledge that you can approach building your habits with the "I don't care if this ever becomes fun… I'm going to stick it out!" mentality. As Mark Twain wrote, "Twenty years from now, you will be more disappointed by the things that you didn't do… than by the ones you did so. So, throw off the bowlines. Sail away from the safe harbor. Catch the trade winds in your sails. Explore. Dream. Discover."

Success Is Boring

Traveling across the bridge to "have" is, for the most part, a boring journey. This one factor is the most widely unaccepted truth about success. Yet, in the same breath… it is the very reason why so many people have failed to achieve what they themselves define as "success."

Now, I am not saying that your lifestyle has to become boring in order for you to accomplish your goals – absolutely not! It's the actual process of what it takes to arrive at the final destination that can be very boring. Success is certainly not boring… but the process of *achieving* it can be.

Remember back when I talked about single hits in baseball? Well, single hits are… boring – at the very least, they are not exceedingly exciting.

Hey, remember when I said at the beginning of this book that success is often overlooked because of its simplicity? Again, the simple action-steps that must be taken to persist through the "do" stage in order to finally arrive at the "have" stage are boring, too.

We often miss out on our chances for success because we don't feel exhilaration while doing the daily habits that get us there. Many of us stop practicing those habits because we think that success is supposed to be exhilarating… and we quit too soon.

You never really "feel" like you're succeeding… *just when you're about to succeed!*

This can be a hard hit for us. Especially when you've bought into the idea that success means "signing autographs" or having your name appear in lights. Hey, even Hollywood actors will tell you that the process that led to their fame was a tough road, made them skeptical, and was at times a boring journey. You never really find yourself saying, "Wow, this is it! Now, I am succeeding!"

I have a friend who won a Gold Medal in the 1992 Olympics in Barcelona, Spain. His name is Herb Perez. I ran, kicked, punched, and fought with Herb everyday during that year. I can tell you this:

Herb knows that the process of achieving a Gold Medal is boring one.

When Mr. Perez and I would go jogging in the mornings, I would ask him what he thought about when he becomes tired while training. (Actually, I would ask him what he thought about when *I* became tired!) He would always have a positive response... and, this while doing the most arduous work.

It is amazing that the little subtleties that separate the champions from the spectators have more to do with *attitude* than any other factor.

Every day that Herb would wake up at 5:30 a.m. and go for his five-mile run... That is when he won his Gold Medal... through his habits. Not on the podium in Barcelona.

Your "Gold Medal" will be won in the same fashion. It will be earned at the local level, through your habits, and then won in the public eye.

Pump Blindly

Achieving success is like pumping a well.

You've heard me say before that we've all been millionaires, Olympic Athletes, and highly-effective people. By way of review, I want to remind you why I say this. I'm referring to the actual habits of the *millionaire, the Olympic athlete, and the effective person, not their actual results.* The implication here is that, at one time or another, we've all thought about and decided upon (Be); made a plan & and taken some action (Do)... but then... we quit. And, when we quit – we robbed ourselves of the best part (Have).

One of my instructors, Chung Park, taught me this principle when success continued to elude me during the start of a dojo (martial art school) we both operated.

I was putting in some crazy hours... sleeping at the school, passing out flyers every day, and pretty much teaching my guts out day in and day out. After some time passed... coupled with no rewards from these efforts, I decided,"It's just no use." I was demoralized, bedraggled, and ready to "pack it in."

Master Park, on the other hand, was just warming up! When he noticed my defeatist attitude, he sat me down and said, "Palangi, I don't think, *now*, is a good time to quit." Then he paused and said, "I think all we need to do is *pump blindly* for a few more seasons – and we'll be very happy that we stuck it out."

"Pump blindly, sir? What's that?"

"It means that, no matter where you go… there is always water beneath the surface of the ground. The trick is, Scott, in not trying to assume or guess how far under the surface the water lies. When you try to figure out how far the water is from the surface, you'll always be disappointed." Master Park continued with, "Scott, so many people finally wake up one day and realize that life has more to offer. Then, in a huge explosion of determination, they get a *great idea*. And then, they get outside help; they find resources; they learn more; they get excited; and they include their friends and family in on the big idea… But then they do everything except for this…" Master Park sat up straight in his chair, folded his arms across his chest proudly, and began to tap his foot.

I looked down to see if he was indeed tapping his foot and, after seeing his shoe go up and down slowly on the surface of the carpeted floor, I looked back up at him with my eyebrows raised. He had a huge grin of his face. He knew I got the message.

"Have you ever pumped water from a well, Mr. Palangi? I'm talking about one of those old-fashioned type of wells that have a handle and are connected directly to a water source deep within the ground. You know what I'm talking about? Well, Scott, we are all pumping a proverbial well. And the problem is… when we first start to pump, it feels good! Our arm is moving up and down… *we get into it…* we enjoy the action of doing something, and we are actually pretty happy just to *be pumping*. We sort of *hope* there's water in this well, but soon enough – our true nature surfaces. (That is, of course, if we're willing to look at it that way.) We become impatient: "Where are my results?!".

You see, usually when you are not getting the reward for the actions you're undertaking – you tend to want to blame the *pumping apparatus*: "This pump is too old. It's rusty. It's worn out… We need an updated version," etc. After that, we start to blame the *location of the well*: "There's no water in this well! I should know. After all, I've been pumping *for a whole three minutes!* If there was water in this well, somebody else would have discovered it already!" And, too quickly, you start to say things like, "Well, I guess I didn't really want water in the first place. Water sucks. I've pumped water before – it just *doesn't work.*"

He then said, "Now that's only three negative reactions that have occurred so far… all because you people do not like the action of pumping the well! So far you're blaming: the pump itself, the location of the well, and then… *the actual water, too!* Sounds crazy, right? But, that's how we humans operate!

"But wait, there's more!" Now, Master Park was getting his groove on. He got really serious and spoke in a low, calm voice… "Guess what else happens while we stop our pumping to bitch about the well? The water… it goes back *down* – down to the bottom of the well… All along, it was ready to come out and reveal itself to you! *And you quit too soon!*

Now, can it get any worse? Absolutely. Next, someone *else* comes along… someone who *knows* the theory of the well… and is *willing* to pump blindly… And they … get <u>*your*</u> *water!!!*"

Menial tasks performed over and over much resemble the pumping of a well. The similarities are so obvious with regard to what it takes to succeed that this simple fact is overlooked 100% of the time. The attitude you must adopt is that your well, whatever it may be, is going to require some blind pumping.

We Always Think "The Well Is Dry."

Colleagues of ours, who are achieving stellar results, can be a source of lousy modeling if you do not understand what they actually did to get those results. It's only natural to see the fruit of someone else's labors and wonder why our *seemingly identical labors don't* offer the same harvest. We will always think the grass is greener on the other side if we take our eye off the pump.

Our peers are usually unaware of how much they can influence our stick-to-it-iveness. When we see their well, and taste or sample their water, we cannot help but think that maybe we got the wrong well.

Psychologists say that the root of much mental illness is derived from people measuring themselves against others, You've got to resist comparing your results with those of people who have struck gold. Besides, you will rarely ever know how hard someone has to work at their well. Your friends and associates will sometimes want to portray the appearance that it was easy for them, like *success is a breeze.* In part, what they are trying to do is make you think that if you do not achieve success *out of the gate,* it must mean there is something wrong with you.

I know it may sound like I'm saying you've got lousy friends. but we've all done it. Sometimes we do not initially want to admit how hard we've had to work in order to get our results. We think that maybe -- when people finally hear how hard we had to work to get our results... maybe, they will think the reward wasn't worth the effort, that the effort to reward ratio doesn't balance.

So, another rule to keep in mind, along with pump blindly, is to remember to use the *"blind"* element of that statement: *Put on blinders.* Don't watch the Joneses. Keep your eye on your pump, your well, and hopefully your water, too.

Pumping Someone Else's Well

Goals that you do not choose to consciously set for yourself will be set for you. Remember, we are all working on goals – sometimes they are someone else's. Many times you will have to pump someone else's well. This is just part of learning what it takes to succeed. Don't listen to people who tell you that, "You have to work for yourself in order to get ahead." Although there is some truth, much truth, to this statement – you can learn a lot by pumping someone's well or by working for someone else.

Make a conscious decision to act like the well you're pumping is your own well. You can't pump someone else's well forever and live out your dreams, but you can earn a hell of an income and get all the "kinks" worked out of your *own* plans in the meantime.

It can be discouraging to work on someone else's goals, while yours seem to be on the back burner... Do not worry. You will be compensated for your efforts. If not monetarily, at the very least you will have strengthened your own work ethic. Then, when the opportunity presents itself – you'll posses the needed work muscles and habit reflexes to get *your* job done well.

Then, when you do begin to get your well pumped up and running... and the water is coming out predictably and abundantly... Remember to let your crew take a drink! If you make it to the point where you need to enlist the help of others, *remember to take good care of them, too!*

Distractions While Pumping

Conquering the urge to quit is not easy... especially when you have friends and family who can't "see" the water you are pumping for. They will always remind you of how invisible the water seems to be! If you aren't careful to school them on the pumping principle, the things they say will negatively reinforce what you feel when you hit those sticking points.

We talked a little bit about this and it would be good idea to revisit. It's tough when you are trying to cross the bridge from Do to Have and everyone else is watching the faucet. "So, how's it going... any water yet? Hmm, I told ya..." You've got to be tough for them, too. You not only have to lead your life – you've got to lead theirs. Too. If you don't teach them the things you know about success – they will just bring you down. The sad thing is, they don't even realize this.

On the other hand, if you associate with high-achieving individuals... you will not get that type of feedback. Instead you will get the support and encouragement to stick it out. Whenever someone tells you about a lofty goal, you too should remember that you serve as a potential distraction when you aren't positive and encouraging.

One of the best ways to keep people positive and, at the same time, turn them from potential distractions into supporters, is to educate them about the cycle of Be, Do, and Have. It will solidify your resolve to persevere and enhance your ability to lead people. Most importantly, people will begin to respect your goals and believe in your ability to accomplish them.

You cannot ignore distractions – but you sure can influence them!

Most People Want The Water First

Pre-payment of success does not exist. Never become the person who wants water prior to doing any of the pumping. It seems a little obvious, but haven't you seen the type of people who will not lift a finger until you at least give them a "sip" first? What a pathetic state of existence. These people believe that applying some effort before getting a result is like paying the check at restaurant before getting a menu. They want to "taste the food" and make sure it's worth the price. They want an absolute promise, a 100% guarantee that their efforts will pay off. They don't see that the act of the effort itself is where the real virtue is found.

I think that many of us "want proof" before trying a lot of things. In some cases, however, research becomes the only action people ever take! They'll keep looking for evidence that the water is going to be there. "I don't want to waste my time" is their rationale. What they fail to realize is: "Until you are willing to waste your time in pursuit of your dreams, *all of your time is being wasted!*" Don't try to look that one up, folks; it's original.

Hey, let me tell you something, any time you are guaranteed a clear-blue-sky, you find out two things fast:

There is no clear-blue-sky.

You never work as hard when you're results are guaranteed.

A funny thing happens when you are promised success… You never really work very hard to achieve it when you know that it's guaranteed. But, when you aren't sure and still take action – your faith grows -- and, as a consequence, your results *triple!*

Show me any successful person and I'll show you someone who will kick down doors to get what's on the other side. Conversely, you could put a plastic bag of cash behind a glass wall… and, still, many people would say, "That's not real. It's a scam. It's probably just fake money!" They want it delivered and they want to be able to spend it first – before ever moving an inch. So, I am here to tell you this:

Even if you gave people the money first, even if you let them spend a few bucks to prove to them it's real… When it came time for them to work for what you'd pre-paid them, they would tell you, "Uhmm, can you give me a minute or two, I got a full stomach. Uh, can I work this money off tomorrow? I want to go to the mall."

Never ask for the water first.

Back To The Drawing Board (Journal)

Self-awareness is the key to discovering what it will take to put the finishing touches on your success. While we've been talking extensively about the dynamics of the space between your Doing and Having, it is important to revisit the *power of the pen.* The journal offers you a speedy shot of self-awareness if you are willing to put in the time to use it. If you make the deliberate effort to "think on paper" about how you feel about your journey, you'll become aware of the way you are thinking about... the things that you are thinking about. It sounds like a parable, I know; but journaling allows you to reflect on the events that have transpired... almost in a more objective and unbiased way.

It is sort of like looking *at* the glasses – instead of looking *through* the glasses. Here's why: Let's say you have done some "to-do's" that are supposed to take you closer to your goals... but your goals *still* seem a million miles away. Well, if you were to just sit and stew over "what you've put in vs. what you got out" (like so many of us do when we're not seeing any progress) and replay this over and over in your head like a horrible movie – this changes your internal dialogue. The end result is: No gained self-awareness and worse feelings about the tasks you still have left to do *and* the miles you still have to travel!

Now, if you were to "talk" to your journal, rather than talk to yourself... or worse, your friends... you get to "rid" yourself of any anxieties that much quicker. Conversely, if you take the route of talking to your friends about your "tough road," nothing will get accomplished. Usually, your friends end up trying to offer you their version of solutions, or you just end up carrying on and on, repeating yourself over and over... not making much sense at all.

When you begin the habit of journaling, your relationships improve. You now spend your time together having more productive conversation, because you "come to the table" ready to be a friend rather than need a friend.

Putting your thoughts down on the events that are transpiring allows you to look at the actions more clearly. For some reason, when you put your thoughts on paper, you step into another state of consciousness. You'll notice that the thoughts: "It seems like I am going nowhere... My goals are still so far away... Will this work?" end up translating into something more objective like, "I think I am feeling frustrated, because the road to success seems like a treadmill. My level of persistence is being tested." Then, when you go back and read what you're writing, you'll see that sometimes you just need to be stronger. The problems, once they're on paper, sort of stay on paper.

Now, your mind is freed up for more productive thinking.

Journaling And Emotions

Obstacles that try to knock you off your path will not be as challenging as the emotions that those challenges spawn... emotions that can remain long after the obstacles are overcome. By journaling, you'll learn to leave your goals at the playing field. You'll lose the tendency to wear your heart on your sleeve as well.

Emotions will surface during your journaling that, otherwise, would have remained dormant. One of the many reasons people tend to skip journaling is because it sometimes makes you confront not-so-pleasant, yet necessary-to-deal-with, emotions. If you've been having a problem with someone and you journal about it, as opposed to think about it, you'll often realize that you might not have been treating that person the way you should have. Other times, when you feel like quitting, you'll come to recognize your impatience and lack of will power.

What we sometimes forget to realize is that, by confronting the emotions that arise during the journaling process, we deal with them much more effectively. Left alone, unaddressed feelings may rear their ugly heads at ill-opportune times.

For example, if you've been having a tough time with a family member while trying to achieve some important goals, the journal will give you a chance to isolate what you're feeling. Whereas, if you do nothing, you may have the tendency to lash out at others. Journaling regularly will help you clarify what's really going on beneath the surface. You'll also become more rational and more level-headed.

Journaling Methods

Consistency is the most important factor in journaling. There are of course "techniques and tricks" that you may find useful; and you'll learn them here too, but consistency is more important than method. By sticking to a consistent schedule with your journaling efforts, you'll avoid the typical venting that usually results from hold things inside. The consistency gives you a regular release, much like a steam valve so you can avoid sporadic outbursts. Also, consistency will prevent the long-winded ranting that you'd be more likely to engage in if you neglected to write regularly. This brings me to my next point.

Timing. It is highly recommended that you stick to the same time schedule; plan a regular time daily to write your entries. This element of consistency teaches your brain to "give you its best stuff." After a while of doing this, you'll actually begin to have more productive and clearer thinking. Like going to lunch, you're teaching your brain to get on schedule, to build up an appetite for writing. Schedule your journaling just like lunch, working out, or any other important appointment.

Story form. Try writing your journal entries in a story format. People who've done this before report that it journaling becomes more fun this way. It also takes the *emotional charge* out of any really upsetting parts of your life.

One of the biggest phenomena reported by people using this method is that, after some time doing it this way, you begin to realize that your life really is a story! More importantly, you are the author of that story!

It's almost like your brain *knows* that you're going to be recording a lousy story later on, so… to resolve that, your brain makes you act in the best way during the present moment. This gives you the necessary strength, patience, and fortitude to most effectively ensure that you give your life story a happy ending!

The Plateau

The process of success is not a gradual climb.

Learning, whether it be in school, through real world experience, or with a physical skill – follows a process that is very similar to achieving your goals. By taking a look at the parallels between "learning" and "achieving," we can enhance the depth of our appreciation for the cultivation of persistence.

The process of learning is often referred to as a "curve." It implies that learning follows a steady, gradual, and upward climb. Like this:

In one sense, by looking at learning in this way, you come to realize that the more you learn, the tougher it gets, right? After all, if learning involves a gradual incline of steady progress – and progress goes upward – then, it must mean that we should prepare for hard work. The problem is that, if it were a steady incline, it really wouldn't be that hard to persist. But, it *is* hard to persist. It's hard to persist because learning does not follow a so-called "curve."

Learning, and all progress for that matter, tends to emulate a plateau, with a bump of progress occasionally, and then another plateau. Then eventually, another bump of progress, followed immediately by another plateau. There is no curve at all. Again, if progress were always upward, it would be easy to stick with things even when they became more difficult. Why? Because, even though the "upward-ness" of progress gets difficult... at least you have positive feedback or rewards to motivate you to keep going!

It is relatively easy to persevere as long as your labor is producing "fruits." But that is not what happens, is it?

Progress seems smaller because of time elapsed and growth occured

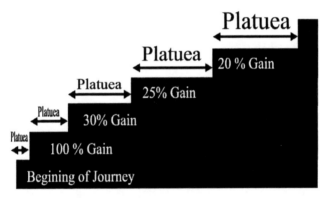

Achieving success is more like this:

Achievement is more like *steps* of progress, but then a long "plateau" before taking the next step.

Take learning how to throw a baseball, for example: Let's say that you have never seriously learned to throw a baseball before. And, for whatever reason... you now have to learn how to throw one.

Well, your first day out, your throwing 30 mph. Not great, but it something that can be built upon with some practice. So, you decide to practice throwing all day long. How good could you be the next day? Maybe you could throw 50 mph. Perhaps with a little coaching, you could even throw 60 mph... the very next day! Right? Yes, it's very possible.

Now, you are on the next level... a level twice as high as the previous day.

237

But, could you repeat that process over and over? I mean, could you have a 30 mph increase in speed *every single day? Forever?* Of course not, because that is not the way of progress. Initially, you can achieve some impressive gains – but not everyday. If that were possible, you would hear of stories of people throwing baseballs at 3000 mph!

Your progress always is greatest in the beginning, but then "the frequency of the surge" happens less frequently.

There is also a second factor to consider. Look at the diagram again. Notice how each "step" of progress is equal to one another. Yet, compared to what they are individually… when held up against their "past progress," the steps become less and less significant – EVEN THOUGH THEY REPRESENT THE SAME SIZE OF IMPROVEMENT!!

This is the missing link, the answer to "why we quit too early." We are always comparing our last "improvement" to the one that is either not occurring – or – just about to occur!

It's no wonder why we are great starters but poor finishers! Our concept of our improvements, in relation to the time it takes to achieve the next improvement, often gets the best of us.

The Philosophy To Adopt To Live Between The Steps

Treating all of your growth, success, and achievements, with the "stair model" instead of the "gradual climb" model will allow you to make allowances" for more time to elapse and, subsequently, allow for more progress.

Remember, the distance between each step requires some "walking" in to get to the next one. In the beginning, you had only to take that first step up the stairs… but now, each step is farther and farther apart. Accept the fact that, if you're willing to put one foot in front of the other – repeatedly – your goal is guaranteed.

Don't resent the fact that each new step only seems to require more and more walking.

Surrender to the idea that the real goal is to just enjoy the process of walking in between steps – not just enjoying the "high" of going up the next step.

Besides, ever notice how short the time is when you are actually being elevated? The time flies by. It's gone before you even get to enjoy it! Here is where everybody really misses out on the true growth of success... they always correlate more joy to "conquering the next step" but, in reality, that time is only a manifestation of your ability to keep on traversing the "plains" until you become elevated again.

Most people attach their joy with these brief moments of progress.

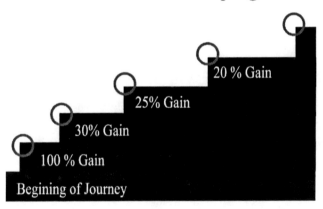

What is to be learned from this model is important: if you make it a condition to be motivated... and to be spirited, only while going to the next level – you'll literally rob yourself of the opportunity to really grow. Persons of high persistence and follow-through... who can stick with things until they transform accomplishment, understand that there is a better way to look at this inevitable "stairway to success." A way in which... you look at the "Process" as the "Goal" itself.

How Masters, Experienced People, and Experts View The Process

People who've achieved mastery in any field are more apt to replicate success with ease. Because they have a reference of the cycle involved, the "steps" of success, they are less likely to quit when they're on that boring plateau part of the current step. This is a true sign of maturity… They do not blame the goal for how long it takes to manifest. They also do not blame the process or curse the very the nature of high-achievement. Instead, they approach all of their aspirations with total certainty that the goal they've affixed in their consciousness… is theirs for the taking, if they can only manage to "take a step in the right direction" every single day.

If you'll remember a few pages back, I asked you to call upon your "past templates" to remind yourself that you've already used the Be, Do, Have theory of goal achievement. Now, take a look back at those things you've done… Can you see that your progress occurred quite similarly to what is portrayed in the diagram above? Can you see how it was like an instant jump of improvement followed by a flat spot, and then, finally, another jump of improvement… but only after you'd "paid the price" on the flat spot?

Deciding to "hang around" on the flat spot does not mean you are going to be allowed to "coast" either. It's not going to be easy just because you're not theoretically going up hill. You will still have to work as diligently as you did during the times when you experienced obvious progress! And that's sort of a bummer, too! It would seem more fair if, while on the flat spot, you could simply: relax, take a break, or take your eyes off the ball. But that would be like resting (and you know better now) as the water is *just about to come out the pump*, right?

Just keep plugging away. Wake up; check your schedule; look at your most important 3 goals we discussed in the "doing' section of this book. And make damned sure that you've got something in that daily planner that is at least an "attempt" at taking you closer to your top 3 goals. Remember... you've got to chip away at success. Only by choosing the attitude of a master, will your goals manifest.

Masters eventually, and always, achieve their next goals. They know that the Be-ing part *can* be done... They know that the Do-ing part *must* be done... But, most importantly, they are aware that the Having *will* come -- as long as they choose the attitude of perseverance. They never lament that the next level may seem far, far, away.

We Are Hard-Wired For "Successful Failure"

Mankind has made some incredible strides in the past thousand years. Unfortunately, human beings have, pretty much, remained the same. Our DNA, or our instincts if you will, are set to "get what we need." Then, as long as we have existed, this somehow seems to shift to "just keep what you got" once we have the thing you needed. Why is that? This is where we find that #1 enemy of achievement: "the comfort zone." This is a problem – your biggest roadblock, especially if you want to live up to your full potential.

Now, one's comfort zone can be a good thing... but only if you know how to use it as a tool. Use your comfort zone while you reflect upon things you've already accomplished; be grateful for what you've got, as well as for what you have the potential to do.

Even scientists acknowledge that people have a comfort zone – meaning, *a mechanism in our brain that makes us do only the things we've already done or the things we're already 'comfortable with.'* – This served us well back when we were cavemen and a primitive bunch. Our species was used to eating, used to sleeping, and so on... If we didn't have these hard-wired instincts, humans may have perished. This is why I say we are hard-wired for "successful failure." You are programmed to "successfully" do the things that will sooner or later perhaps keep you breathing – butt… will stop bringing you success!

We have this natural tendency to quit because, back in a time when we didn't know where our next meal or "kill" was coming from. we had to conserve as much energy as possible. No wonder we see so many men want to watch TV after a hard day at the office!

The good news is… by examining the various ways our minds play tricks on us, we obtain a keener insight into conquering the "default settings" of our minds.

Your Mind Will Play Tricks On You

You decide to start an exercise program. Your strategy is… everyday after work, you're going to get to the gym by 7 pm.

As you're pulling in the driveway after work, you notice that your lawn has really starting to get a bit out of control. You say to yourself, "Well, I really should take care of this lawn thing; my home is important to me… and, this weekend I promised to take the girls to that play in the city – so I definitely won't have time to mow it then. Maybe I'll call someone to take care of it… Yeah, that's what I'll do. Besides, nobody mows their own lawn anymore. I could be doing more things if I didn't have to cut my lawn… Hmm, where's that guy's number who does everyone's lawn? Gee, I know what I'll do… I'll go on the internet and do a "quick search" for his phone number." And, what happens? You've been there. No lawn gets mowed. No workout gets accomplished. You end up on the internet for hours… and the worst part is – you say to yourself, "Well, there's always tomorrow."

Your mind plays tricks on you!

You decide to start eating healthier. You've thought about it... Your doctor has encouraged you, even warned you, that your diet has to change... Your life depends on it.

Then, as you open the fridge, before your salivating eyes lies a piece of chocolate cake. A little to the right of the cake, however, is a small bag of carrots... And what does your brain say? Take the cake! You can eat those carrots tomorrow. Wrong!

I hope you haven't gotten sick of hearing me say this over and over, but our habits, our mind, and our ability to "re-train ourselves" are the master keys to perseverance. And, see? I certainly haven't gotten sick of telling you!

Every Instinct You Have Is Wrong

Have you ever heard someone say, "You just have to listen to your instincts and live accordingly?" I mean, we all hear people say, "My gut tells me such and such." But, remember the instincts are only as good as the data. Most people are broke. Many people are less happy more frequently than they are happy. So much for instinct...

Animals have certain instincts that ensure and promote their survival. Their instincts override their intelligence – or lack thereof. These instincts allow animals to "know" what they need to do survive. Humans so not have such natural, unimpeded instincts. In fact, our natural instincts, if we have any that is, are usually what get us into trouble.

For example, someone cuts you off in traffic. Your brain says, "Kill 'em!" Someone upsets you at work. You become happy when things don't go that person's way, or even happier if they screw up. Most of our natural instincts gear us up for comfort, apathy, and procrastination. Bad stuff if you want to finish what you've started!

There are many people who lament that we are not all "natural-born achievers." They feel contempt and even disgust that our Creator did not give *us* perhaps the same natural instincts as *someone else,* anyone who appears to be a little more successful.

What they do not realize, however, is that this is actually a blessing. You see, we can develop *new* instincts. We can slowly, gradually override the lousy instincts that tend to have been our knee-jerk reactions. Yet, it requires time and effort to become more self-aware... and more responsible.

How, you ask? Well, the first step is to simply *know* that this is a universal truth, this "wrong instinct" stuff... The simple realization that your instincts are wrong gives you a chance to suspend your certainty that your impulse is the most beneficial one to apply to the task at hand.

Let me explain: the best time to second-guess your self is when you are ready to *quit, procrastinate*, or *curse* the process that it takes to cross the bridge of achievement.

The Better Brain

Conscious mind tells the subconscious mind to get to work on the things you think about most. This is your better brain. It has the ability to stand outside of itself and look inward. It is exactly this function that is going to get us to where we want to go.

But, we must train it. We must be vigilant in our application of willpower and teach ourselves to "ignore" the instincts that will take us off our path.

It is this better brain that told you to purchase this book. It is the better brain that told you to go on diet, start an exercise program, and to pick this book up and read it right now. These things require self awareness.

They involved the use of your *will.*

Just as we used this better brain functioning to begin these new habits, we must also use it to remind ourselves to stay on track.

It works like this:

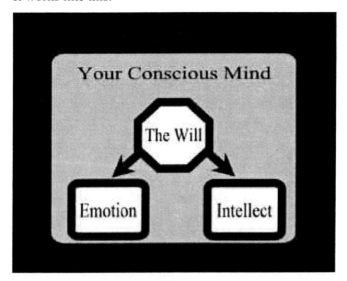

The shaded box resembles your conscious mind. Remember? That's the part of our mind in use when we are: conscious (of course), selecting, deciding, thinking, and most importantly... doing! Still though, the whole point in doing is *having,* so what is needed is a way of controlling (or, more realistically, influencing) our minds so we will stay on track! Our conscious mind is comprised of three components:

The Intellect

The Emotions

The Will

The Intellect

Logical functioning of the mind stems from our intellectual processes. These involve the calculation, reasoning, and contemplation of facts. The Intellectual part of our conscious mind is the part that listens to the "voice of reason." And, rightfully so. Without it, we wouldn't be able to measure the consequences of our actions, or decide whether we should take the elevator down to the first floor... or jump!

Some people live solely through the use of their intellect. They do not want to hear about "feelings, theories, or philosophy." Their motto is: "Just give me that facts, man - only the facts."

The Emotions

Our emotions dictate the vast majority of which actions we choose to take. Emotional states can bring us to high levels of excitement and enthusiasm or... to the very gates of Hell, if allowed to run rampant.

It has been said by psychologists that we humans make our decisions based on "emotion backed up by logic." For example, you get hungry. You feel like "going out for pasta tonight." You've always loved its taste. The ambiance of the restaurant puts you in a great mood. You've recently seen a cooking show featuring a dish with fresh basil, garlic, and tomatoes... and – you haven't eaten Italian in over a month. You're about to stuff your face... based on emotion. But wait: you are also going for a 12-mile jog tomorrow. You need your energy. And this pasta meal will serve as your "carbohydrate loading." (You just peppered your emotion with some logic.) Moments later, its "Yes, I think I'll have some fresh parmesan, thank you."

Those in the marketing industry understand the concept of emotion backed up by logic better than anyone.

The Will

You will use the power of your "will" to negotiate the fine line between starting, and sticking-with things. Without the will - the consciousness to say "I will do this rather than that" - man is no different from any of the other animals. The unique human endowment of "will power" is fascinating once you start to absorb the concept and apply it in your life.

You will not create much success in your life without conscious, skillful, and deliberate use of your will. I know of no successful person who has succeeded without the use of *will*. Further, I know of no failures who have and apply lots of will power. This common denominator of "will' will be evident throughout all successes. Whether starting a new business and getting it off the ground or achieving an athletic endeavor, the *will* is what you'll use to fasten your actions into results.

Lack of willpower is often the reason many goals don't even get out of the starting gate. People, not having succeeded in anything before, may be reluctant to chart a new course, a path different from their past memories of *goals-not-gotten*.

Don't worry if you think you lack the will to succeed. That's natural! Take comfort in the fact that you can build it. It isn't biological, the will. Also, the fact that you can't "see" it, should strengthen your belief that the will can be changed, altered, improved upon. Take your height, for example – that's genetic. Your will, on the other hand, has no genetic makeup. You can change it whenever you decide. For many, the will becomes stronger just by becoming aware of this very fact. It's like someone has just given you the permission to more willful and so you become so.

If you'll recall from earlier chapters, I said to be grateful for the Law of Cause and Effect. This is because the law suggests that, although your results are your "fault," it also means that anytime you want – you can change your results at your own discretion. Same thing goes with the will.

We are born lacking in will. Remember the path of least resistance? It is human nature to gravitate towards the easy, quick, and free when the long, arduous, and mundane must be done. That's just the way it is.

But, pretend that your will is a huge machine. Everyone has one and all machines have identical specs. Successful people simply put more fuel into the engine and, of course, then go farther and faster than those who use less fuel.

What is this proverbial "fuel?" *Awareness*.

Become more aware of how you are operating at all times. For example, right now, are you operating more out of a sense of intellect or emotion?

This is an important question to ask because Logic is great fuel. Emotion, too, is a great fuel. However, when those two fuels are mixed with the power of "will," you unleash a powerful force... a force stronger than your moods and stronger than emotions or intellect alone. Much like the example of 1+1=3... the "will" causes a detonation that turns promises into actions, actions into habits, and habits into results.

Deliberate usage of the will can take you more quickly to your destination than any other single component. We are all born with pretty much – a lousy will. Sometimes, though, we are lucky enough to discover its power through mentoring, parenting, or self-discovery.

Where is the will built?

Dialogue. Inner dialogue. This may too simple for you to comprehend, but you can even ask a three-year-old and they'll tell you that I'm right. The fact is that, with all the stuff you've ever and will ever quit... a mental, internal, and - in some cases – even a verbal dialogue is occurring.

All the things you've ever quit ceased beginning with something like this: "This sucks!"... "I hate this" ... "There must be an easier way."

Now, many people will agree with this concept. It fits through their window. Consider this seriously though: this perspective works the same way for helping you to work through the stuff that sucks, but that takes you to your goals.

Saying to yourself, "I can do this" or "This is tough, but I'm a whole lot tougher" will do wonders for you. I have applied this tactic many times, right as I felt like puking during hard training, during a tough negotiation or a personal problem, and with many other things that "suck!" It always works.

A great, simple story highlights this perfectly:

A and B were fighting. A and B possessed equal skill, experience, and strength. As they fought, they both became equally tired, equally sore, and equally frustrated while trying to win.

Meanwhile, as they fought, A always thought to himself, "I can't do this any longer. I'm tired." Yet, B thought to himself, "Just one more blow; just one more blow."

And thus, he gave A one more blow, downing his fatigued opponent. Not because of greater skill. Not because of greater experience, knowledge, or even education in "fighting." B simply chose to talk to himself differently. And… succeeded because of it. Remember the power of your inner dialogue!

Now, of course that story is similar to the one we all learned when young about the "little train that could." The concept still holds true today.

Find anyone with a superior "will" and you'll also be looking at someone who knows how to talk to themselves in the most empowering ways.

The will begins with inner dialogue. Use your will to balance the calm, cool, "Doctor Spock"-type of mindset. Use the power of your emotions to give force to your intellect. Most of all, use your will to enhance them *both,* so that the conscious mind becomes your servant – not your master.

Success Has A Price

Karate Master Peter Urban has a sign in his school of martial arts that reads:

The Three Rules of Karate:

Everyone Works

All Start At The Bottom

Nothing Is Free

I love that slogan!

Number 3, *nothing is free,* is the most often overlooked principle in goal achievement.

Similar to the person who wants the water before pumping the well – many times, we want a taste of success before paying for it.

It's of no use to delve into *why* this is true. It could be because when we were children, our parents gave us what we wanted to "shut us up" or to "bribe us." It could be that, at heart... we are a *lazy* species!

Nonetheless, as soon as we develop the skill of "paying the price," we will... as the saying goes – get what we paid for.

What Price Will You Have To Pay?

Two prices are always paid in order for you to accomplish your goals. And this is often why people cannot stay on the "road less traveled" in order to finalize their goals. They miss this "Dual Payment" Law.

Now, granted, most people don't want to pay or aren't willing to pay *any price* for success so, subsequently, – they prevent themselves from getting what they want. But... those are not people who are reading this book! Those are the people who are reading the newspaper or, worse, watching the "ball game" on TV.

Let's get a grasp on this payment concept. Most people accept the fact that at least ONE price will be paid. This is called THE FIRST PAYMENT.

The first payment is one with which most people are familiar. Work, effort, the "single-action steps"... and, the *doing*, if you will. Even in childhood, we're sort of taught to pay the first price. Most of the people you work with are probably familiar with the First Payment.

The First Payment, however, is only the *starting* point, and is the reason we can achieve a little bit of success. This first payment involves the *creating*.

The Second Payment

The second payment is the reason we have a difficult time persisting. It is also the reason we become greedy, impatient, and grossly unfocused on our path to achievement. Whereas the first payment requires you to "GIVE"... The Second Payment asks you to GIVE UP.

When I say "give up" I mean stop doing, cease focusing on, and quit! I know what you're thinking. "But we are supposed to persist. I thought quitting was bad!" And it is, but it's perfectly okay—even mandatory in some form—if you are to achieve your goals! What does this involve? It involves identifying what the "little extra" entails, that will help you reach your goals.

For example: If you want to achieve a single-digit body fat, or enhanced health and well being, the first price you'll pay is that of intense exercise.

And, many people CAN get that part done. That's the first payment, the one that is considered a "given."

But, the second payment... The most crucial payment... and, the payment that will absolutely guarantee you get the total benefits from the exercise is: "Diet!"

Well, what's that payment consist of? Will it involve *giving up* something? Might it include *quitting something?* You bet!

Now, by itself, the second payment doesn't have much impact. But when it is included as a follow-up to the first payment, YOU QUADRUPLE both your chances for success, and the SPEED of your success, too!

If you want to double-quadruple your success rate, you could dig a little deeper and find a possible third, and even a fourth payment. The Third Payment could be "giving up late night TV" so that your body recoups and is ready for the next First Payment! A fourth payment could be "less hanging out with the *gang.*" You will also rapidly increase your success rate, by choosing to "do other things" besides hanging out with people who are not also "sharing your vision." This is the central theme of all support groups.

You see, you may have been good at the first payment your whole life – but, when someone comes along and says, "Hey, that's just the start!" That is when you realize that you've got to search for that second payment and PAY THE PRICE for success.

Conflicting Goals

One of the biggest contributing factors in not *having* after *doing* is because we tend to have conflicting goals. Just as fast as we are heading towards our goals, we are also engaging in behavior that is taking us faster and faster away from those same dreams.

Like the saying "have your cake and eat it too," we fail to adhere to the simple wisdom of the second payment – the sacrifice.

Show me any person who has tons of so-called "potential" but never manages to realize their dreams, and I'll show you a real-life example of someone who's traveling north and south at the exact same time! And, the kicker is... they can't even see it!

If you have teenagers, you've witnessed tons of evidence to support this theory. You will see your child get straight A's – but meanwhile are caught up "trying to be cool." Then, what happens? Well, once they manage to graduate college, if they've not become accustomed to the "second payment," they will interview poorly, have lousy habits, and always "come close – but no cigar!" in the real world.

This conflicting goals stuff is the source of much debate, too! Look at the trouble President Clinton got himself into by not making the second payment! There are groups of people in this country who believe that no second payment is necessary. They believe you can go north and south simultaneously.

Dr. Steven Covey, in his "First Things First" seminar says, "A double-minded man is wrong in all his ways." Another famous philosopher said, "Man cannot continue to do good in one area of life whilst succeeding to bad in another area." It has a little slant towards "morality," but please understand, morality has nothing to do with my point here. In many cases, it simply boils down to the issue of "time."

There simply isn't enough time to pursue "building a business" AND "going to the Yankees game!" At least, not initially. And, if you *are* to be "out of balance" with this discipline... better to be out of balance in the direction of goal achievement, right?

You Can Pay Me Now or Pay Me Later

252

More often than not, we avoid paying the price for success because we'd *rather* do something else.

Have you ever seen the bumper sticker "I'd rather be fishing"? Many people live out their lives in this manner, not realizing it is the cause of much of their own disappointment. After years of watching the clock, and hours of trying to squeeze in some time to "go fish," these people find themselves blaming something or someone for their situation. When you run into these people, just say, "Yeah, but look at the bright side... at least you got to go fishing!"

Sooner or later, we are going to have to pay the price - the first one and the second one – so why not pay now?

By avoiding the pain associated with paying the price for success now (be it the effort put in, or the things sacrificed), you'll pay much greater prices for your delays. First, there's the pain of missing out on the fruits of the success you could've already had. Secondly, you'd still have to pay the price for the thing you want to achieve!

So, why pay twice? The procrastination of *not* finishing what you start is much greater than the pain of JUST "Do"ING IT!

Remember the Aamco commercial? The man says, "You can pay me now or pay me later!" He tries to show the contrast of the pain of getting your car maintenance now versus later – a bit of routine maintenance or you can wind up getting your transmission replaced!

The pain of regret associated with missed opportunities, procrastination, and giving up... is so much worse than the pain of paying the price for success today!

Difficulty Is Relative

All things are equally hard. The path you're traveling right now, even if it doesn't appear challenging, *is still hard.* And this is actually an awesome thing! You see, all of it is hard.

My friend Fred Mertens, a self-made millionaire says, "It's hard being broke... and, it's hard being rich – you just get to take your pick."

Another one of my mentors, Master Keith Hafner, also a self-made millionaire asks, "Is it hard to earn a fortune? Yes. Is it hard to not have a fortune? Yes. Is it hard to raise kids with high self-esteem? Yes. Is it hard to have kids with low self-esteem? Yes! Is it hard to achieve your goals? Yes. Is it hard living with the fact you never achieved your goals? Yes!" And in the exact same words he says, "You get to take your pick."

You, too, have probably noticed that, on the continuum of success... either end of the spectrum is equally hard!

This begets the question: *If* all things *are* equally hard, then *why not pick the better situation?*

It's like going to work. Is it hard to go to work and break your butt to achieve the company's goals? Yes. But isn't it also hard, maybe even harder... to sit around and *watch the clock* all day... looking for opportunities to "cut corners" and *shirk your work?* Definitely. The effort you'll invest in dodging responsibilities at work eventually becomes... well, work!

The main reason we don't deliberately choose the better situation is because we actually believe that one lifestyle is easier, less stressful, and/or more *laid-back* than the one that commands us to move outside of our comfort zone.

We tend to think that, for some reason, one lifestyle is easier to live than the other. And since we're humans and gravitate towards the path of least resistance – we'd just as soon pick the path of lesser effort over the greater.

In fact, not only will we choose the lesser – many times... we'll defend it. We'll use comments like, "Hey, who wants all that stress anyway?"

"I just want enough to get by."

"We are NOT materialistic people; we're more the down-to-earth type." Hey, call it what you want. I've used that crap before and it's all rhetoric.

When we are children, we have dreams. For some reason along the way, we released our vision of those dreams. Perhaps no one told us that both lifestyles are equally hard. Perhaps we made attempts and, because it was *too hard*, we gave up *too early*.

Whatever the case may be, most of us die with our music still in us. Is it that we refuse to accept the notion that maybe, just maybe, we fall short of our goals simply because we believe that life is easier by having less?

Don't you believe that for a second.

Of all the people I've met in my travels, every single soul who ever admitted "I only want enough to get by" – NEVER *had* enough to get by. Not enough money, not enough health, not even enough peace of mind.

After a few years pursuing this routine, we will then build up a series of excuses. And we'll cling to these excuses as long as we believe they'll keep us "safe." Rationalizing that we don't like the so-called "unpredictability" that *living on the edge* appears to require. Yet, in reality... nothing is more unpredictable than NOT living up to your full potential! We become so used to mediocrity, that we forget that a life of mediocrity IS JUST AS HARD AS THE LIFE OF EXCELLENCE!

That's the big secret! It's all equally hard!

Now, there is one caveat to this... Or perhaps better put – one problem.

If I am right, and all things are equally hard... Your next question should be, "How do I stay motivated enough to keep on *plugging away* so that I can achieve my goals?"

Simple.

Life Always Gives You A Nine

Experts involved with human motivation have proclaimed that the reason we usually *quit things* is because the reward of our actions is not *big enough*. However, *you*, having read this far, *should never again buy into that sort of excuse*! You already know that the rewards of high achievement take time to unfold. You also know that - much like the farm... most of your time is spent waiting for the harvest (that is, if you've paid the *agricultural price, of course!).*

People with triumphant attitudes will not be susceptible to quitting because of a perceived *"reward lack."* Hell, no! More likely, you will want to quit because of the *pressures* associated with sticking with things! Following-through and sticking-things-out... *sucks!* Anyone who tells you differently is severely medicated or should be medicated!

While attaining your dreams, you will meet with that "inner dialogue" that tells you, "This Sucks!" You'll also think that life is too hard. And... just as Murphy's Law states, "Whatever can go wrong – *will go wrong." My point? Be ready for lots of stuff to go wrong!*

Old Man Persistence can be downright *mean* just as you're about to cross the proverbial finish-line! You can become discouraged and want to quit for a myriad of reasons. Another funny thing about persisting on the "bridge to have?" You will find that every time - without exception - the more important the goal, *the bigger the challenge* life will throw your way!

Please understand this. I want you to *really* get this. I swear, it's almost like some kind of conspiracy! Life will usually give you at least one "trick" *right before the finish line*, right before the proverbial water is about to spew out of that damn well you've been pumping blindly!

I've seen it happen so often that the irony is shocking. It's as if people in your life subconsciously want to test you. Crises can occur when you least expect them.

What's your solution? Well, I'll tell you what the solution is <u>not</u> first.

Prevention is out of the question! You cannot prevent someone else's crises. You've got your hands full with your own – and that's how it should be. To attempt that feat is an effort in futility, yet millions of people try to live their entire lives trying to put out other people's fires or help them to avoid them. Not you. When you're trying to seal the envelope of success, it's time for everyone in your circle of influence, including friends, family, and co-workers – to solve their own problems.

Avoidance is for the weak, but will be very tempting! (But, that's not for you any longer, right?) You just learned that "paying the price" must be done (and remember, there's more than one price tag, too!). You have also accepted the fact that the reason you have the problems you're having is because the only people with no problems are dead ones!

Complaining won't do much good. Most people don't want to hear about your problems and the few who you do "trick" into lending their ear.. probably have bigger problems than you!

And, to top that off... here's yet *another* dose of brutal honesty: most people are secretly *glad* you've got your problems in the first place!

Additionally, if you've become the high-powered, goal-setting machine that I think you're becoming – you *do not* (at least, *you should not*) have time for complaining!

In his book, <u>The Road Less Traveled</u>, author Scott Peck opens with...

Life Is Difficult

Can you remember the commercials for Budweiser that utilized the slogan, "Life is good?" Let me refresh your memory a bit.

Three men are sitting around a fire. There's food, music, women, and, of course... Bud. No dialogue. No story to tell. No problems to be solved.... Then, the screen fades to black while, at the same time – small, white words show up on the screen very subtly as a deep, confident voice says, "Life – Is – Goooood!

What? Life is good? Hey, if your idea of living up to your full potential is merely heat from a campfire while drinking beer with the gang... then, life is indeed good. Question is... good for what? Or, better yet – good for whom?

Partying, celebration, and "high-fives" are great to relieve stress. But, if we treat everyday of the week like it's the weekend, what the hell will the term *partying* define for us on the weekend?

Yes, it's true. Life is good. But it's only good after we first accept that it is – difficult. Accepting that life is difficult first will allow you – or even give you the mental permission to sit by that fire, "hang with the gang," and enjoy that brew.

There is one other side-benefit of buying into the concept of "life is difficult." And there's no better person to ask than the man who made the phrase famous. Scott Peck, author of <u>The Road Less Traveled</u> put it perfectly. Here are his exact words:

"Life is difficult. When we learn to accept that life is difficult – life ceases to be difficult."

Now, as much as I love Scott Peck - and though there is a subtle power to that simple truth... The problem now becomes, "What do I do, now that I accept that life is difficult?"

We need a strategy... a philosophy to use... or a *way of looking at things* if you will. And, since Scott Palangi only deals with what works... here's a more empowering outlook on the issue of "life." This outlook will reveal its power to you each and every day if you are *strong enough* to look past the so-called "difficulty." Turn the page to find out...

Life Always Gives You a Nine!

How bad can your life get? That may sound like a negative question for a person to ask you, but seriously... How bad can it all get? How bad does something have to become for you to say, "That's it, I quit; I've come this far, but I can't go on any longer?"

Goal achievement is not a matter of solving problems once and for all. It's a matter of solving problems every day, forever! Often, we feel like "coasting" a little bit. We manage to overcome a huge obstacle and then we sort of want a breather, or a little rest break. That is how 99.9999% of people operate throughout their lives. They only want a few big speed bumps once in while... and, if life throws them a barrage of "big ones," the old "why me" thinking will start to kick in.

Ask these folks, "How's it going?" You'll usually hear them talk about their life as if "everything is great... except for this *one* thing."

This type of thinking is dangerous. If you are striving towards your achievements "crossing your fingers" that there won't be any more calamities along the way, life has this funny way of robbing you of your confidence.

But, if you look at every setback positively – not just as an opportunity to grow, but as an ABSOLUTE MANDATORY NEXT STEP – your self-esteem skyrockets! You become unstoppable.

Here's why:

Let's say that you have some issue that you're struggling with. Any issue. Think of one right now. Got it? Good. Now give that issue the "mental number of 9."

Now, stay with me... think of something WORSE, something unimaginable that has not happened to you ever... but *could* happen. Got that picture? Good, call that one a 10.

Now, think of all the little situations that you often see other people moan, and groan about – the ones that, when YOU think about, you mentally say to yourself, "What are they complaining about? That's no big deal." Let's call those things an 8 or below.

So then, you've got your 10 (real bad), your 9 (bad), and your 8 and under ((trivial). Where does your growth lie?

The 9's!

Life will always give you something to live up to, to strive towards. You are always getting nines. And, just as soon as your current nine is conquered... *stay ready* – because another one's on the way! Don't shun it or lament about it. Take it and embrace it -- because the only time you stop getting your 9's is when you're dead or when you cease pursuing your dreams... which is pretty much the same as being dead anyway.

Life will not give you a ten. It won't. However, you will find that as you grow in your ability to handle life and all of it's uncertainties – the amount and intensity of those uncertainties will remain pretty much constantly... a NINE!

It's like lifting weights. The stronger you get – the more you have to lift in order to get stronger. Like aerobic exercise, if your "threshold" for endurance is 3 miles... you'll always have to conquer or surpass that three miles before you can reach the next level or plateau.

We readily accept this fact in exercise because the "pain" or resistance, if you will, is self-inflicted. Yet, when "that thing called life" does inflicts it upon us, our knee-jerk reaction is to say, "Hey, that's not fair!"

However, if you begin to look past all the troubles you face with your current challenges, aren't they challenges usually resulting from "self-infliction" as well? Aren't you experiencing the certain things you "hate" in life as a direct result of choosing the particular set the goals you have? Are they not similar to the sweat and the struggle you'd incur while leading up to that *three miles* which you can already run? Of course they are.

Do you see? It's all 9's! My 9's may be your 7's – who knows. Your neighbor's 9's may only be 5's to you! But remember, they're 9's to him! Everyone's 9's are different. So, be compassionate. Be compassionate especially towards yourself.

Give yourself credit for stepping up to the plate and swinging at your nines – but never wish them to go away! Receiving your nines is a sign that you're growing. Don't wish you were more "ready" when they come to you. You are getting them because you are ready for them!

Keep Your Enemies Far... And Your Friends Farther

... or Make your friends an offer they can't refuse.

In the movie "The Godfather," Michael, the leading character, is discovering the human dynamics of the underworld. He begins to realize that things are not always what they appear to be.

There's betrayal, backstabbing, duplicity, and so on. What's worse? It's all in day's work.

At one point, Michael is given advice from the Godfather (his Dad), to *keep his friends close and his enemies closer*. The lesson being: if you're going to succeed in a world of crime, you'd better be aware of who to keep close by your side, and also who belongs... well, a little closer, maybe even "in your pocket." Michael's ability to discern between friend and foe turns out to be a matter of life and death.

What was the Godfather's teaching to Michael?

A Strategy.

Now, granted... *your* dream list may not include: "Become the Godfather" as a primary objective... But you will *still need* a "relationship strategy" – and this will influence the difference between your success and failure while you are trying to live up to your full potential.

I will offer you one sure-fire, guaranteed strategy, to navigate the "underworld" of achievement shortly. But first, let's spend a little time looking at "what happens" *when you...*

Challenge The Status-Quo!

Often times, when we set out to achieve some worthy end, or some lofty goal, the people who will hold us back will not be our enemies, but rather those closest to us.

It's not that they are out to get us. Not at all. But our friends, unfortunately and usually, see us for "what we are" right now – not for "what we can become" tomorrow.

Call me a pessimist. Call me negative. Even tell me I look at friends the wrong way if you want... But, if you were to tell some of your closest friends and family members that you were going to become the President of the United States, a marathon runner, a Nobel Prize Winner, or a successful home-based business owner – you might not receive the support that would best empower you on your quest towards those goals.

The people who sometimes support us the least can be those who sit right across the dinner table from us! Be tolerant though. It's typical for people who love us to want to protect us from making a mistake or perhaps failure.

What they don't realize (and what *you* must realize) is that, by attempting to protect you from failure, they are really serving to prevent you from success.

Let that one sink in a little... because, in reality, if you knew what you were truly capable of accomplishing, *it might scare the daylights out of you!* And, rest assured, if it scares the daylights out of you, it's probably the type of goal *most people* will doubt you can achieve.

Don't worry, though. I have a plan for you. I'm not the Godfather; but if it's success you want, I'll make you an offer you can't refuse. And, yes, it will make the difference between your success or failure.

Somone Sets a Goal

Let's say we are on a bowling team. There are six of us: 3 women and 3 men. Let's also say that we play in a league. Nothing too competitive – we're just having fun. We get together on Wednesday nights to have a good time, shoot the breeze, have a few laughs, and enjoy a little recreation.

But one day, we all show up at the alley and, to our surprise, our teammate Sarah has arrived a little early...

Sarah's getting a private lesson with a pro! She's gotten a little more serious about her game; she's now trying to improve herself.

What would be a typical response from most of our team members?

It might be something like: "Ahhhhhh, look what Sarah's *doing...* *Hmmm.* Well, haven't *we* become ambitious?" At least, that's what we're willing to verbalize. On the inside, it may be a bit more like, "Bitch!"

Seriously though, when we set a goal, isn't it true that many times, the knee-jerk reaction of our colleagues is to offer *at best* a superficial "Wow-good-for-you" type of support?

You will frequently encounter this type of subtle resistance while crossing your *personal bridge* to success. To keep your enthusiasm high and your motivation unshakeable, you'll need a deliberate strategy with which to defend yourself. This might mean making some new friends. It may even mean saying goodbye to some people you've known, but the newfound friend you'll get intimate with will be – you!

Keep Your Goals to Yourself

Secrecy is important if you plan to sustain motivation. If you run around announcing your "grand plans" to the world, you will quickly discover that this is a bad strategy. It's tough to do, too!

When you get a "wild hair," you will want to shout about it and "tell the world." Use caution here.

There are several reasons that make this a lousy plan. I'll give you 5 good ones just to convince you:

Your friends, if they haven't yet achieved any of their desired goals, will tell you it's a bad idea; you can't do it; and furthermore, you're crazy.

If you tell someone who has tried to achieve what you wish to achieve (but has failed at it)... they will likely be there to remind you of how tough your goal will be to achieve. They won't even be able to warn you of potential pitfalls intelligently... because the thought of you attaining your goals (where they could not) makes them eat their hearts out.

Most people are not naturally ambitious and do not believe in the power of goals. This especially holds true if your particular goals involve monetary objectives. In a self-righteous way, your friends may not give you the best support you so desperately need (even if that entails "self-support" by shutting your own mouth about your agenda) during the initial phase of your quest.

The first phase of your goal, the groundwork phase, is often the hardest. At the very least, it entails the most obvious challenge in terms of "no visible payoff." And your trusty comrades will be there to remind you of your lackluster to-date results in a hurry!

What if you perhaps want to change your mind? Now, not only did you not receive the support you had hoped for, but should you choose to abandon ship – they'll call you a quitter!

Some self-help experts will advise you to "make your goals public." Their theory is that, just in case you feel like jumping ship, changing your sails, or hey... let's say you get into something and find out you're not quite ready for this - for whatever reason - and you now want to postpone your goals? Guess what? You get to explain yourself 30 thousand times. It's not fun. You'll feel dumb, and may look even dumber!

Hey look, if you absolutely must run your mouth to your friends and colleagues about what you're doing or trying to accomplish, tell em' only the mundane stuff. If you want to let them know

264

you're going to the restroom, to the store, or to the movies... fine. But keep stuff like your new invention, your first million, and your killer movie script to yourself.

Look at it this way; what's more impressive? You never accomplish all you say you're gonna' do, and come up with stories of excuse – or – you "disappear" from the social circuit and your peers, colleagues, and family who then get to see your results? If you ask me, the second option is much better for your reputation, personal sense of integrity, and levels of self-confidence while you are striving to achieve the goal you've been keeping under lock and key.

One thing's for sure, though... if you never say you're going to be movie-star, and we see you on the silver screen? When you later say you're running for president, we'll not doubt you then!

Keep it to yourself.

The Up-Lifters

There is one group of people with whom you can share your dreams. They are the group of people who have taken "The Road Less Traveled" themselves.

When you tell these types of people about your goals, they *lift you up* rather than pulling you down under the guise of "Hey, I'm just looking out for you." These Up-Lifters know what it's like to face the skeptics, the nay-sayer's, and the people who live their lives without pursuing dreams of their own.

The Up-Lifters share in your excitement, are aware of the opportunities that can be found with risk-taking, and encourage the fact that you're "going for it!" As you tell them of your sojourns, the obstacles you face, and your own concerns associated with achieving worthy ends – they are glad to see that someone else, "gets it." They can encourage you, and give you a more sincere "heads up" even if you are making unwise decisions, because the place they are coming from is one of experience – not resentment, or doubt. (The latter two you are more likely to encounter when sharing your dreams with the "T.V. Watchers.")

Lean on the Up-Lifters for support. Draw your strength from them. Do not think for a second that you're bothering them either... They understand that, although "success is never achieved alone," it can indeed be a lonely journey sometimes. These folks know what it's like to "skip the parties" that you'll be invited to along on the road to your dreams.

Searching for these Up-Lifters is the challenging part, especially if your goals are unique, grandiose, or "new" to the world. I have found two methods that work quite well:

Letter Writing

Becoming an Up-Lifter yourself

Letter Writing

This can be labor intensive but, once you get good at it, you'll resort to it frequently. Oddly, few people do this anymore! I have no idea why, either... because it is so effective.

You'd be surprised how many people who want to become actors never write letters to successful actors to find out what they are thinking about and how they achieve their goals. Perhaps it's because, if they did, they might write something stupid like, "I want to be rich and famous just like you... can you hook me up?" It sounds nuts, but this is the type of question high-achieving men and women get asked all the time.

A better approach -- one that would do you more good *and* probably get you contacts as a by-product -- would be, "I am having a tough time pursuing this goal of mine... I can't stop thinking about quitting. I have no idea whether or not I am doing the right thing. What did you think about during such times?" This kind of questioning will often result in an inspiring, contact-building, return letter TEN TIMES more powerful than any run-of-the-mill "What's your favorite color? Do you work-out with free-weights or machines? Is it boxers or briefs? I'm a Sagittarius too!" kind of rhetoric!

Most of your role-models will take your sincere letter to heart and respond quickly. If they do not, don't worry; they are probably just busy. I usually get a great response from such successful folks. Even better, the more you write to them, the better you will get at writing letters that bring responses.

Make your list; get some stamps; and go for it! Believe me, the letters you get back... you'll have framed and hanging on your wall to re-inspire you from time to time!

I have three letters that I reflect upon all the time. One, from Scott Alexander, is only four words in length! Scott wrote the self-published book, Rhinoceros Success, a book that sold 3 million copies. I called him to tell him about the philosophy of Be, Do, and Have... One week later, I received a hand-addressed envelope in the mail. Inside was a picture of a Rhinoceros, with a caption in big, bold letters saying, "Keep Charging!" On the back, was a handwritten message that read, "GET THAT BOOK WRITTEN!"

I would be remiss if I didn't tell you that what you hold in your hands is a result of that card.

Becoming an Up-Lifter yourself.

You may have heard it said that, "The best way to change the people around you is to change yourself." It is absolutely true in this sense as well. The fact is, if you want to be surrounded by uplifting people... the best way to do so, is to become one yourself!

Brian Tracy, one of the most prominent, if not THE MOST PROMINENT self-help gurus of our time calls this, "The Law of Correspondence." Brian maintains that "like attracts like." In this sense, it's not that your negative associates will evolve to become more like you (although it's very possible). Rather, you will miraculously begin to "find" uplifting types of people almost everywhere you go!

Begin immediately to develop the supportive language, mannerisms, and outlook towards others that will help them achieve their goals, too.

The supportive framework you'll provide family and friends will begin to empower them towards achieve their own goals. At the same time, you'll be able to develop your own innate powers of persistence.

Nothing will empower *your* ability to be persistent more than becoming the type of person who encourages others to bridge the gap between their own "Do" and "Have" with an optimistic outlook. When your friends tell you about their dreams say, "Go for it! Do it!"

The minute you decide to become that uplifting source for others, you instantaneously eliminate negative influences in your own life and begin to build new and healthier associations… associations that will ensure your chances for persisting through tough times.

Your Second Graduation

People of high-achievement are oftentimes faced with several "graduations" in life. Now, typically speaking... when we think of a graduation, we think of a "party," but the graduation I'm talking about here is not so much a *party* as it is a ***part-ing.***

The fact of the matter is, don't we all sooner or later "graduate" from many of our relationships? It seems as though, whether it's work or play, we eventually outgrow our current circle of friends and influences.

It seems a little obvious, but we usually do this much too late or in sort of a haphazard way... waiting, thinking, and procrastinating until finally, we've had enough!

Well, this isn't always fun, but it you want to rapidly accelerate your rate of success and, at the same time, increase your ability to persevere in the face of setbacks, you'll need to make a to-do list of people and influences to say "goodbye" to.

Bruce Lee once remarked that becoming a great martial artist wasn't so much a "gaining of skill" as it was an "elimination of habits." Likewise, some of the associations you've maintained in your life are holding you back. They are in a sense your *bad habits.* Finding exactly which ones have to "go" is the tricky part.

Here is a list of questions to think about:

- Who could you do without?
- Who should you do without?
- What do they do that holds you back?
- Would they benefit, too, if YOU were to leave them?
- Why have you waited so long to turn them loose?
- How can you "romance them out the door" so as not to offend them?

The Most Powerful Word In The English language... NO

I was once taught that the word "no" was negative... Let me tell you something, all your failures have occurred, in part, because you can not say "NO." You will never be able to perform the finishing touches necessary for you to accomplish your goals until you improve your ability to say "NO."

You've already learned that, in the past, you've started and quit things that more than likely... would have taken you to all your goals if you'd stuck with them. We've looked at the fact that we *know enough things.* We've looked at the fact that *there is enough time.* We've also observed that if only we could have *"stuck things out"* in the past – chances are, we'd be in a completely different place than where we're at currently. Probably a much better place at that.

What was the problem? Well, when you get right down to it, we all need to improve our ability to say "NO."

If you can master one thing from having read this book, let it be that the power of saying "NO" at the right time... to the wrong thing... is a master key to success.

The next thing then is to identify which things will be told "NO."

Saying "NO" in the context of achievement means exercising your self-awareness, your will-power, and your courage to say "NO" to:

People, Places, Things, and most importantly... *Good Ideas.* Yes, you heard me right... good ideas! You will be shocked when you discover that at the core of many distractions is a "good idea." First, let's look at each category and see if we can awaken our "NO" awareness.

People

If all the people in the world to were to go on vacation at once and leave you alone, you would have no choice but to... get the things done that you have to do. Now, of course, there are some people who would get very lonely, bored, and kill themselves. But don't worry about them. They are not our concern. Chances are, if you're reading this book, you know what I am talking about.

Now, I am not even talking about your ability to say "NO" yet either! I'm saying that if you added back all the time that's stolen from you via: telemarketers, drop-in visitors, old friends from the neighborhood, and a few current friends from the new neighborhood... you'd have yourself a big chunk of time with which to twiddle your fingers until finally getting to work.

The amount of time consumed by people in our lives is staggering. If people would just leave you alone, the truth is, you'd get a lot more done.

Now, exactly what you'd get done is another story. Hopefully, by now, you've become the kind of person who is writing down your goals, thinking of better ways to do things, learning more, improving yourself, and so on. Why do I say hopefully? Well, I know some people who, if they did not have other people "infringing upon" their time, would simply play with their dog a little more, browse through a few more magazines, chat on the phone about last night's game and, quite honestly... do more of the "other stuff" they really need to say "NO" to.

The upside for these people is... playing with their dog, browsing magazines, chatting on the phone, and finding more time to do all of that stuff... IS THEIR GOAL! So, in that regard – they are already successful, and the joke is on us.

Some people don't say "NO" because they don't have anything else to "YES" to. Now that you have some goals from filling in the dream list and your daily planner, you have got to master the ability to say "NO" to people when they want to "do lunch" or "do nothing" or worse... "do nothing at lunch!"

Most underachieving men and women are great at making all of their friends happy. Every time they are asked a favor they'll say, "YES." But, in the process they are also saying "NO" to themselves, though they don't see it that way. Now, I'm not saying you should be a selfish, non-helping friend who never cares about anyone. No. Quite the contrary. All I am saying is:

If you are not working steadily toward achieving your goals, you will NOT become a happy person. If you are not a happy person, you cannot be a great friend. By saying "NO" to your friends, you are actually being a good friend.

Will your friends see it this way? Initially, no. But eventually, they will come to respect your time, your goals, and more importantly... you as a person whose time is too valuable to waste. Remember, BE precedes all. By saying "NO," you *become* the kind of person whose time does not get wasted. Remember when I asked earlier in this book, "How come when everyone has nothing to do... they always want to do it with you?" Well, that applies here as well.

Don't tell them you've got stuff to do. It won't help. If my friends invite me to the diner, *even when I am doing nothing at that very moment,* I say, "I'm sorry, but I won't be joining you." I will not say, "I'd love to go... but I got this "thing I gotta' do" or "I gotta' get up early tomorrow." They will invariably say, "Hey, so do I... I gotta' get up, too. Plus I have three deadlines to meet by tomorrow morning – let's go." Just say, "I'm sorry, but I won't be joining you. Tonight, I have to say no."

People screw up with this principle quite often. They say, "I don't see the harm in saying "YES" if I am not doing anything at the

271

moment... what's the big deal?" Don't be one of these idiots. When you've "got nothing to do," take advantage of it. *Do* nothing. Do not even think about squandering your "nothing-to-do-time."

At first it will be difficult. Your friends will be going out to dinner, they may have even arranged a group babysitter for all the "kids," but just say "NO"! Your time is too valuable, especially if you have a dream list you're working on.

When you begin saying "NO", you have deliberately decided to spend your extra time working on your goals by reading about things you need to learn, writing letters you need to write, making calls you need to make, or simply doing some planning – the benefits of these actions are immeasurable. Believe me when I say that most of your ability to finish what you start is derived not from the stuff you'll do, but rather, in the stuff you *do not* do!

I repeat: *People* are NOT the problem... Our ability to say *NO* them is the problem!

Places

Fortunately, people are associated with places and this one factor can sneak up on you! The people who want to steal your time often like to link it to a place where it's easier to waste it (this way it won't seem so time consuming), like going to the mall, to lunch, out for a drink, or even coffee.

One great way to avoid going to places is to create a mental list of places you will go only if it's necessary. For men – Home Depot is the culprit. Every husband has said to his spouse, "Honey, I just need to make a quick trip to Home Depot and I'll be right back" (three hours, and three-hundred dollars later, of course!). Be smart and realistic about how much time can be sucked up by going to places.

For women, of course, the mall is the trap! Shopping is not a healthy virtue if you've got a goal that needs to be tackled. Closely linked with shopping is "running errands." Get in the habit of clustering your errands together. Trips to the nail salon, supermarket, Baby Gap, Bath and Body Works, all rob you of valuable time. Realize that, until you discipline yourself to wait until you can knock-off three or four tasks in one run, you would be flushing time right down the toilet.

The secondary benefit of saying "NO" to places is that it forces you to stay put and work! If you say "NO" to places that are not essential, you'll quickly speed up your rate of accomplishment.

Things

Gadgets, electronics, do-dads, and anything that is inanimate or outside yourself falls under the category of "things." Please note this includes the so-called time-saving "things," too. You know, the ones where, *when you finally learn how* to save so much time using them, several days have elapsed?

Men in particular love "things." There's just something about us that makes us love "things." Of course, our female counterparts call them toys and for a good reason, too. They are aware that we get distracted by all sorts of things that we should just be saying "NO" to.

Saying "NO" to things is difficult because we rarely think we are wasting time on "things." Take fixing up the house, for example. Many times, you will set a goal to fix up something around the house, and right when you are 85% done – you get sidetracked doing some "other thing" like learning how to use a new tool that supposedly will make the job "easier."

Watch out for things… they have a more subtle way of sneaking into your life.

You may be wondering why I decided to throw this saying "NO" stuff into the persistence section of this book as opposed to the "time management" section. Let me explain. The reason we quit is usually because we aren't seeing desired results quickly enough and, therefore, tend to get discouraged. But the real reason we don't see results is because we end up saying "YES" to something that we could and should be saying "NO" to.

That makes "NO" a persistence issue, period.

Distracted people quit more readily than non-distracted people. And distracted people always say "YES" to... Yep, you guessed it:

People, Places, and Things!

But there is one more type of pesky distraction. And it is, without a doubt, the biggest issue by far.

A Good Idea

Disguised as something that will propel you faster towards achieving your goals, and coming along at what appears to be "the perfect time" – will be the infamous "Good Idea" that you must learn to say "NO" to. The reason this one trips people up so frequently is because it is usually veiled as a legitimate "assistant" to help you along the path. Why is this one so important? Because it is a subtle invader. And why must you master saying "NO" to the Good Idea? The biggest reason is because anyone can so "NO" to a "Bad Idea!"

Bad ideas are obvious! Drugs, dangerous activities, gambling... all of these are pretty simple to see coming and are pretty simple to "detect" as distractions. But the Good Idea? That one will often times appear to be too good to be true. If your "NO" muscles aren't developed, you could set yourself back another several days, weeks, or months.

Besides, if an apparently "good idea" is really as good as it seems... You should always have the option of coming back to it later on. The advantage to saying "NO" here is two-fold. One, you stay on track with your current projects. Two, you'll be able to revisit this "good idea" with a more objective outlook and mindset later.

Whenever I tell people that one of the major deterrents to success we will face is the wisdom to say "NO" to a good idea, they invariably respond, "Why? If it's a good idea, we should do it, right? Why say no?" Think about this for a moment... Can you remember a time when you were doing just fine, and then, along came some cockamamie idea that just sort of weaseled its way into your life?

274

Perhaps one of the strangest paradoxes is, the more you work towards finishing what you start, and the more success you achieve – the greater and greater the "Good Ideas" become that you have to train yourself to say "NO" to.

I have a friend who is a very successful real estate agent who shared his distractions with me. He said, "Just when I am making some progress establishing myself in a neighborhood, gaining some popularity, and scratching the surface of success, some "great opportunity" will present itself. Usually in the form of a *time- or money-saving* thing that will be hard to resist. Or, maybe someone will try to convince me to look at a better "territory." The temptation to get distracted in the name of, "Wow, this is just what I was looking for" is incredible!"

You see, whereas "bad ideas" will obviously hurt you and distract you, the good idea can distract you—*long before you are wise enough to see that it can hurt you.* Not physically, of course, but isn't missing out on your dreams because you are always "acting on" good ideas painful? You bet it is.

One For The Ladies

The need for saying "NO", does not discriminate. However, men and women have a tendency to lack "NO POWER" in different departments.

Following the old-fashioned and much outdated phrase, "Ladies first"...hang on to your seats, and get ready to take your medicine *like a man!* Here comes your #1 problem. Get your highlighter, your 3 x 5 cards, and all your note-taking paraphernalia.

You need to improve your ability to say "NO" to your friends.

It seems that the girls are sort of hard-wired to say "YES" to friends without thinking things through. What's worse, they will often be saying "YES"... while inside their hearts and minds, they are screaming "NO"!

Girls will get off the phone after saying "YES" to being invited to some social event with their friends (knowing that they have vitally important things to do) and think to themselves, "Why did I say yes? I can't manage to do all this stuff and meet Nicole for dinner! Why can't I just say NO!"

It's like they hate disappointing people or something. Probably it's just a motherly instinct or feminine empathy. Remember being a kid? "Mom, can I have someone over for dinner?"

"Yes"

"Mom, can I stay over at John's house?"

"Ok, Honey."

"Mom, I want these new sneakers. Can I get em'?"

"Yes, dear."

Have you ever seen a women take on so much responsibility that they just can't jam any more into a 24-hour day... and then... Pow! They explode with overwhelming emotion? Then, it seems like the only antidote is... CHOCOLATE.

You could say that women aren't as emotional as us men make them out to be... They just have a hard time saying (not to mention – hearing) the word "NO". Just about anybody *would* be emotional if they said "YES" to all the people, places things, and all "the good ideas constantly fighting for one's attention!

I bet if they did a point-of-sale survey at the cash register of a Godiva store, you'd find that some of the busiest women in America bought chocolate that day! But, seriously girls, try my "NO" strategy for a week and see what happens. It's actually quite simple, only a two-step strategy. Here's how you do it:

Identify which friend you most need to learn to say "NO" to. It could be "NO" to shopping, gossiping, doing lunch, or play dates. Find out who it is and then look at all the other things you could be doing... all the little chunks of time that would be consumed, and all the potential goal-time that you are literally flushing down the toilet. Do it now!

Okay, now here is the tough part: RESOLVE TO SAY "NO" the next time you are being lured into a "hang-out!"

That's it. If you ladies can develop the skill of disappointing your friends a little more... you will not be disappointed!

I must add that it's kind of good the girls are hard-wired to say "YES." Men are more the opposite; we lean toward saying "NO" just because we're more pigheaded about stuff. We will often say "NO" when we should have said "YES". Maybe that's why men and women need each other so much.

Moving on... Let's talk about MEN.

One For the Boys

On page 140 or so, I introduced to you the concept of home runs, remember? Well, the part that I left out was that, MEN are more specifically geared to live by this principle!

Just as women are genetically pre-disposed to saying "YES"... We men cannot seem to say "NO" to procrastination!

Think I'm wrong? Take a look at how most men operate during their daily lives! Do you think comedians who crack the jokes about how men "hate filling up the gas tank" just make that stuff up? Heck no! It's true. We will put off, and put off, and put off doing what quite easily could be done right now!

Home maintenance, cleaning the cars, fixing the kids' bikes, paying the bills, getting our teeth cleaned... the list goes on. Better to mow that lawn now, remember?

Hey, how about when we are lost? We will put off asking for directions for hours, just to be able to say... "See, honey? I know where we're going!" Meanwhile, our spouse is eyeballing the fuel gauge wondering how far she'll have to push the car!

Why do you think retailers invented Valentine's Day anyway? So that we men would have a way of trying to make up for months of procrastinating the display of love we should be showing for our spouses!

A funny thing about human nature is... after all this neglect and putting things off... we men then try to save the day with some huge display of effort! With one big swing, we try to "hit it out of the park." Then, of course, we stand around ready to sign autographs and receive accolades for our wondrous feat. To make it worse, we then accuse our spouse of not giving us any credit for our fantastic deed. They stare at us expressionlessly. Now, we tend to think that they are being unappreciative. But, what's really going on is that they're thinking, "What the hell were you waiting for, idiot? NOW you want a pat on the back?" And under their breath they are saying, "What took you so long?" and "Hmm, we'll have to see how long this'll last!"

Men, sorry if I sound like a "sellout," but we need to say "NO" to the home run.

We need to say "NO" to the habit of the "I'll get around to it soon" mentality.

There Is A Season For Success

You've no doubt learned by now that the #1 ingredient for success is perseverance. By way of review, you'll recall that there are many people with talent... great ideas... and God-given gifts. You'll also recall that all of those people will remain absolutely useless (every last one of them) if they lack even an ounce of persistence.

In the words of the most winning coach in the history of football, Vince Lombardi said, "Don't give me a guy with talent; give me a guy who'll go for the hard-ones."

You've got to be that person who'll "go for the hard ones." The best way of becoming this kind of person is to learn all you can about "the season" that is germane to your goal.

Here's what I mean:

Let's say you're from Manhattan and I gave you a kernel of corn to plant... You probably wouldn't know "the season" that would be relevant for harvesting a kernel of corn! You could model the actions of the highest award-winning agriculturists in the world, but it would not help your harvest one darn bit. That is, until someone tapped you on the shoulder and said, "Hey dummy, make sure you give it a year or two!"

Not having this "insider info" with regard to the law of farming, you would not be able to produce an abundant harvest. You would create the image of a bountiful crop in your mind (Be). Then you would get your trusty "how-to" manual and take the precise action steps necessary (Do)... but it would not be until you discovered (by instruction, insight, or painful experience) that:

There is a season for success!

Each and every goal in the universe has a "season." And you can't expect much except for some hard work and waiting until that season arrives

Staying with this metaphor, so often we buy the best seed, make sure our soil is fertile, take out the weeds, water the seeds... and then forget to do the most important part... we forget to *tap our foot!*

You must find out what the "right season" is for your goals to transpire and then make some allowances for time to pass during their accomplishment.

If the season for a kernel of corn is 8 months, and you apply that strategy for planting bamboo (which takes years to grow roots!), you would get frustrated, start blaming everything except for your philosophy – and quit!

Albert Einstein said, "People love chopping wood... in this activity results can be seen immediately!" Imagine trying to apply the formula for chopping wood to running a marathon. It seems ridiculous, though you'd be shocked at how many people live like this!

I once coached a woman who was trying to build a massage therapy practice. She wanted some support during her related challenges, so we went to lunch for a "pep-talk". She opens with a comment I hear all too frequently (and usually among younger people, however this woman was 50). She said, "You know what,

Scott... remember that goal of building my massage therapy practice? Well, it's just not paying off. I mean, I got my certification. I passed all my tests. I jumped through all the hoops you have jump through to do this stuff. Heck, I even bought some fancy frames for my diplomas so I could hang them in the front office! But, it just isn't happening... and I've already been "at it" for a *whole year*."

After hearing this, I wanted to send her a diploma for being a certified loser. But, being the uplifting and encouraging soul that I am, I decided to give her advice she was NOT ready to hear:

"Wow! Are you serious? A whole year?," I said.

"Hmmm," I went on, "That's horrible. Certainly, the world should give you what you want after 365 days of trying. Yes indeed. That's no fair. Not fair at all... In fact, anyone who wants to have a prosperous and abundant career for 20-plus years should certainly get exactly that after putting in a whole year's worth of work!"

Her face grew tight, as she became disgusted with my brutally honest sarcasm. She informed me that she was going to go back to college to finish her degree (another thing she'd quit) and then get a "steady."

You know what a "steady" is, right? It's a job you have where you are guaranteed a paycheck regardless of your performance or results. A job, often times created *for you* by someone else who steps up to the plate... who takes all the risk, puts up capital, credit, sometimes their home, and takes on the responsibility of paying you while keeping promises to the end-users of the high-quality service you (are supposed to) provide.

Now look, there's nothing wrong with getting a steady, but even the Corporate or Tenured "stress-free, 9-5 grind", packed with benefits and security... still has a season for success!

In FACT, I'll go as far to say that any goal that can be accomplished in less than a year is not really a goal at all.

I once heard Tony Robbins say this about time... It is the most profound, and insightful wisdom you'll ever hear about adopting a persistent attitude. Tony says:

"Most people OVERESTIMATE how much they can accomplish in *one year* and UNDERESTIMATE how much they can accomplish in *five years!*

I'll repeat that little tidbit and then give you some examples to drive home this critically important point as we round the corner to the close of this book:

"Most people OVERESTIMATE how much they can accomplish in *one year* and UNDERESTIMATE how much they can accomplish in *five years!*

Something's not right about that. I mean, after all you've done…

As soon as you stop utilizing the "wood chopping" formula for growing your business, building your reputation as a professional, raising a family that is healthy in mind and body, or dropping 50 pounds – your success is guaranteed!

Get a 3 x 5 card and write down these words. Now, go tape it on your bathroom mirror at home.

"I quit way too early… Until NOW!

In the past, using again the example of the well, you've stopped pumping just shy of getting water! Only to let someone else come along, pick up where you left off, and get what should have been *your* water quickly! Keep on pumping!

The harder you try - the harder it is to quit.

When karate students quit, it is always because they didn't feel they were getting any benefits… but they if they didn't get any benefit, it's because they weren't try hard enough in the first place.

Remember: Can't is an animal too lazy to TRY.

Your solution? When you feel like quitting, ask yourself: "Is it possible that I have not tried hard enough?" Then, distrust your first answer. Remember, every instinct you have is wrong. Now, ask yourself the question again.

Your Self-Esteem Meter

The degree to which you persevere is in direct proportion to your belief in yourself. People who believe in themselves always stick with things. People who do not believe in themselves quit. It really is that simple.

The major problem with quitting is not the actual quitting, though. It's quite all right to quit something, as long as you know WHY you quit. Too many times, however, we make excuses for why we quit something. Instead of owning-up to the fact that we don't believe in ourselves, we'll rationalize and say, "Oh well, that just wasn't for me..." or "I decided to try something else."

The excuses we come up with for quitting something are often times just as convincing as the reasons we had for starting it. Every time someone quits something, if you went "back in time" to the moment they made their resolution to do that particular thing in the first place, you'd have heard a much different story. If people could only "re-hear" themselves when they made a decision to "Do" something and start it! If they could replay that initial conviction when they feel like giving up, they'd feel like the lazy-asses they truly are.

In almost an immature way, when we are pumping the well, we will often say, "There's no water here."

When you declare to the world, "I will be successful," Old Man Persistence will check your attitude. Be prepared.

Grab a 3 x 5 index card right now and write across the top: "I QUIT WAY TOO EARLY... UNTIL NOW!"

Keep foremost in mind: the harder you try, the harder it is to quit. Remember what Lombardi said about "going for the hard ones." As a karate teacher, you tend to take it personally when a student quits. This is a good attitude to adopt, too. It's best to look inward before looking for the external reasons for why people may quit. It follows the premise of "good teacher – good student."

However, there is one caveat to the above statement. It has been my observation that the students who stick with things the longest are NOT the ones who possess superb skills, attain "great results," or receive the most attention from the teacher. Nor are they the ones who stay the most motivated and enthusiastic either. The one commonality among those who stick it out is that they *try their hardest*. And that is IT.

Nothing else.

Remember this the next *time you feel like quitting something*. Often times... you'll discover that you will want to quit only when you're not trying your hardest!

PART V: PUTTING IT ALL TOGETHER

Great Ideas Happen... Implementation Is The Hard Part.

You've learned that happy, healthy, and successful people assert the proper attitude more frequently than the wrong attitude to "set the stage" for their success.

You've learned that a Positive Mental Attitude will not guarantee success – but that success is impossible without it.

You've learned that the mind, just like the body, is exposed to "the elements" and subsequently, can "get dirty"... and hence, much like bathing – you continually, constantly need to bath your mind by feeding it positive and uplifting material.

You've learned that life is difficult but ceases to be difficult when we embrace, look forward to, and confront each and every obstacle as if it were "necessary medicine." Consider each obstacle the absolute "perfect lesson" we need to learn in this school of life.

You've learned that, amidst all the bad stuff that happens to you, including: your upbringing, the way people have treated you, even *tragic events* – between all that... and your response to them, THERE IS A SPACE FOR YOU TO CHOOSE YOUR RESPONSE. In the beginning, of course, it won't be a very big space, but through self-awareness, independent will, and the power of attention, you can lengthen that space and begin to choose the responses that will lead to your growth and happiness.

Next, you've learned that wants and/or desires create skills. Not the other way around. You may have been programmed for years to believe that your priorities should be aimed at what you *need*

285

and not on what you *want*. Such mis-thinking is the reason many people die with their music still in them.

We've observed that "To want is not only good, but the opposite is insanity." We've seen that it takes a little effort to get what you need but, by focusing on what you *want*, you get what you need as a by-product. The best part is... you can create a want "on purpose" (even if you don't feel like wanting it!). *Wants* offer us an addendum to the age-old adage of, "Where there's a will, there's a way" - with "Where there's a Want, there's a Will!"

You've learned that all things are created twice, first mentally – then in physical reality. We looked at how all things... every building, every garden, every person, and every dollar in circulation was first... *an idea.*

You learned that the pen has power. Coupled with the "dual creation" philosophy, you learned some specific planning methods that work much better than other planning methods. By following the methods of the world's greatest planners, you can rapidly transform your thoughts (goals) into reality (accomplishments). You also know that, by failing to plan – you're actually, and *deliberately*, planning to *fail* (whether you realize it or not!).

You learned that every single living (and dead) human being has, at one time or another, possessed the HABITS THAT COULD LEAD TO SUCCESS, HEALTH, and HAPPINESS. If they failed to achieve their full potential, it was because they lacked the perseverance that fastens those habits to success!

You learned that there is a formula for success. Copy the right formula – reap the same results. Better yet... copy the principle *behind* the formula and you will have a longer lasting result... because your actions will stem from a spirit of Be rather than simply the action and labor of Do.

This is especially important if your goals deal with innovation or are goals that have never before been accomplished by anyone else. You can always model *principle*... the thinking or theory behind the action. People like Edison, Ford, and Einstein would be "back on top" in their field in no time today, in spite of all the technological advances they would be unaware of, because they lived their lives by focusing on the Be-ing aspect. (Probably the same reason they were so damned persistent, too!)

You learned many strategies that, when implemented, will inspire you to persevere while on life's "endless plateaus" and that they are part of what we commonly call - *a journey*. You have realized that the excitement which comes from the "bursts" or breakthroughs of progress were only the result of our ability to **stick it out on the plateaus!** (...even when it seemed like we were going nowhere.)

You learned that by saying "Yes" to a *good thing...* you are, many times, saying "No" to the *great thing!* Improving your ability to say "No" is a virtue. You'll never quite get to the point where this becomes easy – you just get more aware of how much you need to *do it!*

You learned that, in the words of Calvin Coolidge: "Nothing can take the place of persistence." Not talent, education, or genius.

I want to leave you with a story that, quite honestly, served as the major theme of this book. But first, I'd like to let you know that I have not *always* had a bias for action... but that I do see the power in having it.

The story of "Garcia" says it much better than I ever could, so I have reprinted it here, in its entirety, for you to enjoy.

A Message to Garcia

The Story of Garcia:

In all this Cuban business, there is one man who stands out on the horizon of my memory like Mars at perihelion. When war broke out between Spain & the United States, it was very necessary to communicate quickly with the leader of the Insurgents. Garcia was somewhere hidden in the mountain vastness of Cuba- no one knew where. No mail nor telegraph message could reach him. The President needed to secure his cooperation, and quickly.

What to do!?
Someone said to the President, "There's a fellow by the name of Rowan who will find Garcia for you; if anybody can, it is he."

Rowan was sent for and given a letter which he was to deliver to Garcia. How "the fellow by the name of Rowan" took the letter, sealed it up in an oil-skin pouch, strapped it over his heart… How in four days, he landed by night off the coast of Cuba, stepped from an open boat, disappeared into the jungle… How in three weeks, he came out on the other side of the Island, having traversed a hostile country on foot, and delivered his letter to Garcia, are things I have no special desire to tell in detail at this time.

The point I wish to make is this: McKinley gave Rowan a letter to be delivered to Garcia; Rowan took the letter and did not ask, "Where is he at?" By the Eternal! <u>There</u> is a man whose form should be cast in deathless bronze and the statue placed in every college of the land. It is not book-learning young men need, nor instruction about this and that, but a stiffening of the vertebrae which will cause them to be loyal to a trust, to act promptly, concentrate their energies, and DO the thing- "Carry a message to Garcia!"

General Garcia is dead now, but there are other "Garcias."

Any man, who has endeavored to carry out an enterprise where many hands were needed, has been well-nigh appalled at times by the imbecility of the average man and his inability or unwillingness to concentrate on a thing and do it. Slip-shod assistance, foolish inattention, dowdy indifference, & half-hearted work seem to be the rule; and no man succeeds, unless by hook or crook, or threat, he forces or bribes other men to assist him; or mayhap, God in His goodness performs a miracle, & sends him an Angel of Light for an assistant. You, reader, put this matter to a test: You are sitting now in your office. Six clerks are within call.

Summon any one and make this request: "Please look in the encyclopedia and make a brief memorandum for me concerning the life of Correggio."

Will the clerk quietly say, "Yes, sir" and go do the task?

On your life, he will not. He will look at you out of a fishy eye and ask one or more of the following questions:

Who was he?

Which encyclopedia?

Where is the encyclopedia?

Was I hired for that?

Don't you mean Bismarck?

What's the matter with Charlie doing it?

Is he dead?

Is there any hurry?

Shan't I bring you the book and let you look it up yourself?

What do you want to know for?

And I will lay you ten to one that, after you have answered the questions, explained how to find the information, and shared why you want it, the clerk will go off and get one of the other

clerks to help him try to find Correggio - and
then come back and tell you there is no such man.
Of course, I may lose my bet; but according to
the Law of Averages, I will not.

Now if you are wise, you will not bother to
explain to your "assistant" that Correggio is
indexed under the C's, not the K's, but you will
smile sweetly and say, "Never mind," and go look
it up yourself.

It is an incapacity for independent action, moral
stupidity, infirmity of the will, unwillingness
to cheerfully catch hold and lift… these are the
things that put pure Socialism so far into the
future. If men will not act for themselves, what
will they do when the benefit of their effort is
for all? A first-mate with knotted club seems
necessary; and the dread of getting "the bounce"
Saturday night, holds many a worker to his place.

Advertise for a stenographer, and nine out of ten
persons who apply can neither spell nor punctuate
- and worse, do not think it necessary to be able
to do so.

Can such a one write a letter to Garcia?

"You see that bookkeeper," once said the foreman
to me in a large factory.

"Yes, what about him?"

"Well he's a fine accountant, but if I'd send him
up town on an errand, he might accomplish the
errand all right. On the other hand, he might
stop at four saloons along the way, and by the
time he reached Main Street, have forgotten what
he had been sent for."

Can such a man be entrusted to carry a message to
Garcia?

We have recently heard much maudlin sympathy
expressed for the "downtrodden denizen of the

290

sweat-shop" and the "homeless wanderer searching for honest employment." Often accompanying it all are many hard words for the men in power.

Nothing is said about the employer who grows old before his time in a vain attempt to get frowsy ne'er-do-wells to do intelligent work. Nothing is mentioned about his long-patient striving with "help" that does nothing but loaf when his back is turned. In every store and factory, there is a constant weeding-out process occurring. The employer is constantly sending away "help" that have shown their incapacity to further the interests of the business, and others are being taken on. No matter how good times are, this sorting continues. If times are hard and work is scarce, the sorting is done finer - but out and forever out, the incompetent and unworthy go.

It is the survival of the fittest. Self-interest prompts every employer to keep the best - those who can carry a message to Garcia.

I know one man of really brilliant parts who has not the ability to manage a business of his own and yet, is also absolutely worthless to any one else. Why? Because he carries with him constantly the insane suspicion that his employer is oppressing, or intending to oppress him. He cannot give orders; and he will not receive them. Should a message be given him to take to Garcia, his answer would probably be, "Take it yourself."

Tonight this man walks the streets looking for work, the wind whistling through his threadbare coat. No one who knows him dare employ him, for he is a regular fire-brand of discontent. He is impervious to reason; and the only thing that can impress him is the toe of a thick-soled No. 9 boot.

Of course, I know that one so morally deformed is no less to be pitied than one physically crippled. But in our pitying, let us drop a tear, too, for the men who are striving to carry on a great enterprise, whose working hours are not limited by the whistle, and whose hair is fast turning white through the struggle to hold in line those of dowdy indifference, slip-shod imbecility, and the heartless ingratitude which, but for their enterprise, would be both hungry & homeless.

Have I put the matter too strongly? Possibly I have; but when all the world has gone a-slumming, I wish to speak a word of sympathy for the man who succeeds - the man who, against great odds, has directed the efforts of others... and having succeeded, finds there's nothing in it: nothing but bare board and clothes.

I have carried a dinner pail & worked for day's wages. I have also been an employer of labor; and I know there is something to be said for both sides. There is no excellence, per se, in poverty; rags are no recommendation; & all employers are not rapacious and high-handed... any more than all poor men are virtuous.

My heart goes out to the man who does his work diligently when the "boss" is away, as well as when he is at home. And the man who, when given a letter for Garcia, quietly take the missive, without asking any idiotic questions, who with no lurking intention of chucking it into the nearest sewer, or of doing aught else but delivering it, never gets "laid off," nor has to go on a strike for higher wages. Civilization is one long, anxious search for just such individuals. Anything such a man asks shall be granted. His kind is so rare that no employer can afford to let him go. He is wanted in every city, town, and village - in every office, shop, store, and factory. The world cries out for such: he is needed, and needed badly- the man who can carry a message to Garcia.

The End.

The Story of Garcia brings me to my final point...

A point that, as with all advice, *is easier said than done;* and, much like the "fat doctor," I need to take my own medicine just as quickly as I prescribe it for others.

I have said for a long time: "I am not standing on a mountain shouting *'Hey, look at me... C'mon up here where it's awesome!'*" No, not at all. Rather, I am standing beside you saying, "You see that mountain over there? Well, that's the one we should climb... Let's take the journey together."

The Stunning Conclusion

I almost forgot...

You might be wondering....

"How do I know all this'll *work*?"

"How can I be *sure* that this *Be, Do, and Have* stuff will really *create results in my life?*"

"And... how exactly, can you *guarantee me* that my future levels of success, health, and happiness will begin and end in the *mind*."

Most importantly, you should be thinking:

"How can I be certain it will *work* for *me*?"

It's already working.

You're already living the life of your "dreams..

This has been the predominant force in your life.

The difference is, now, you have some tools to control it… to live your life *deliberately.*

ABOUT THE AUTHOR

Scott Palangi is the founder of Palangi Martial Arts, a hybrid system of self-defense that emphasizes the *lifestyle* benefits of martial arts through self-improvement.

He resides in Englewood, NJ and continues to teach martial arts to men, women, and children. Scott also speaks to organizations about time-management, leadership, and success skills. To have Scott speak at your organization, visit **www.scottpalangi.com**